# The Nature of Life

# The Nature of Life

## Readings in Biology

Foreword by Lynn Margulis and Dorion Sagan

Selected and Edited by

Nancy Carr

Joseph Coulson

Mike Levine

Gary Schoepfel

Donald Whitfield

and

Mark Stefanski

*Advanced Placement Biology instructor,*
*Science Department, Marin Academy*

Published by the Great Books Foundation

with support from the College of the Humanities and Sciences

Published and distributed by

**The Great Books Foundation**

*A nonprofit educational organization*

35 East Wacker Drive, Suite 400
Chicago, IL 60601
www.greatbooks.org

9  8  7  6  5  4  3

Library of Congress Cataloging-in-Publication Data

The nature of life : readings in biology.
    p. cm.
   Includes bibliographical references.
   ISBN 1-880323-86-9 (pbk. : alk. paper)
    1. Biology. I. Great Books Foundation (U.S.)

QH311 .N33 2001
570—dc21                2001033681

Cover design: William Seabright
Book design: William Seabright; Think Design Group LLC

But nature is a stranger yet;
The ones that cite her most
Have never passed her haunted house,
Nor simplified her ghost.

To pity those that know her not
Is helped by the regret
That those who know her, know her less
The nearer her they get.

—Emily Dickinson

Lynn Margulis is Distinguished Professor in the Department of Geosciences at the University of Massachusetts Amherst.

Dorion Sagan is the author of *Biospheres: Metamorphosis of Planet Earth* and coauthor with Lynn Margulis of *Slanted Truths: Essays on Gaia, Symbiosis, and Evolution.*

The College of the Humanities and Sciences is a great books distance-learning college established in 1998 that offers undergraduate and graduate education in the humanities with concentration in imaginative literature, natural sciences, philosophy and religion, and social science. The College of the Humanities and Sciences promotes student-faculty scholarship through research, discussion, and the development of collaborative publications. For more information go to www.chumsci.edu or call 1-877-248-6724.

Advanced Placement Program Biology teachers, working in cooperation with the Great Books Foundation, contributed to this book's development and participated in a pilot of the materials. Advanced Placement Program is a registered trademark of the College Entrance Examination Board, which was not involved in the production of this book.

## The Great Books Foundation

**President**
Peter Temes, Ph.D.

**Editorial Director**
Joseph Coulson, Ph.D.

**Director of School Programs**
Bill Siegel

**Director of Adult Programs**
Donald Whitfield

**Production Editor**
Anne Gendler

**Copy Editors**
Beth Duncan
Katherine Faydash
Mary Klein

**Editorial Assistant**
Brendan Malone

**Production Assistant**
A. C. Racette

# About the
# Great Books Foundation

## What is the Great Books Foundation?

The Great Books Foundation is an independent, nonprofit educational organization whose mission is to help people learn how to think and share ideas. Toward this end, the Foundation offers workshops for leaders of and participants in Shared Inquiry discussion and publishes collections of classic and modern texts for both children and adults.

The Great Books Foundation was established in 1947 to promote liberal education for the general public. In 1962, the Foundation extended its mission to children with the introduction of Junior Great Books. Since its inception, the Foundation has helped thousands of people throughout the United States and in other countries begin their own discussion groups in schools, libraries, and community centers. Today, Foundation instructors conduct hundreds of workshops each year, in which educators and parents learn to lead Shared Inquiry discussion.

## What resources are available to support my participation in Shared Inquiry?

The Great Books Foundation offers workshops in Shared Inquiry to help people get the most from discussion. Participants learn how to read actively, pose fruitful questions, and listen and respond to others effectively in discussion. All participants also practice leading a discussion and have an opportunity to reflect on the process with others. For more information about Great Books materials or workshops, call the Great Books Foundation at 1-800-222-5870 or visit our Web site at www.greatbooks.org.

# Contents

## Readings and Questions

# Foreword

Abright, red sun decorates the ceramic brick-tile embedded at eye level on Boltwood Walk, across from the town hall in Amherst, Massachusetts. This unique public artwork bears the following inscription: "First-rate men and women will not and cannot work under conditions fixed by those who are afraid of ideas—Henry Steele Commager, 1991." A famous scholar who taught at the nearby college and died shortly after the brick-tile was unveiled, Commager was most noted for his widely distributed textbooks on the history of the United States. He recognized, as do the editors of this anthology, the singular importance, and the danger, of the clear idea.

That people are members of the mammalian class (animals with hair and mammary glands) and the primate order (lemurs, apes, monkeys, and their kin) and are angels on neither their mother's nor their father's side of the family is a big idea. That the center of the universe is not Earth, or even the sun, is another big idea. That one can travel the globe westward and arrive in the Far East is still another. Big ideas have consequences in actions; they may lead to revolutions, new inventions, and even war. Textbooks tend to avoid ideas entirely. They seek refuge in trivia and fail to recognize muddle and inconsistency. Even Commager's excellent textbooks suffered the usual excess of facts, dates, and pages. More is not always more; it is often less. A clear idea, like an exquisite line of poetry, organizes the immensity of experience and its details: the idiosyncrasies, the patterns, and the confusion snap into sharp focus.

From its inception, the Great Books Foundation has been a curator of the ideas that have shaped Western civilization. By emphasizing the importance of the texts in which they were originally expressed, the Foundation helps us understand that the power of ideas is often intimately related to, if not inseparable from, the words by which these ideas initially entered the world. This anthology, in which you will find many of the big ideas in the science of life, stands as a case in point. It is the antithesis of the ordinary textbook. Instead of facts to remember, or an attempt by one person or several to portray the final truth of a scientific field, the selections in this book show science in action, with its conflicts and quirks, its enlightenments and enchantments, all reported in the first person. The book enables you to see how biology, like all science, is a human enterprise; being fallible, humans make mistakes. Science, in fact, is a continuous record of mistakes, a mistake-making process, like evolution itself. The errors and self-corrections of science are equivalent to evolution's mutations, infections, starvations, and environmental crises. Evolution's mistakes and casual encounters create new beings, just as science's mistakes push the search for truth to the next level.

The road to truth, or, at any rate, to verifiable description, seldom mirrors a sociologist's or philosopher's caricature of careful hypothesis followed by meticulous experiment, then widespread acceptance by the enlightened international scientific community of open minds. As Claude Bernard points out, we are structurally limited by being smaller than the universe we study. Perception is not perfect but Procrustean (after Procrustes, the robber of Greek mythology who cut off his victims' legs to make them fit his too small bed). Our perception, always grossly limited, never takes in everything. Although we carry in our minds a three-dimensional map of the world, for example, our eyes are not on the sides or back of our heads, but only in the front.

Because science is an intensely social activity, a group enterprise based on observation and consensus, methodical checking and rechecking, it compensates for limited individual perception and cultural superstition. Science admits occasional flashes of insight with which a new, more fruitful way of looking at the world is transmitted first to scientists and eventually to their public. As Bernard says,

knowledge of the inmost nature or the absolute, in the simplest phenomenon, would demand knowledge of the whole universe. . . . In living bodies
absolute truth would be still harder to attain, because, besides implying
knowledge of the universe outside a living body, it would also demand
complete knowledge of the organism. . . . Absolute knowledge could,
therefore, leave nothing outside itself, and only on condition of knowing
everything could man be granted its attainment.

Thus the wisdom of philosophical humility, an awareness of what we
do not know, stands out clearly in these readings. We recognize the tendency for us as humans to see, to a large extent, not the untrammeled truth,
if it even exists, but what we want to see. The social aspect, the need to communicate results to others who are superficially or intimately engaged in
scientific inquiry, leads, perhaps, to a less flattering but more realistic
impression of the progress of science. The process by which a new theory
comes to be accepted can be divided into three all-too-human phases:
(1) "Your theory is absolute nonsense"—the community of sciences rejects
what may be a startling new way of looking at the evidence, often mini-
mizing or disregarding the evidence in order to do so; (2) "Your theory is
true but trivial"—the theory is reluctantly accepted because of its explanatory power or its ability to generate fresh and compelling investigation, but
the originators do not receive their due; and (3) "The theory is both true
and important, but actually it is not yours—we knew it all along"—a still
more unflattering characterization of the march of science suggests that new
theories are really accepted only after the deaths of the scientists of the
previous generation.

However one looks at it, a funny thing happens on the way to the textbook. Instead of portraying scientific knowledge as the product of a living,
thriving, messy process, of an asymptotic search for understanding that
relies on fresh perspectives, new tools, and careful methodologies, textbooks present it as revealed truth. Instead of the ultimate triumph of this
process over refractory hierarchies and academic intransigence, scientific
knowledge appears as a body of static information to be memorized by
high school and college students and their teachers.

Most popular science books and many textbooks contain the educational equivalent of food concentrated at the top of the food chain: con-
densed thoughts garnered from a synthesis of received ideas. In place of

primary research or original theory, these books present only conventional representations thereof. This approach, a sort of literary heterotrophy, has its advantages. Feeding the mind on the conventional understanding of complex work allows for a kind of easy digestion of key concepts and the most important bits of information. However, in its avoidance of the appearance of conflict and its emphasis on unanimity, the resulting perspective on the scientific process neglects an essential point—fertile diversity of thought, intellectual contentiousness, devastating criticism, and repeated observations from different viewpoints all lead to new ideas. This anthology includes some wrong and intellectually stultifying ideas, but it does not suggest an illusory consensus, a monoculture of theory.

Encountering the writings of the thinkers themselves, the sources of the ideas that have propelled scientific history, is exciting, fun, and even inspiring. In explaining the rarity of big fierce animals, Paul Colinvaux provides us with an ecological analogy to this experience. Lions and tigers and bears must feed on smaller organisms, which themselves feed on smaller organisms; energy, derived from the sun, is inevitably lost along the food chain. Some beasts, however, are exceptions. The baleen whale, for example, maintains its enormous size by filter feeding on huge numbers of krill and other plankton. Like the reader of this anthology, the whale goes right to the source. Rather than depend on the digestion of a slew of intermediary organisms, the hulking baleen whale refines raw material. And in doing so it remains less likely to be destroyed by a biological magnification of toxins accumulated in increasing concentration as species devour one another. The baleen whale enjoys its independence, a freedom from undue influence, and the robust health of a vegetarian.

It is our belief that this anthology offers readers the kind of planktonic purity, the sort of directness of resource enjoyed by the baleen whale. But with the freedom to gain one's intellectual nutriment closer to the source of the educational food chain comes a corresponding obligation: hard work, the engaging but not always comfortable task of thinking for oneself and facing the sometimes cacophonous music of intellectual discourse. The baleen whale eats no frozen steak for dinner. Rather it continuously feeds on the microscopic animals, which themselves are only one step away from the primary metabolic process of photosynthesis.

This brings us to big ideas too new to be found in this anthology. We mention them not just because they are contentious, and therefore illustrative of primary intellectual process as opposed to textbook unanimity, but also because they seem to us both true and major new developments in the scientific way of looking at life. The first of these ideas is that all of nature, both animate and inanimate, can be seen as possessing a unifying, earthly purpose.

In addressing the question of the purpose of both animate and inanimate nature, modern biologists have accepted Aristotle's contention that physiological development is itself a natural end but rejected his belief that the inanimate world shares a similar purpose. It is not because they were instilled with a purpose by a deity that living beings display purposeful behavior; rather, those beings that fail to do so die before they are able to reproduce. In this view, the matching of structure to function becomes evidence for adaptation and the basis for natural selection. The filtration of urine by the kidneys, the efficacy of thought generated electrochemically in the brain, or the ideal match between the orchid and its arthropod pollinator have been honed by millions of years of failure.

Today, however, we suggest that a purpose common to both animate and inanimate nature can be described by the second law of thermodynamics—the same law that prevents life from taking all the energy it wants from the sun and that tends to clump animals at various sizes. The second law of thermodynamics says that entropy, a measure of disorder, increases in isolated systems. But living matter is not isolated; it is continuously energized, feeding on the sun and those who feed on the sun. A broader statement of the second law, in view of a purpose common to all of nature, is that nature abhors a gradient. A gradient is a difference across a distance. A difference between high and low atmospheric pressure is resolved by the appearance of a highly complex, swirling storm system, such as a tornado or a hurricane. Differences in chemical potential gradients are resolved by inanimate chemical clocks, long-lasting and cyclical chemical reactions. Without any attribution of divine intervention, it is possible to argue that such systems fulfill the function, or exist for the purpose, of eliminating preexisting gradients.

From their ancestors among the earliest oxygen-eschewing cells on earth, living systems have been, and still are, gradient reducers. Only life—unlike momentary cycles of chemicals or storm systems—has been able to continuously fulfill this prosaic purpose, its material thermodynamic imperative, for over three thousand million years, by cellular organization safeguarded by gene-based reproduction. In our view, the scientific understanding of nature's purpose may go a long way toward healing the open wound that remains between organized religion and experimental science.

Religious practitioners are often ignorant of scientific thought, and scientists, in dismissing the primary data of experience, too frequently deny feeling. We each know we are sentient, thinking, willing, emotional, and incompletely determined beings. However imperfect, the living ability to imagine the future and act with an eye toward it must—from a thoroughgoing evolutionary viewpoint—have a basis in inanimate phenomena. The immensely fruitful metaphor of ourselves as machines is a limited metaphor. It comes, like many creation stories, from the real human experience of building things, putting them together from the bottom up. But there is no a priori reason to believe that nature was put together, like Tinkertoys or LEGO bricks, from the bottom up. Living beings, all of us, are better seen as selves, cellular enclosures originating in top-down fashion from an energetic and ancient environment. We are open thermodynamic systems. Our anthropomorphism and anthropocentrism, both in modern science and in the traditional religion supposed to be its antithesis, tend to obscure our perception.

That living beings, along with their artifacts and local environments, display a physiology within and beyond their borders that fulfills the natural purpose of gradient reduction at the whole-organism level is one new idea. A second new idea is that life is the geological force that retained water and initiated plate tectonics on Earth, the third planet from the center of our solar system. We mention these ideas here to provide not only a preview of what may be part of biological science of the future, but also to demonstrate with example the necessity to think for oneself, to stay ahead of the curve of convention, to be both critical of and yet open to new concepts. For the reader who comes to it with intellectual hunger, *The Nature of Life: Readings in Biology* presents a bountiful feast of rich ideas, from ancient to modern times.

*Lynn Margulis and Dorion Sagan*

# Introduction

How did life begin? How is it changing? How are human beings related to other forms of life? This collection of readings will introduce you to some of the questions that scientists have posed about the nature of life, and to provisional answers. While the questions they pose and the answers they give often vary greatly, each selection included here exemplifies the disciplined curiosity that informs the scientific process.

All the selections were written by scientists, many writing about their own work and discoveries. Among others, you will find Gregor Mendel describing patterns of inheritance in plants, Charles Darwin explaining the mechanism of natural selection, James Watson detailing his codiscovery of the structure of DNA, and Lynn Margulis reconstructing the conditions under which life came into being. Biographical information is included with each author's selection, and suggestions for further reading about the authors and the subjects they write about can be found in the bibliography.

An anthology of this size cannot aspire to be either exhaustive or fully representative; rather, our intent is to suggest the range and vigor of work in biology. Our selection criteria included the historical significance of the work, the quality of the writing, and the stature of the author in the scientific community. To ensure this collection's relevance to biology coursework, we also chose readings that correspond to the eight major themes the

College Board uses to organize its Advanced Placement Program Biology curriculum. While you can learn much from independent reading of these selections, we hope that you will also have the opportunity to discuss your thoughts about them with others.

Three groups of questions follow each selection. The **content questions** will help you think further about the scientific information contained in the readings and see relationships between the selections and your classroom activities. The **application questions** draw on a wider base of information than is contained in the selections alone and sometimes require additional research; they are designed to give you opportunities to work more extensively with the concepts you encounter in the readings. Finally, the **discussion questions** ask you to formulate your own responses to the issues raised by the selections and connect your study of biology with other subjects and with your beliefs and convictions. We have called these *discussion questions* because they may be reasonably answered in more than one way and, therefore, are particularly worth talking about.

Consider your reading and discussions an experimental voyage: just as scientists form a hypothesis, test it, and reconsider it, you will read, question, and develop your own understanding about major issues in biology. We hope that your encounters with these writers will inspire a life-long interest in the questions that remain to be answered, or that must be asked anew.

# Theme Notes

The readings in this anthology were chosen in part because they correspond to the eight major themes the College Board uses to organize its Advanced Placement Program Biology curriculum. In the pages that follow, you will find an explanation of each of these themes, along with a table indicating which themes are addressed by which selections.

## I. Science As a Process

Science is generally understood to be cumulative. Year after year, the quantity of knowledge increases as scientists make observations, conduct experiments, and formulate theories. The ongoing result of this activity guides continuing work and makes possible the accurate prediction of future events. At any given time in history, the approach to understanding the natural world in a way that can be called scientific is based on deeply embedded assumptions about what kind of knowledge of the world is possible and how it can be acquired. Each age, including our own, cherishes its scientific ideas about the way things are. In addition, each age has its own ideas about what procedures to follow in investigating the natural world.

However, all the sciences have changed profoundly again and again throughout history. This process of change happens not simply because more knowledge is acquired, but because new knowledge continually raises new questions, sometimes at such a fundamental level that the entire set of assumptions underlying science shifts to a new pattern of understanding.

Each of the selections in this anthology deals with a specific set of questions or problems in biological science, while at the same time saying something about science as a process. Therefore, science as a process should be kept in mind as an overarching theme.

On one level, this theme is exemplified by the experimental procedures described in detail by many of the writers. For example, Mendel sets out what he had in mind in devising his plant experiments, combining careful observation with the deduction of results from the mathematical theory of probability. Watson describes how thinking carefully about the geometric arrangement of certain molecules suggested how DNA is shaped and replicates. In these two cases, the process of forming hypotheses and deducing results led to far-reaching changes in what we understand about living organisms.

On another level, reading and discussing many of these selections can lead to insights about the historical process by which biological science develops. Aristotle and Lucretius offer evidence for their understanding of the world of living organisms that may seem outmoded to us at the beginning of the twenty-first century. But if we carefully consider how their deep assumptions influence their scientific outlook, we may gain a clearer view of those assumptions that underlie science in our own time. In doing so, we become better able to ask the searching questions that can lead to further scientific progress.

**The writers in this anthology who deal most explicitly with science as an investigative process are Aristotle, Darwin, Mendel, Bernard, Lorenz, Watson, Colinvaux, Gould, and Margulis. The selection from Bacon occupies a special position. It sets forth a way of investigating the natural world that is sometimes called the foundation of the modern experimental method and sometimes considered an oversimplification of the way science actually works. Therefore, it was included to stimulate discussion about the theme of science as a process.**

## II. Evolution

The theory of evolution is the great unifying idea of biological science. In the century and a half since Charles Darwin's revolutionary work, evolutionary theory has enabled biology to achieve the status of a mature science, possessing great explanatory power over the numerous phenomena of the world of living organisms.

Drawing on an immense body of evidence, including the record left by fossils, studies in comparative anatomy, and molecular research, evolution offers the principles by which living things have come to be as they are now, since the beginnings of life on earth. One of the reasons evolutionary theory is so disturbing to many people is that, in showing the descent and kinship of all organisms, including humans, it posits a world of change rather than stability.

From the earliest prelife chemical forms through the complex organisms living today, the interplay of environment and heredity has led to the succession of life forms that make up the earth's biosphere. Evolutionary theory explains how organisms adapt to their environments and how successful adaptations of structure, physiology, and behavior are perpetuated generation after generation. Understanding the mechanisms by which characteristics persist and change has been a central concern of biological research, from Mendel's early experiments with hybrid plants to the Human Genome Project.

Evolutionary theory explains the relationships among species in a straightforward way: descent with modification through time. In doing so, it further explains the great diversity of life on earth, past and present, and challenges humans to identify their biological relationship with the natural world. Ultimately, evolutionary theory poses searching questions about the shared place of humans in the biosphere.

**The great importance of evolution as a theme for the study of biology is reflected in the fact that most of the readings in this anthology have some bearing on it: Lucretius, Darwin, Mendel, Eiseley, Lorenz, Watson, Dawkins, Colinvaux, Wilson, and Margulis.**

## III. Energy Transfer

The concept of energy, or the capacity for doing work, is fundamental to the understanding of all natural phenomena. One of the most important insights in the development of biological science was that the basic laws of thermodynamics govern the processes of living organisms. According to the first two laws of thermodynamics, energy can be neither created nor destroyed, and the effect of physical and chemical changes increases the disorder (entropy) of the universe.

However, living organisms are the preeminent example of orderliness in nature: reproduction, metabolism, and growth are characterized by highly complex and ordered processes. Plants are able to trap energy in sunlight and transform it into chemical energy, a form useful for life on earth. As animals eat plants or other animals that have eaten plants, each stage in the food web produces waste heat, which joins the pool of energy released into space. Thus, this small portion of the sun's energy that is temporarily trapped and stored sustains the high level of organization we call life.

At the cellular level, available energy is transformed into ATP, the primary carrier of chemical energy for all living matter. Photosynthesis and cellular respiration are the major processes by which this energy transfer takes place. At the level of populations and ecosystems, the amount of available energy in the complex networks of food chains is a major determinant of the density and distribution of individuals and species. In addition, energy availability ultimately places a limiting value on the size of organisms.

**Among the readings in this anthology, those by Carson, Watson, Colinvaux, Wilson, and Margulis probe different aspects of biological energy transfer.**

## IV. Continuity and Change

In biological science, continuity and change are not in opposition, but complement each other. The theme of continuity and change gives us a way of understanding how both similarities and differences among living organisms arise, are established, and continue to shift over time.

Much of the sense that we can make of the world of living organisms comes from the fact that each reproduces according to its own kind. An individual organism's continued resemblance to itself throughout life, as well as its resemblance to its parents, results from the mechanisms of heredity by which characteristics are maintained from generation to generation. These mechanisms, operating at the cellular level, are based on the accurate replication of genetic information encoded in the structure of DNA.

There are numerous sources of genetic variation, including mutations of all kinds as well as the variations that arise from the ordinary combining of maternal and paternal DNA that occurs in sexual recombination. Some variations, expressed in new structures or functions, may be harmful to an individual organism's ability to fit into its environment. Other variations may lead to more successful adaptability and greater advantage for survival. Because heredity ensures the continued inheritance and maintenance of characteristics, it conserves beneficial changes and establishes them as predominant.

The ideas of continuity and change allow us to chart the course of evolution of homologous structures (such as paws and hands) from a common ancestor. In addition, they show us the meaning of the interrelation between conservative biological processes, such as mitosis, and sources of variation, such as genetic mutation.

**Many writers in this anthology are concerned with the theme of continuity and change, since it is so closely tied to evolutionary theory: Aristotle, Lucretius, Darwin, Mendel, Eiseley, Lorenz, Watson, Dawkins, Colinvaux, Gould, Wilson, and Margulis.**

## V. Relationship of Structure to Function

While much of biological science deals with complex processes involving abstract concepts such as energy transfer and homeostasis, underlying everything are the shapes and physical properties of the material that constitutes living organisms.

Although an easy analogy is often made between man-made objects designed for a specific purpose, such as a hammer or a building, and living structures that are well adapted to perform some function, there is an important difference to keep in mind. The living structures evolved over long periods of time as a result of the interplay between random genetic variations and changing environmental pressures, with natural selection accomplishing the preservation of those characteristics most suited to survival. The fit between biological structure and function is not purposeful but rather necessary, given the conditions under which it has come to be.

Structural adaptations occur at all levels—from the molecule to the organism. Because a molecule naturally has a particular shape, it may come to serve a biological function in a way that reflects its configuration. On a larger scale, parasites have evolved morphological adaptations to their hosts to enhance their survival.

Thinking about biological problems in structural terms can often lead to great insights. For example, the geometric configuration of DNA strands suggested to Watson and Crick how genetic material can replicate.

**In this anthology, Aristotle, Darwin, Eiseley, Watson, Dawkins, Colinvaux, Gould, and Margulis are concerned with the relationship of biological structure to function.**

## VI. Regulation

Living forms, whether cells, individual organisms, or entire populations, can maintain their stability in a constantly changing world only through biological mechanisms that resist internal change. Because living forms continually take in energy to carry out the processes of life, they are in perpetual change; at the same time, to function in an orderly way, they must keep internal conditions relatively uniform and stable.

The regulatory mechanisms in living forms are responses to signals from their environments and operate at all levels of life (molecule, cell, organism, population) and at many different time intervals—from fractions of seconds for biochemical reactions to hundreds or thousands of years for large population adjustments. These self-regulating, or homeostatic, mechanisms are essential to survival and have developed through the evolutionary process of natural selection.

One of the most important kinds of biological self-regulation takes place at the cellular level, where the proper balance of enzymatic activities and homeostasis of body fluids is maintained. In this way, a living organism achieves a constant internal environment. In addition, regulatory mechanisms control the expression or suppression of genetic information, the growth and development of an organism, and the body's responses to disease.

At the level of populations and communities, homeostatic regulation comes into play in predator-prey relationships, the limits to community growth as a result of crowding, and a vast array of behavioral patterns in response to changing environmental conditions. The close study of these patterns has important implications for how our species can successfully operate in a biosphere that hosts increasing human population growth.

**In this anthology, Darwin, Mendel, Bernard, Carson, Lorenz, Colinvaux, Gould, Wilson, and Margulis address questions related to biological regulation.**

## VII. Interdependence in Nature

In biological systems, whether considered at the molecular and cellular level or in terms of complex communities of individual living organisms, myriad interactions take place. Some of these interactions increase the likelihood of survival; others have the opposite result. While in a very general way everything in the biosphere depends on everything else, all life woven together in a network of innumerable links, biological science carefully attempts to distinguish various kinds of interactions. One of the most significant of these is the relation of interdependence.

At the molecular level, both within a single organism and among different kinds of organisms, many biochemical processes complement and balance each other. Examples include the carbon dioxide–oxygen cycle involving plants and animals, and the way in which the hydrolysis of ATP provides initial energy for the oxidation of organic fuels, which in turn provides for the synthesis of additional ATP.

Since no living species lives in complete isolation, numerous adaptations in structure, physiology, behavior, and life history have evolved among populations within an ecosystem. Adaptations such as competition, mutualism, commensalism, predation, and parasitism form the stable web that is conducive to the perpetuation of an ecosystem. These interdependencies have profound implications for how we understand biological evolution. Because organisms provide for each other the living interactive environment in which characteristics are expressed in the struggle for survival, each is the product of the other in the process of natural selection. Often the continued coexistence of all members of a community is necessary for the survival of each. These relationships are often subtle and surprising. One of the most important achievements of biological science is to discover and articulate them so that humans can proceed to live in the biosphere with knowledge and care.

Among the authors in this anthology who address the theme of inter-dependence in nature are Darwin, Eiseley, Carson, Lorenz, Dawkins, Colinvaux, Wilson, and Margulis.

## VIII. Science, Technology, and Society

Biology and technology have a complex interrelation. Biology uses technologies that make possible the investigation of the natural world. In turn, the insights and discoveries provided by biological research lead to the creation of new technologies that are applied to the solution of an immense range of problems. Finally, biology is essential to assessing, understanding, and solving environmental problems caused by technologies of all kinds.

Sometimes a new technology is developed as a direct response to the need for an improved way of making observations and conducting experiments. For example, new techniques of microscopy were developed to advance the understanding of the basic structure and function of cells. Other times, a technology that developed independently of any specific scientific need will be adapted to a new purpose, making possible new kinds of scientific investigation. The many innovations in computer technology are examples of this development.

As scientists apply biotechnology to a range of problems, such as the treatment of diseases and the development of better agricultural yields, they raise questions that cannot be answered by science alone. These ethical questions must be answered by both scientists and nonscientists thinking as philosophers and acting as responsible citizens, particularly in a democratic society. Philosophy has its own methods for investigating problems, and political systems have specific decision-making processes. However, it is always important that people seeking to answer these questions are well informed about the scientific principles involved.

Biology is central to understanding and solving environmental problems caused by the increasing impact on the biosphere of technologies of all kinds. To some extent, humans have always altered the environment out of which they have evolved. In doing so, they create new conditions that strongly influence the course of natural selection and adaptation for themselves and other living things. Because of the greatly accelerated rate, beginning in the last century, by which technology creates altered living conditions, one of the greatest challenges to biology is understanding and assessing environmental imbalances caused by the choices humans are making. Sometimes these choices are deliberate and have foreseeable consequences; sometimes they are made without forethought and knowledge of the consequences.

**In this anthology, Bernard, Carson, Lorenz, Dawkins, Gould, and Margulis are particularly concerned with the relationships of science and technology to society. Bacon raises other questions important to this theme.**

# Thematic Table

This table provides an overview of the major themes and subject areas addressed by each of the selections in this anthology.

| Theme | I. Molecules and Cells | II. Heredity and Evolution | III. Organisms and Populations |
|---|---|---|---|
| **1. Science As a Process** | | | |
| Aristotle | | | Aristotle |
| Bacon* | | | |
| Darwin | | Darwin | Darwin |
| Mendel | | Mendel | |
| Bernard | | | Bernard |
| Lorenz | | Lorenz | Lorenz |
| Watson | Watson | Watson | |
| Colinvaux | | | Colinvaux |
| Gould | Gould | | |
| Margulis | Margulis | Margulis | Margulis |
| **2. Evolution** | | | |
| Lucretius | | Lucretius | |
| Darwin | | Darwin | Darwin |
| Mendel | | Mendel | |
| Eiseley | | Eiseley | Eiseley |
| Lorenz | | Lorenz | Lorenz |
| Watson | Watson | Watson | |
| Dawkins | Dawkins | Dawkins | Dawkins |
| Colinvaux | | Colinvaux | Colinvaux |
| Wilson | | Wilson | Wilson |
| Margulis | Margulis | Margulis | Margulis |
| **3. Energy Transfer** | | | |
| Carson | Carson | Carson | |
| Watson | Watson | Watson | |
| Colinvaux | | Colinvaux | Colinvaux |
| Wilson | | | Wilson |
| Margulis | Margulis | Margulis | Margulis |
| **4. Continuity and Change** | | | |
| Aristotle | | | Aristotle |
| Lucretius | | Lucretius | Lucretius |
| Darwin | | Darwin | Darwin |
| Mendel | | Mendel | |
| Eiseley | | Eiseley | Eiseley |
| Lorenz | | Lorenz | Lorenz |
| Watson | Watson | Watson | |
| Dawkins | Dawkins | Dawkins | Dawkins |
| Colinvaux | | Colinvaux | Colinvaux |
| Gould | Gould | Gould | |
| Wilson | | | Wilson |
| Margulis | Margulis | Margulis | Margulis |

| Theme | I. Molecules and Cells | II. Heredity and Evolution | III. Organisms and Populations |
|---|---|---|---|
| **5. Relationship of Structure to Function** | | | |
| Aristotle | | | Aristotle |
| Darwin | | Darwin | Darwin |
| Eiseley | | Eiseley | Eiseley |
| Watson | Watson | Watson | |
| Dawkins | Dawkins | Dawkins | |
| Colinvaux | | Colinvaux | Colinvaux |
| Gould | Gould | Gould | |
| Margulis | Margulis | Margulis | Margulis |
| **6. Regulation** | | | |
| Darwin | | Darwin | Darwin |
| Mendel | | Mendel | |
| Bernard | | | Bernard |
| Carson | Carson | Carson | Carson |
| Lorenz | | Lorenz | Lorenz |
| Colinvaux | | | Colinvaux |
| Gould | Gould | Gould | |
| Wilson | | | Wilson |
| Margulis | Margulis | Margulis | Margulis |
| **7. Interdependence in Nature** | | | |
| Darwin | | Darwin | Darwin |
| Eiseley | | Eiseley | Eiseley |
| Carson | Carson | Carson | Carson |
| Lorenz | | Lorenz | Lorenz |
| Dawkins | Dawkins | Dawkins | Dawkins |
| Colinvaux | | Colinvaux | Colinvaux |
| Wilson | | Wilson | Wilson |
| Margulis | Margulis | Margulis | Margulis |
| **8. Science, Technology, and Society** | | | |
| Bacon* | | | |
| Bernard | | | Bernard |
| Carson | Carson | | Carson |
| Lorenz | | Lorenz | Lorenz |
| Dawkins | Dawkins | Dawkins | |
| Gould | Gould | Gould | Gould |
| Margulis | Margulis | | Margulis |

\* Although not specifically concerned with biology, the selection from Bacon's *Novum Organum* is included to raise general questions about the inductive scientific method.

# About Shared Inquiry

Shared Inquiry is the effort to achieve a more thorough understanding of a text by discussing questions, responses, and insights with others. For both the leader and the participants, careful listening is essential. The leader guides the discussion by asking questions about specific ideas and problems of meaning in the text, but does not seek to impose his or her own interpretation on the group.

During a Shared Inquiry discussion, group members consider a number of possible ideas and weigh the evidence for each. Ideas that are entertained and then refined or abandoned are not thought of as mistakes, but as valuable parts of the thinking process. Group members gain experience in communicating complex ideas and in supporting, testing, and expanding their thoughts. Everyone in the group contributes to the discussion, and while participants may disagree with each other, they treat each other's ideas respectfully.

This process of communal discovery is vital to developing an understanding of important texts and ideas, rather than merely cataloging them. By reading and thinking together about important works, you and the other members of your group are joining a great conversation that extends across the centuries.

## What does Shared Inquiry contribute to the study of science?

Shared Inquiry focuses on the interpretation of texts, in the belief that many readers working together can achieve a more complete understanding than any one reader can alone. We hope that reading and discussing the selections in this anthology will not only increase your knowledge of biology, but also enhance your appreciation of the scientific process. By reading scientists' own explanations of their work, you can see the evolution of their ideas and the way in which they build on the work of colleagues both present and past. And because science advances by asking questions, posing hypotheses, and testing them, the parallels between the scientific method and Shared Inquiry discussion are strong.

## Guidelines for leading and participating in discussion

Over the past fifty years, the Great Books Foundation has developed guidelines that distill the experience of many discussion groups, with participants of all ages. We have found that when groups follow the procedures outlined below, discussions are most focused and fruitful:

1. **Read the selection before participating in the discussion.** This ensures that all participants are equally prepared to talk about the ideas in the work, and helps prevent talk that would distract the group from its purpose.

2. **Support your ideas with evidence from the text.** This keeps the discussion focused on understanding the selection and enables the group to weigh textual support for different answers and to choose intelligently among them.

3. **Discuss the ideas in the selection, and try to understand them fully before exploring issues that go beyond the selection.** Reflecting on a range of ideas and the evidence to support them makes the exploration of related issues more productive.

4. **Listen to others and respond to them directly.** Shared Inquiry is about the give-and-take of ideas, a willingness to listen to others and to talk to them respectfully. Directing your comments and questions to other group members, not always to the leader, will make the discussion livelier and more dynamic.

5. **Expect the leader to ask questions, rather than answer them.** The leader is a kind of chief learner, whose role is to keep discussion effective and interesting by listening and asking questions. The leader's goal is to help the participants develop their own ideas, with everyone (the leader included) gaining a new understanding in the process. When participants hang back and wait for the leader to suggest answers, discussion falters.

## How to make discussions more effective

⌒ **Ask questions when something is unclear.** Simply asking someone to explain what he or she means by a particular word, or to repeat a comment, can give everyone in the group time to think about the idea in depth.

⌒ **Ask for evidence.** Asking "What in the text gave you that idea?" helps everyone better understand the reasoning behind an answer, and it allows the group to consider which ideas have the best support.

⌒ **Ask for agreement and disagreement.** "Does your idea agree with hers, or is it different?" Questions of this kind help the group understand how ideas are related or distinct.

⌒ **Reflect on discussion afterward.** Sharing comments about how the discussion went and ideas for improvement can make each discussion better than the last.

## Room arrangement and group size

Ideally, everyone in a discussion should be able to see and hear everyone else. When it isn't possible to arrange the seating in a circle or horseshoe, encourage group members to look at the person talking, acknowledging each other and not just the leader.

In general, Shared Inquiry discussion is most effective in groups of ten to twenty participants. If a group is much bigger than twenty, it is important to ensure that everyone has a chance to speak. This can be accomplished by either dividing the group in half for discussion or by setting aside time at the end of discussion to go around the room and give each person a chance to make a brief final comment.

# Using the Questions
# for Each Reading

## Content Questions

These questions will help you grasp more fully the scientific information in each selection. You will be able to answer content questions on the basis of the selections themselves; no additional sources are needed.

## Application Questions

Going beyond the material covered in the reading is the distinguishing factor of these questions. They require you to bring in and apply information from other sources, and they may entail some research. Application questions will enable you to work more concretely with the ideas expressed in the readings.

## Discussion Questions

These questions may be reasonably answered in many different ways because they ask you to express your own ideas about the issues raised in the selections. Discussion questions offer you the opportunity to weigh evidence, consider your own convictions, connect your study of biology to other subjects, and respond to scientific thinkers with your own reasoned judgment.

# Aristotle

Aristotle (384–322 BCE) is one of the founding thinkers of Western civilization. Although he is most often thought of as a philosopher, his works cover a vast range of human concerns, including ethics, logic, physics, psychology, and politics. Aristotle was also profoundly influential as a scientist: he was the first to develop the idea of scientific disciplines and to write systematically about scientific phenomena, and he was the first experimental scientist to record his work. His surviving works include five major treatises on biology.

Aristotle's interest in science began at an early age, since his father was court physician to the king of Macedonia. Aristotle was part of the highest echelon of Greek learning, studying under Plato in Athens and tutoring the future Alexander the Great. He founded the Lyceum, his answer to Plato's Academy, in 335, establishing it as a center for research into multiple fields of knowledge. The surviving works of Aristotle appear to be mainly lecture notes from courses he gave at the Lyceum.

Aristotle's contributions to biology can hardly be overestimated. As leading biologist Ernst Mayr remarks in *The Growth of Biological Thought,* "no one prior to Darwin has made a greater contribution to our understanding of the living world" than Aristotle. His work in comparing and drawing distinctions between natural phenomena and proposing their classifications was groundbreaking. In addition, Aristotle was passionately interested in the causes of life, asking what enabled complex living beings to develop and grow. He posited an *eidos,* or formative principle, that determined what an organism became. As Mayr notes, this corresponds to the place the genetic program of an organism now holds in biological understanding.

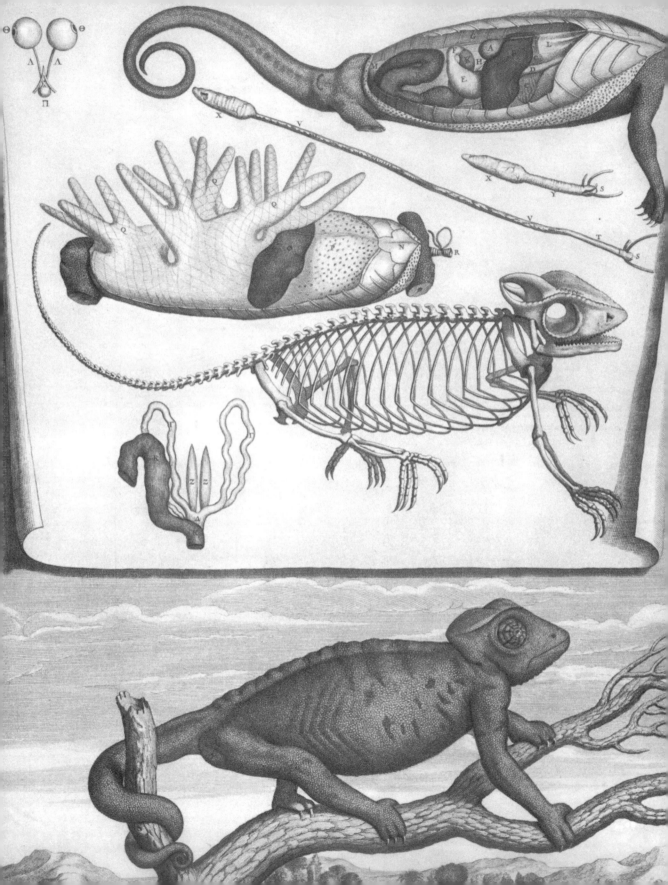

# Parts of Animals

*(selection)*

Of the works of nature there are, we hold, two kinds: those which are brought into being and perish, and those which are free from these processes throughout all ages. The latter are of the highest worth and are divine, but our opportunities for the study of them are somewhat scanty, since there is but little evidence available to our senses to enable us to consider them and all the things that we long to know about. We have better means of information, however, concerning the things that perish, that is to say, plants and animals, because we live among them; and anyone who will but take enough trouble can learn much concerning every one of their kinds. . . . Of "things divine" we have already treated and have set down our views concerning them; so it now remains to speak of animals and their nature. So far as in us lies, we will not leave out any one of them, be it never so mean; for though there are animals which have no attractiveness for the senses, yet for the eye of science, for the student who is naturally of a philosophic spirit and can discern the causes of things, nature which fashioned them provides joys which cannot be measured. . . .

First of all, our business must be to describe the attributes found in each group; I mean those "essential" attributes which belong to all the animals, and after that to endeavor to describe the causes of them. It will be remembered that I have said already that there are many attributes which are common to many animals, either identically the same (e.g., organs like feet, feathers, and scales, and affections similarly) or else common by analogy only (i.e., some animals have a lung,[1] others have no lung but something else to correspond instead of it; again, some animals have blood, while others have its counterpart,[2] which in them has the same value as blood in the former). And I have pointed out above that to treat separately of all the particular species would mean continual repetition of the same things, if we are going to deal with all their attributes, as the same attributes are common to many animals. Such, then, are my views on this matter.

Now, as each of the parts of the body, like every other instrument, is for the sake of some purpose, namely, some action, it is evident that the body as a whole must exist for the sake of some complex action. Just as the saw is there for the sake of sawing and not sawing for the sake of the saw, because sawing is the using of the instrument, so in some way the body exists for the sake of the soul, and the parts of the body for the sake of those functions to which they are naturally adapted.

So first of all we must describe the actions *(a)* which are common, and those which belong *(b)* to a group, or *(c)* to a species. By "common" I mean those that are present in all animals; by "those which belong to a group" I mean those of animals whose differences we see to be differences "of excess" in relation to one another: an example of this is the group Birds. Man is an example of a species; so is every class which admits no differentiation of its general definition. These three sorts of common attributes are, respectively, (1) analogous, (2) generic, [and] (3) specific.

Now it is evident that when one action is for the sake of another action, then the instruments which perform the two actions differ exactly as the two actions differ, and if one action is "prior" to another and is the "end" of that other action, then the part of the body to which it belongs will be "prior" to the part to which the other action belongs. There is also a third possibility, namely, that the action and its organ are there simply because the presence of others *necessarily* involves them. (By affections and actions I mean generation, growth, copulation, waking, sleep, locomotion, and the other similar ones that are found in animals. Examples of parts are nose, eye, face; each of these is named a "limb" or "member." And the same holds for the rest too.)

1. [Almost always used in the singular by Aristotle.—Trans.]
2. [By "blood" Aristotle means red blood only. "Blooded" and "bloodless" animals do not quite coincide with vertebrates and invertebrates, for there are some invertebrates which have red blood, e.g., mollusks *(Planorbis)*, insect larvae *(Chironomus)*, worms *(Arenicola)*. In other invertebrates the blood may be blue (Crustacea) or green (Sabellid worms), or there may be no respiratory pigment at all (most insects).—Trans.]

Let this suffice concerning the method of our inquiry, and let us now endeavor to describe the causes of all these things, particular as well as common, and, according to the principles laid down, we will begin with the first ones first.

↬   ↬   ↬

We may now make what is practically a fresh beginning. We will begin first of all with the things that come first in importance.

An animal can neither exist nor grow without food. Therefore in all living creatures of perfect formation there are two parts most necessary above all: one by which food is taken in and the other by which residues are eliminated. (Plants—which also we include under the head of living things—have, it is true, no place for the useless residue, but this is because their food, which they get out of the earth, is already concocted before it enters them, and instead of this residue they yield their fruit and seeds.) And in all creatures there is a third part intermediate between these indispensable two, and this is the seat of the source and principle of life. Plants, again, are so made as to remain in one place, and thus they do not exhibit a great variety of nonuniform substances; they have few actions to perform, and therefore but few organs are needed to perform them. For this reason we must consider plants and their formations separately. But with creatures that not only live but also have the power of sensation, the formations are more varied, and there is more diversity in some than in others, the greatest variety being found in those creatures which in addition to living have the capability of living the good life, as man has. Man is the only one of the animals known to us who has something of the divine in him, or if there are others, he has most. This is one reason why we ought to speak about man first, and another is that the shape of his external parts is better known than that of other animals. Another and obvious reason is that in man and in man alone do the natural parts appear in their natural situation: the upper part of man is placed toward the upper part of the universe. In other words, man is the only animal that stands upright.

## Content Questions

1. What does Aristotle mean by a "group" of animals? (23–24)

2. Why does Aristotle say that some attributes are more significant than others in describing groups? (23–24)

3. What does Aristotle mean by "essential attributes"? (23)

4. Why doesn't Aristotle want to treat the particular species separately? (24)

5. What does Aristotle mean by "generic" and "specific" attributes? (24)

6. On what basis does Aristotle set plants apart from animals? (25)

7. What does Aristotle mean when he says that formations are more varied in creatures with sensations? (25)

## Application Questions

1. How does the current biological basis for grouping organisms differ from Aristotle's?

2. How is Aristotle's understanding of plant nutrition different from the current view?

3. Aristotle states that "the parts of the body [exist] for the sake of those functions to which they are naturally adapted." (24) How does this view compare with our current understanding of the relationship between biological structure and function?

4. Within the context of our current understanding of biological evolution, how does the position held by human beings *(Homo sapiens)* compare with the position Aristotle gives our species?

## Discussion Questions

1. Why is it important for Aristotle to discover the causes of things as well as to describe them?

2. What does Aristotle mean in saying that a "philosophic spirit" is needed to discern the causes of things? (23)

3. In the following two quotations, does "nature" mean the same thing or different things: "it now remains to speak of animals and their nature" and "nature which fashioned them provides joys which cannot be measured"? (23)

4. Are groups of animals found in the world, or are they constructed by humans practicing scientific observation? Are there natural groups that preexist human classification of them?

5. What are some of the meanings of the word *cause?* Which meanings might Aristotle have had in mind when he speaks of cause?

6. What does it mean to say that "each of the parts of the body . . . is for the sake of some purpose"? (24) Is what Aristotle means by "purpose" the same as or different from what we mean when we say that the actions and intentions of a person have a purpose?

# Lucretius

Lucretius (98?–55? BCE) is a Latin poet and philosopher known for his single, multi-volume poetic work *De rerum natura (On the Nature of Things)*. However, virtually nothing is known about his life. Lucretius's importance to science lies in his synthesis of earlier Greek theories about life and matter, which he presents in a form intended to be pleasing as well as instructive. Specifically, *De rerum natura* helped preserve and popularize the scientific ideas of Democritus (460?–370? B.C.) and Epicurus (341–270 B.C.).

From these philosophers Lucretius derived his most important assertions: matter is composed of atoms; the human soul is material and mortal; and there are determinable, natural causes for earthly phenomena. Democritus was the first to articulate an atomic theory of the universe, and his ideas presaged later theories about the indestructibility of matter and the conservation of energy. Epicurus, who gave his name to a school of thought focused on the pleasures of earthly life, had the greatest influence on Lucretius. Epicurus's teachings about human mortality, the mechanistic nature of the universe, and the unimportance of the gods are strongly reflected in Lucretius's work.

# The Way Things Are

*(selection)*

Things which we see are sentient, we must now
Acknowledge, have their origin in things
Quite without sentience. Many things we know
Neither refute this nor give argument
Of any force against it, but they tend
Rather to give it credence and support.
They lead us by the hand, almost, to show
That animals are born from senseless stuff.
Haven't you seen live worms come crawling out
From a manure pile after heavy rain
Has drenched earth rotten? The same thing occurs
In the same way with all other things:
Rivers and leaves and forage are transformed
To animals, and animals to men,
And our own bodies oftentimes sustain
The strength of predatory beasts and birds.
Nature turns all the foods to living flesh
And out of this creates all sentient things;
In the same way she makes dry tinder break
In flame, thus turning everything to fire.

The most important point—I hope you see—
Consists in the arrangement of the atoms,
Their order, their reciprocal give and take.

Now what's all this that shakes and moves your mind,
Turns your perceptions hither and yon, forbids
Acceptance of belief that sentient things
Are born, or may be, out of things insentient?
Stones, wood, earth, all of them combined, can never
Produce a living sense, but bear in mind
I do not say that consciousness derives
All helter-skelter from all creative force,
From all the elements that make up matter.
I do insist that we must recognize
How small the primal atoms are that make
A sentient object; I insist again
That we must know their order, shape, design.
In wood, in clods, we see them not at all,
Yet, when the rain rots wood and crumbles clod,
The little worms are born. The reason is
That a new cause, in this case rain, has broken
The old arrangement, so disturbed the atoms
That new things have been brought to birth, and must be.
Now, those who argue sentient things are formed
From other sentient things, and these derive
From others still, would have to claim that atoms
Are somehow soft, and therefore must be mortal.
Sensation, as we know, inheres in things
Like sinews, bowels, veins, and all of these
Consist of soft and perishable stuff.
Well, even so—suppose such particles
Are everlasting; they would have to have
The feelings proper to one part alone
Or else be thought, each by itself, to be
The likeness of a fully sentient creature,
But parts can't have sensation by themselves;

They are dependent, rather, on each other.
Does a hand feel handlike, or have any feeling
When severed from the body? Why, of course not!
So that takes care of half of that dilemma,
Leaving us to conclude that atoms must
Be like ourselves to feel the selfsame things
That we do, share with us the sense of life.
But then how can we call them first beginnings
Or primal motes, exempt from ways of death,
If they are living creatures and, as such,
Mortal by definition? Resolve the paradox,
Concede them immortality: what then?
They'll join, they'll meet, they'll reproduce themselves,
Bring nothing forth except a beastly mob,
A common herd, as men and cattle do,
Or wilder animals. If, by chance, they lose
One bodily sensation and gain another,
What good the loss, the gain? We must resort
To the old argument: as eggs become
Chickens, as worms emerge from rotten earth
After a heavy rain, so sentience must
Be born out of insentience.

                                        Somebody now
Will argue that sensation can arise
From nonsensation; all it takes is change,
Something like birth, some such creative process.
The way to answer this is to make clear,
To prove, that birth and change of any kind
Alike depend upon the prior force
Of an—I'd almost say—deliberate union.

You just can't have sensation in a body
Before its creature's born, while all its matter,
The elements of its makeup, are dispersed
All over the world, in river, air, and earth,

As well as in earth's created growing things,
And have not come together, in a way
Suited to movement, brought to light and life
The all-perceiving, all-protective sense.

Sometimes some heavier blow than natural
Strikes down some living thing, confusing all
Its senses, whether of body or of mind.
Because of this, the arrangements of the atoms
Are sundered, all the vital movements blocked,
Until the shock, diffused through all the limbs,
Loosens the bonds of spirit from body, sends
That spirit, shattered and fragmented, forth
From every portal. What else can a blow
Succeed in doing, except shatter and break?
Sometimes less violent blows are struck, and then
The vital forces win, they win, they quell
The riots, they recall to normal ways,
Expel the dominance of the tyrant death
From lording it over the body, light again
The fires of sense, almost gone out. How else
Can consciousness come back from the very door
Of death, reverse its almost-finished journey?

Since pain exists when violence attacks
Material particles within the body,
Shaking them loose, troubling their residence
In flesh and bone, but, once they settle down
In peace again, a calm delight ensues—
From this we know that atoms cannot ache
With any pain or grief, cannot rejoice
With pleasure, since they have no elements
To be disturbed, upset, or restored
To profitable sweetness. They must be,
It has to follow, quite sensationless.

All animals have feelings, that we know,
But still, it makes no sense that every mote,
Every particular atom in their makeup
Has, in its essence, the same kind of feeling.
As for the human race, well, what about it?
Do those peculiar atoms, out of which
We are compounded, shake their sides with mirth,
Bedew their cheeks with tears? Are they smart enough
To talk about the way things mix together?
Do they investigate their own beginnings?
If they're composed of other elements,
And those of others still, and so on, and so on,
There's just no place where you can dare to stop.
As long as you keep saying that a thing
Is talking, laughing, being wise, I'll hound you
Until you stop insisting things are made
Of particles like themselves. That's foolishness,
Sheer lunacy. Surely, a man can laugh
And not be made of laughing particles;
He can be wise, talk sense, and reason well
Without one philosophical atom in him.
It is only proper, then, to realize
That every sentient creature which we see
Is made of particles with no sensation.

We all have come from heavenly seed; we all
Have the same father, and our mother earth
Receives from him the fertilizing showers.
So pregnant, she brings forth the shining grain,
The trees that make us glad, the race of men,
The generations of wild beasts, the food
By which they feed, increase, and multiply.
She is rightly called our mother, and the sons
Of earth return to earth, but any part
Sent down from heaven must ascend again,
Recalled to the high temples of the sky.
And death does not destroy the elements

35

Of matter, only breaks their combinations,
Joins them again in other ways to cause
Changes of form and color, to bestow
Consciousness, or withdraw it in a moment.
It makes a world of difference in what order
Atoms form combinations, how they are held,
And how they move together. Do not think
They hold forever in their keeping things
Which in our sight float over surfaces,
Are born, meet sudden death. In my own verse
It makes a difference in what ways I set
My words, my parts of speech. No two may be
Alike exactly, but they share alike
Many a letter common to them both.
The order makes the difference. So it is
With more material objects: change the order,
Motion, position, combination, shape,
And all will have to change.

When the male seed and female seed are fused,
One partner may be dominant, overpower
The other in a burst of violence.
If this should be the woman, then the child
Will have her features and her qualities.
The same thing happens if the man assumes
The role of dominance; the children then
Will be more like the father. When you see
Daughters and sons whose build and looks appear
The heritage of both alike, be sure
That in the act of procreative love
A parity existed, neither one
Being lord or slave, victim or conqueror.
At times, again, resemblances can skip
A generation or more and reproduce
A distant ancestor. The cause of this

Lies in the fact that hidden in all bodies
Are many first beginnings, primal motes
Passed on by the successive generations,
And out of these the goddess fashions forms
Whose lot is various, on a child bestows
Ancestral traits of voice, complexion, hair.
Sons may be like their mothers, and the girls
More like their fathers; this is natural,
Since all things born are made from double seed,
Although in mixed proportion; this is clear
Whatever the sex of the new generation.

~ ~ ~

                                    In the beginning, earth
Covered the hills and all the plains with green,
And flowering meadows shone in that rich color;
Then into air the various kinds of trees
Luxuriant in rivalry arose,
And just as feathers, hair, and bristles grow
First on the bodies of all beasts and birds,
So the new earth began with grass and brush
And then produced the mortal animals
Many and various. Creatures such as these
Could not have fallen from the sky, nor come
Out of the salt lagoons. They are earthborn,
And truly earth deserves her title *Mother*,
Since all things are created out of earth.
Even today creatures arisen from earth
Are shaped by rain and by the warmth of sun;
No wonder then that in the past when earth
And air were younger, more and larger things
Came into being, first the fowls of the air,
The various birds that break their shells in the spring,
As locusts do in summer when they leave
Their crinkled husks in search of livelihood.
In that time past earth was indeed prolific,

With fields profuse in teeming warmth and wet,
And so, wherever a suitable place was given,
Wombs multiplied, held to the earth by roots,
And as each embryo matured and broke
From fluid sac to air, nature would turn
In this direction pores or ducts of earth,
Channels from which a kind of milklike juice
Would issue, as a woman's breasts are filled
With the sweet milk after her child is born.
Earth gave her children food, the atmosphere
Such clothing as they needed, and the grass
A soft rich bed; that new and early world
Held no harsh cold, no superfluity
Of heat, no storm of wind; such forces also
Were in their infancy. . . .

                              In those old days
Many attempts were failures; many a kind
Could not survive; whatever we see today
Enjoying the breath of life must from the first
Have found protection in its character,
Its cunning, its courage, or its quickness,
Like the fox, the lion, and the antelope.
And there are many animals we guard
With our protection, for their usefulness:
The watchdog, beasts of burden, woolly sheep,
Horned cattle, all those eager refugees
Who left the wilderness in search of peace
And provender they had not planned to earn
But which we gave them for their services.
But those to which nature made no such gift,
Neither their own innate capacity
For living nor their usefulness to us,
For which, in turn, we'd give them food and safety—
Such creatures, in the shackles of their fate,
Lay easy victims of their predators
Till nature brought the species to extinction.

## Content Questions

1. Why does Lucretius consider it important that senseless stuff transforms into sentient things? (31–33)

2. According to Lucretius, how can rivers and leaves eventually provide food for predatory birds? (31) What does this process illustrate about the order of nature?

3. Why does rain-soaked wood produce worms, in Lucretius's account? (32)

4. What does Lucretius mean when he says that we all come from "heavenly seed"? (35–36) Does he believe that sentient creatures are all made of the same stuff? Why or why not?

5. How does Lucretius explain why some children look more like their fathers, while others look more like their mothers? (36–37)

6. According to Lucretius, why do traits sometimes skip a generation or more? (36–37)

7. What does Lucretius mean when he says that "all things born are made from double seed, / Although in mixed proportion"? (37)

## Application Questions

1. How similar is our current understanding of the atom to Lucretius's ideas about it? How does our understanding differ?

2. Lucretius asserts that "animals are born from senseless stuff" and that "many things we know / Neither refute this nor give argument / Of any force against it." (31) Give examples of scientific evidence collected since Lucretius's time that refute his assertion.

3. Compare Lucretius's view of heredity with our current view. What are some of the important observations we have made that have influenced the way in which we understand how traits are passed from one generation to the next?

## Discussion Questions

1. When Lucretius says that "the order makes the difference," is he implying that human consciousness is only an accidental product of the particular arrangement of atoms that constitutes a person? (36)

2. In Lucretius's explanation of heredity, how would you characterize the difference between his theory that the dominance of one parent in the act of procreation results in the child resembling that parent, and his theory that a goddess controls the presence of traits possessed by a child's ancestors, not its parents?

# Francis Bacon

Francis Bacon (1561–1626) is considered one of the Renaissance's most important thinkers. He reacted against the philosophy of scholasticism, which highly valued the authority of the church fathers as well as Aristotle, and was the leading proponent of the inductive method, in which general principles are derived from particular facts. Accordingly, Bacon insisted that learning must begin with close scrutiny of the real world. This close observation involved conducting experiments, gathering data, and striving to interpret the results objectively. Bacon expounded his ideas in a number of works, the most influential being *Novum Organum* (*New Instrument,* 1620), from which the following aphorisms are reprinted.

The son of a councilor to Queen Elizabeth I, Bacon was born into wealth and privilege. He attended Trinity College, Cambridge, at a time when such education was available to very few. When Bacon was eighteen, however, his father died and left him impoverished; his wealthy relatives did very little to help him. Bacon succeeded despite these setbacks, pursuing a legal career and winning a seat in the House of Commons when he was just twenty-three. During the reign of James I, Bacon eventually became lord chancellor. In yet another reversal of fortune, in 1621 Bacon was accused of having accepted a bribe while serving as a judge. He was tried and convicted. He lost both his fortune and his position at court, but continued to conduct research, write, and publish for another five years.

Flor.

# Novum Organum

*(selection)*

## I

Man, being the servant and interpreter of nature, can do and understand so much and so much only as he has observed in fact or in thought of the course of nature. Beyond this he neither knows anything nor can do anything.

## II

Neither the naked hand nor the understanding left to itself can effect much. It is by instruments and helps that the work is done, which are as much wanted for the understanding as for the hand. And as the instruments of the hand either give motion or guide it, so the instruments of the mind supply either suggestions for the understanding or cautions.

## III

Human knowledge and human power meet in one; for where the cause is not known the effect cannot be produced. Nature to be commanded must be obeyed; and that which in contemplation is as the cause is in operation as the rule.

IV

Toward the effecting of works, all that man can do is to put together or put asunder natural bodies. The rest is done by nature working within.

XCII

But by far the greatest obstacle to the progress of science and to the undertaking of new tasks and provinces therein is found in this—that men despair and think things impossible. For wise and serious men are wont in these matters to be altogether distrustful, considering with themselves the obscurity of nature, the shortness of life, the deceitfulness of the senses, the weakness of the judgment, the difficulty of experiment, and the like; and so supposing that in the revolution of time and of the ages of the world the sciences have their ebbs and flows; that at one season they grow and flourish, at another wither and decay, yet in such sort that when they have reached a certain point and condition they can advance no further. If therefore anyone believes or promises more, they think this comes of an ungoverned and unripened mind, and that such attempts have prosperous beginnings, become difficult as they go on, and end in confusion. Now since these are thoughts which naturally present themselves to men grave and of great judgment, we must take good heed that we be not led away by our love for a most fair and excellent object to relax or diminish the severity of our judgment. We must observe diligently what encouragement dawns upon us and from what quarter, and, putting aside the lighter breezes of hope, we must thoroughly sift and examine those which promise greater steadiness and constancy. Nay, and we must take state prudence too into our counsels, whose rule is to distrust, and to take the less favorable view of human affairs. I am now therefore to speak touching hope, especially as I am not a dealer in promises and wish neither to force nor to ensnare men's judgments, but to lead them by the hand with their goodwill. And though the strongest means of inspiring hope will be to bring men to particulars, especially to particulars digested and arranged in my Tables of Discovery (the subject partly of the second, but much more of the fourth part of my Instauration), since this is not merely the promise of the thing but the thing itself; nevertheless, that everything may be done with gentleness, I will proceed with my plan of preparing men's minds, of which preparation to give hope is no unimportant part. For without it the rest tends rather to make men sad (by giving them a worse and meaner opinion of things as they are than they now have, and making them more fully to feel and know the unhappiness of their own condition) than to induce any alacrity or to whet their industry in making trial. And therefore it is fit that I publish and set forth those conjectures of mine which make hope in this matter reasonable, just as Columbus did, before that wonderful voyage of his across the Atlantic, when he gave the reasons for his conviction that new lands and continents might be discovered besides those which were known before, which reasons, though rejected at first, were afterward made good by experience and were the causes and beginnings of great events.

## XCIV

Next comes a consideration of the greatest importance as an argument of hope; I mean that drawn from the errors of past time and of the ways hitherto trodden. For most excellent was the censure once passed upon a government that had been unwisely administered. "That which is the worst thing in reference to the past ought to be regarded as best for the future. For if you had done all that your duty demanded and yet your affairs were no better, you would not have even a hope left you that further improvement is possible. But now, when your misfortunes are owing, not to the force of circumstances, but to your own errors, you may hope that by dismissing or correcting these errors, a great change may be made for the better." In like manner, if during so long a course of years men had kept the true road for discovering and cultivating sciences and had yet been unable to make further progress therein, bold doubtless and rash would be the opinion that further progress is possible. But if the road itself has been mistaken and men's labor spent on unfit objects, it follows that the difficulty has its rise not in things themselves which are not in our power, but in the human understanding and the use and application thereof, which admits of remedy and medicine. It will be of great use therefore to set forth what these errors are. For as many impediments as there have been in times past from this cause, so many arguments are there of hope for the time to come. And although they have been partly touched before, I think fit here also, in plain and simple words, to represent them.

## XCV

Those who have handled sciences have been either men of experiment or men of dogmas. The men of experiment are like the ant, they only collect and use; the reasoners resemble spiders, who make cobwebs out of their own substance. But the bee takes a middle course: it gathers its material from the flowers of the garden and of the field, but transforms and digests it by a power of its own. Not unlike this is the true business of philosophy; for it neither relies solely or chiefly on the powers of the mind, nor does it take the matter which it gathers from natural history and mechanical experiments and lay it up in the memory whole, as it finds it, but lays it up in the understanding altered and digested. Therefore from a closer and purer league between these two faculties, the experimental and the rational (such as has never yet been made), much may be hoped.

## XCVI

We have as yet no natural philosophy that is pure; all is tainted and corrupted: in Aristotle's school by logic; in Plato's by natural theology; in the second school of Platonists, such as Proclus and others, by mathematics, which ought only to give definiteness to natural philosophy, not to generate or give it birth. From a natural philosophy pure and unmixed, better things are to be expected.

## XCVII

No one has yet been found so firm of mind and purpose as resolutely to compel himself to sweep away all theories and common notions, and to apply the understanding, thus made fair and even, to a fresh examination of particulars. Thus it happens that human knowledge, as we have it, is a mere medley and ill-digested mass, made up of much credulity and much accident, and also of the childish notions which we at first imbibed.

Now if anyone of ripe age, unimpaired senses, and well-purged mind apply himself anew to experience and particulars, better hopes may be entertained of that man. . . . In the meanwhile, as I have already said, there is no hope except in a new birth of science; that is, in raising it regularly up from experience and building it afresh, which no one (I think) will say has yet been done or thought of.

## XCVIII

Now for grounds of experience—since to experience we must come—we have as yet had either none or very weak ones; no search has been made to collect a store of particular observations sufficient either in number, or in kind, or in certainty, to inform the understanding, or in any way adequate. On the contrary, men of learning, but easy withal and idle, have taken for the construction or for the confirmation of their philosophy certain rumors and vague fames or airs of experience and allowed to these the weight of lawful evidence. And just as if some kingdom or state were to direct its counsels and affairs not by letters and reports from ambassadors and trustworthy messengers, but by the gossip of the streets, such exactly is the system of management introduced into philosophy with relation to experience. Nothing duly investigated, nothing verified, nothing counted, weighed, or measured is to be found in natural history, and what in observation is loose and vague is in information deceptive and treacherous. And if anyone thinks that this is a strange thing to say and something like an unjust complaint, seeing that Aristotle, himself so great a man and supported by the wealth of so great a king, has composed so accurate a history of animals—and that others with greater diligence, though less pretense, have made many additions, while others, again, have compiled copious histories and descriptions of metals, plants, and fossils—it seems that he does not rightly apprehend what it is that we are now about. For a natural history which is composed for its own sake is not like one that is collected to supply the understanding with information for the building up of philosophy. They differ in many ways, but especially in this: that the former contains the variety of natural species only and not experiments of the mechanical arts. For even as in the business of life a man's disposition and the secret workings of his mind and affections are better discovered when he is in trouble than at other times, so likewise the secrets of nature reveal themselves more readily under the vexations of art than when they go their own way. Good hopes may therefore be conceived of natural philosophy when natural history, which is the basis and foundation of it, has been drawn up on a better plan; but not till then.

## XCIX

Again, even in the great plenty of mechanical experiments, there is yet a great scarcity of those which are of most use for the information of the understanding. For the mechanic, not troubling himself with the investigation of truth, confines his attention to those things which bear upon his particular work and will not either raise his mind or stretch out his hand for anything else. But then only will there be good ground of hope for the further advance of knowledge when there shall be received and gathered together into natural history a variety of experiments which are of no use in themselves but simply serve to discover causes and axioms, which I call *Experimenta lucifera,* "experiments of light," to distinguish them from those which I call *fructifera,* experiments of "fruit."

Now experiments of this kind have one admirable property and condition: they never miss or fail. For since they are applied, not for the purpose of producing any particular effect, but only of discovering the natural cause of some effect, they answer the end equally well whichever way they turn out, for they settle the question.

## C

But not only is a greater abundance of experiments to be sought for and procured, and that too of a different kind from those hitherto tried, an entirely different method, order, and process for carrying on and advancing experience must also be introduced. For experience, when it wanders in its own track, is, as I have already remarked, mere groping in the dark and confounds men rather than instructs them. But when it shall proceed in accordance with a fixed law, in regular order, and without interruption, then may better things be hoped of knowledge.

## CII

Moreover, since there is so great a number and army of particulars and that army so scattered and dispersed as to distract and confound the understanding, little is to be hoped for from the skirmishings and slight attacks and desultory movements of the intellect, unless all the particulars which pertain to the subject of inquiry shall, by means of Tables of Discovery, apt, well arranged, and, as it were, animate, be drawn up and marshaled, and the mind be set to work upon the helps duly prepared and digested which these tables supply.

### CIII

But after this store of particulars has been set out duly and in order before our eyes, we are not to pass at once to the investigation and discovery of new particulars or works, or at any rate if we do so we must not stop there. For although I do not deny that when all the experiments of all the arts shall have been collected and digested and brought within one man's knowledge and judgment, the mere transferring of the experiments of one art to others may lead, by means of that experience which I term literate, to the discovery of many new things of service to the life and state of man, yet it is no great matter that can be hoped from that; but from the new light of axioms, which, having been educed from those particulars by a certain method and rule, shall in their turn point out the way again to new particulars, greater things may be looked for. For our road does not lie on a level, but ascends and descends; first ascending to axioms, then descending to works.

### CIV

The understanding must not, however, be allowed to jump and fly from particulars to axioms remote and of almost the highest generality (such as the first principles, as they are called, of arts and things) and, taking stand upon them as truths that cannot be shaken, proceed to prove and frame the middle axioms by reference to them, which has been the practice hitherto, the understanding being not only carried that way by a natural impulse but also by the use of syllogistic demonstration trained and inured to it. But then, and then only, may we hope well of the sciences when in a just scale of ascent and by successive steps not interrupted or broken, we rise from particulars to lesser axioms, and then to middle axioms, one above the other, and last of all to the most general. For the lowest axioms differ but slightly from bare experience, while the highest and most general (which we now have) are notional and abstract and without solidity. But the middle are the true and solid and living axioms, on which depend the affairs and fortunes of men, and above them again, last of all, those which are indeed the most general; such, I mean, as are not abstract, but of which those intermediate axioms are really limitations.

The understanding must not therefore be supplied with wings, but rather hung with weights, to keep it from leaping and flying. Now this has never yet been done; when it is done, we may entertain better hopes of the sciences.

### CV

In establishing axioms, another form of induction must be devised than has hitherto been employed, and it must be used for proving and discovering not first principles (as they are called) only, but also the lesser axioms, and the middle, and indeed all. For the induction which proceeds by simple enumeration is childish; its conclusions are precarious and exposed to peril from a contradictory instance, and it generally decides on too small a number of facts and on those only which are at hand. But the induction which is to be available for the discovery and demonstration of sciences and arts must analyze nature by proper rejections and exclusions, and then, after a sufficient number of negatives, come to a conclusion on the affirmative instances—which has not yet been done or even attempted, save only by Plato, who does indeed employ this form of induction to a certain extent for the purpose of discussing definitions and ideas. But in order to furnish this induction or demonstration well and duly for its work, very many things are to be provided which no mortal has yet thought of, insomuch that greater labor will have to be spent in it than has hitherto been spent on the syllogism. And this induction must be used not only to discover axioms, but also in the formation of notions. And it is in this induction that our chief hope lies.

### CVI

But in establishing axioms by this kind of induction, we must also examine and try whether the axiom so established be framed to the measure of those particulars only from which it is derived, or whether it be larger and wider. And if it be larger and wider, we must observe whether by indicating to us new particulars it confirm that wideness and largeness as by a collateral security, that we may not either stick fast in things already known or loosely grasp at shadows and abstract forms, not at things solid and realized in matter. And when this process shall have come into use, then at last shall we see the dawn of a solid hope.

## CVII

And here also should be remembered what was said above concerning the extending of the range of natural philosophy to take in the particular sciences and the referring or bringing back of the particular sciences to natural philosophy, that the branches of knowledge may not be severed and cut off from the stem. For without this the hope of progress will not be so good.

## Content Questions

1. What is the difference between "the instruments of the hand" and "the instruments of the mind"? (aphorism II)

2. Why does Bacon say that the "strongest means of inspiring hope [in the progress of science] will be to bring men to particulars, especially to particulars digested and arranged"? (aphorism XCII)

3. For Bacon, what is the relation between experience and experiment? (aphorisms XCIX, C)

4. What does Bacon mean by the term *middle axioms?* Why does he say that on them "depend the affairs and fortunes of men"? (aphorism CIV)

5. Why do the "experiments of light" that Bacon describes never miss or fail? (aphorism XCIX)

6. Why is curbing the imagination's flight important to the advancement of science, in Bacon's view? (aphorism CIV)

7. What does Bacon mean when he says that "it is in this induction that our chief hope lies"? (aphorism CV)

## Application Questions

1. In most current descriptions of experimental biology, a researcher formulates a question, makes observations, and then constructs a hypothesis as a tentative causal explanation. The researcher then conducts an experiment or experiments to test the hypothesis. How does this approach to the scientific method compare to Bacon's description of "experiments of light"? (aphorism XCIX)

2. In what fundamental ways does Bacon suggest that scientific inquiry differs from beliefs based on faith?

## Discussion Questions

1. Why is giving his readers hope for the advancement of science so important to Bacon?

2. Why will natural philosophy, when "pure and unmixed," contribute more to human understanding than what has gone before it? (aphorism XCVI)

3. Why is it vital, in Bacon's view, to "sweep away all theories and common notions" and look at particulars afresh? (aphorism XCVII)

# Charles Darwin

When Charles Darwin (1809–1882) published *On the Origin of Species* in 1859, articulating and supporting the theory of evolution in a way that could be understood by the general public, a long and bitter controversy ensued. Until the mid-nineteenth century, most scientists believed that the earth was only several thousand years old and that species of plants and animals had been separately created and were unchanging. But by the beginning of the nineteenth century, new ideas were fermenting about the earth's age and changes in species over time. The idea that humanity was descended from apes shook the religious faith of many and fired others to resist Darwin's theories fiercely. This mid-Victorian gentleman began a debate about human origins that continues today.

As a child and a young man, Darwin seemed extremely unlikely to cause such cataclysmic change. A mediocre student, he pursued medical training chiefly because his father and grandfather had been prominent physicians. Medicine failed to keep his interest, however, and he found watching surgery in an era before anesthesia unendurable. When Darwin rejected medicine, his father advised him to study for the ministry and, in 1831, he took a divinity degree from Cambridge University.

Darwin's life changed decisively when his science tutor at Cambridge, John Stevens Henslow, recommended that he accompany Captain Robert Fitzroy on his voyage of scientific exploration aboard the HMS *Beagle*. On this five-year trip, Darwin honed his powers of observation, formed his first original scientific theories, and became fascinated by the question of how species develop, which he would explore for the next twenty years. Darwin was strongly influenced by Sir Charles Lyell, whose *Principles of Geology* suggested that the earth was eons older than previously thought; in 1856, Darwin began to write about his own theory of evolution. He was spurred to publish his work when he read an essay by Alfred Russel Wallace that presented the same ideas, though without much supporting evidence. Painfully aware of the controversy his work would create, Darwin nevertheless published both *On the Origin of Species* and, in 1871, *The Descent of Man*. At his death in 1882, Darwin was buried in Westminster Abbey.

# Conclusion to
## *On the Origin of Species*

I have now recapitulated the chief facts and considerations which have thoroughly convinced me that species have changed, and are still slowly changing by the preservation and accumulation of successive slight favorable variations. Why, it may be asked, have all the most eminent living naturalists and geologists rejected this view of the mutability of species? It cannot be asserted that organic beings in a state of nature are subject to no variation; it cannot be proved that the amount of variation in the course of long ages is a limited quantity; no clear distinction has been, or can be, drawn between species and well-marked varieties. It cannot be maintained that species when inter-crossed are invariably sterile, and varieties invariably fertile, or that sterility is a special endowment and sign of creation. The belief that species were immutable productions was almost unavoidable as long as the history of the world was thought to be of short duration, and now that we have acquired some idea of the lapse of time, we are too apt to assume, without proof, that the geological record is so perfect that it would have afforded us plain evidence of the mutation of species, if they had undergone mutation.

But the chief cause of our natural unwillingness to admit that one species has given birth to other and distinct species is that we are always

*This selection is taken from* On the Origin of Species, *First Edition (1859), chapter 14, "Recapitulation and Conclusion."*

slow in admitting any great change of which we do not see the intermediate steps. The difficulty is the same as that felt by so many geologists, when Lyell first insisted that long lines of inland cliffs had been formed, and great valleys excavated, by the slow action of the coast waves. The mind cannot possibly grasp the full meaning of the term of a hundred million years; it cannot add up and perceive the full effects of many slight variations, accumulated during an almost infinite number of generations.

Although I am fully convinced of the truth of the views given in this volume under the form of an abstract, I by no means expect to convince experienced naturalists whose minds are stocked with a multitude of facts all viewed, during a long course of years, from a point of view directly opposite to mine. It is so easy to hide our ignorance under such expressions as the "plan of creation," "unity of design," etc., and to think that we give an explanation when we only restate a fact. Anyone whose disposition leads him to attach more weight to unexplained difficulties than to the explanation of a certain number of facts will certainly reject my theory. A few naturalists, endowed with much flexibility of mind and who have already begun to doubt on the immutability of species, may be influenced by this volume, but I look with confidence to the future, to young and rising naturalists, who will be able to view both sides of the question with impartiality. Whoever is led to believe that species are mutable will do good service by conscientiously expressing his conviction, for only thus can the load of prejudice by which this subject is overwhelmed be removed.

Several eminent naturalists have of late published their belief that a multitude of reputed species in each genus are not real species, but that other species are real, that is, have been independently created. This seems to me a strange conclusion to arrive at. They admit that a multitude of forms, which till lately they themselves thought were special creations, and which are still thus looked at by the majority of naturalists, and which consequently have every external characteristic feature of true species—they admit that these have been produced by variation, but they refuse to extend the same view to other and very slightly different forms. Nevertheless they do not pretend that they can define, or even conjecture, which are the created forms of life and which are those produced by secondary laws. They admit variation as a *vera causa* in one case; they arbitrarily reject it in another, without assigning any distinction in the two cases. The day will come when this will be given as a curious illustration of the blindness of preconceived opinion. These authors seem no more startled at a miraculous act of creation than at an ordinary birth. But do they really believe that at innumerable periods in the earth's history certain elemental atoms have been commanded suddenly to flash into living tissues? Do they believe that at each supposed act of creation one individual or many were produced? Were all the infinitely numerous kinds of animals and plants created as eggs or seed, or as full grown? And in the case of mammals, were they created bearing the false marks of nourishment from the mother's womb? Although naturalists very properly demand a full explanation of every difficulty from those who believe in the mutability of species, on their own side they ignore the whole subject of the first appearance of species in what they consider reverent silence.

It may be asked how far I extend the doctrine of the modification of species. The question is difficult to answer, because the more distinct the forms are which we may consider, by so much the arguments fall away in force. But some arguments of the greatest weight extend very far. All the members of whole classes can be connected together by chains of affinities, and all can be classified on the same principle, in groups subordinate to groups. Fossil remains sometimes tend to fill up very wide intervals between existing orders. Organs in a rudimentary condition plainly show that an early progenitor had the organ in a fully developed state, and this in some instances necessarily implies an enormous amount of modification in the descendants. Throughout whole classes various structures are formed on the same pattern, and at an embryonic age the species closely resemble each other. Therefore I cannot doubt that the theory of descent with modification embraces all the members of the same class. I believe that animals have descended from at most only four or five progenitors, and plants from an equal or lesser number.

Analogy would lead me one step further, namely, to the belief that all animals and plants have descended from some one prototype. But analogy may be a deceitful guide. Nevertheless all living things have much in common, in their chemical composition, their germinal vesicles, their cellular structure, and their laws of growth and reproduction. We see this even in so trifling a circumstance as that the same poison often similarly affects plants and animals or that the poison secreted by the gallfly produces monstrous growths on the wild rose or oak tree. Therefore I should infer from analogy that probably all the organic beings which have ever lived on this earth have descended from some one primordial form, into which life was first breathed.

When the views entertained in this volume on the origin of species, or when analogous views are generally admitted, we can dimly foresee that there will be a considerable revolution in natural history. Systematists will be able to pursue their labors as at present, but they will not be incessantly haunted by the shadowy doubt whether this or that form is in essence a species. This I feel sure, and I speak after experience, will be no slight relief. The endless disputes whether or not some fifty species of British brambles are true species will cease. Systematists will have only to decide (not that this will be easy) whether any form is sufficiently constant and distinct from other forms to be capable of definition and, if definable, whether the differences are sufficiently important to deserve a specific name. This latter point will become a far more essential consideration than it is at present, for differences, however slight, between any two forms, if not blended by intermediate gradations, are looked at by most naturalists as sufficient to raise both forms to the rank of species. Hereafter we shall be compelled to acknowledge that the only distinction between species and well-marked varieties is that the latter are known, or believed, to be connected at the present day by intermediate gradations whereas species were formerly thus connected. Hence, without quite rejecting the consideration of the present existence of intermediate gradations between any two forms, we shall be led to weigh more carefully and to value higher the actual amount of difference between them. It is quite possible that forms now generally acknowledged to be merely varieties may hereafter be thought worthy of specific names, as with the primrose and cowslip, and in this case scientific and common language will come into accordance. In short, we shall have to treat species in the same manner as those naturalists treat genera, who admit that genera are merely artificial combinations made for convenience. This may not be a cheering prospect, but we shall at least be freed from the vain search for the undiscovered and undiscoverable essence of the term *species.*

The other and more general departments of natural history will rise greatly in interest. The terms used by naturalists of affinity, relationship, community of type, paternity, morphology, adaptive characters, rudimentary and aborted organs, etc., will cease to be metaphorical, and will have a plain signification. When we no longer look at an organic being as a savage looks at a ship, as at something wholly beyond his comprehension; when we regard every production of nature as one which has had a history; when we contemplate every complex structure and instinct as the summing up of many contrivances, each useful to the possessor, nearly in the same way as when we look at any great mechanical invention as the summing up of the labor, the experience, the reason, and even the blunders of numerous workmen; when we thus view each organic being, how far more interesting, I speak from experience, will the study of natural history become!

A grand and almost untrodden field of inquiry will be opened on the causes and laws of variation, on correlation of growth, on the effects of use and disuse, on the direct action of external conditions, and so forth. The study of domestic productions will rise immensely in value. A new variety raised by man will be a far more important and interesting subject for study than one more species added to the infinitude of already recorded species. Our classifications will come to be, as far as they can be so made, genealogies and will then truly give what may be called the plan of creation. The rules for classifying will no doubt become simpler when we have a definite object in view. We possess no pedigrees or armorial bearings, and we have to discover and trace the many diverging lines of descent in our natural genealogies, by characters of any kind which have long been inherited. Rudimentary organs will speak infallibly with respect to the nature of long-lost structures. Species and groups of species which are called aberrant, and which may fancifully be called living fossils, will aid us in forming a picture of the ancient forms of life. Embryology will reveal to us the structure, in some degree obscured, of the prototypes of each great class.

When we can feel assured that all the individuals of the same species, and all the closely allied species of most genera, have within a not-very-remote period descended from one parent and have migrated from some one birthplace, and when we better know the many means of migration, then, by the light which geology now throws, and will continue to throw, on former changes of climate and of the level of the land, we shall surely be enabled to trace in an admirable manner the former migrations of the inhabitants of the whole world. Even at present, by comparing the differences of the inhabitants of the sea on the opposite sides of a continent, and the nature of the various inhabitants of that continent in relation to their apparent means of immigration, some light can be thrown on ancient geography.

The noble science of geology loses glory from the extreme imperfection of the record. The crust of the earth with its embedded remains must not be looked at as a well-filled museum, but as a poor collection made at hazard and at rare intervals. The accumulation of each great fossiliferous formation will be recognized as having depended on an unusual concurrence of circumstances, and the blank intervals between the successive stages as having been of vast duration. But we shall be able to gauge with some security the duration of these intervals by a comparison of the preceding and succeeding organic forms. We must be cautious in attempting to correlate as strictly contemporaneous two formations which include few identical species by the general succession of their forms of life. As species are produced and exterminated by slowly acting and still existing causes, and not by miraculous acts of creation and by catastrophes, and as the most important of all causes of organic change is one which is almost independent of altered and perhaps suddenly altered physical conditions, namely, the mutual relation of organism to organism—the improvement of one being entailing the improvement or the extermination of others—it follows that the amount of organic change in the fossils of consecutive formations probably serves as a fair measure of the lapse of actual time. A number of species, however, keeping in a body might remain for a long period unchanged, while within this same period, several of these species, by migrating into new countries and coming into competition with foreign associates, might become modified, so that we must not overrate the accuracy of organic change as a measure of time. During early periods of the earth's history, when the forms of life were probably fewer and simpler, the rate of change was probably slower, and at the first dawn of life, when very few forms of the simplest structure existed, the rate of change may have been slow in an extreme degree. The whole history of the world, as at present known, although of a length quite incomprehensible by us, will hereafter be recognized as a mere fragment of time, compared with the ages which have elapsed since the first creature, the progenitor of innumerable extinct and living descendants, was created.

In the distant future I see open fields for far more important researches. Psychology will be based on a new foundation, that of the necessary acquirement of each mental power and capacity by gradation. Light will be thrown on the origin of man and his history.

Authors of the highest eminence seem to be fully satisfied with the view that each species has been independently created. To my mind it accords better with what we know of the laws impressed on matter by the Creator, that the production and extinction of the past and present inhabitants of the world should have been due to secondary causes, like those determining the birth and death of the individual. When I view all beings not as special creations, but as the lineal descendants of some few beings which lived long before the first bed of the Silurian system was deposited, they seem to me to become ennobled. Judging from the past, we may safely infer that not one living species will transmit its unaltered likeness to a distant futurity. And of the species now living very few will transmit progeny of any kind to a far distant futurity, for the manner in which all organic beings are grouped shows that the greater number of species of each genus, and all the species of many genera, have left no descendants, but have become utterly extinct. We can so far take a prophetic glance into futurity as to foretell that it will be the common and widely spread species, belonging to the larger and dominant groups, which will ultimately prevail and procreate new and dominant species. As all the living forms of life are the lineal descendants of those which lived long before the Silurian epoch, we may feel certain that the ordinary succession by generation has never once been broken and that no cataclysm has desolated the whole world. Hence we may look with some confidence to a secure future of equally inappreciable length. And as natural selection works solely by and for the good of each being, all corporeal and mental endowments will tend to progress toward perfection.

It is interesting to contemplate an entangled bank, clothed with many plants of many kinds, with birds singing on the bushes, with various insects flitting about, and with worms crawling through the damp earth, and to reflect that these elaborately constructed forms, so different from each other and dependent on each other in so complex a manner, have all been produced by laws acting around us. These laws, taken in the largest sense, being growth with reproduction; inheritance, which is almost implied by reproduction; variability from the indirect and direct action of the external conditions of life, and from use and disuse; a ratio of increase so high as to lead to a struggle for life, and as a consequence to natural selection, entailing divergence of character and the extinction of less-improved forms. Thus, from the war of nature, from famine and death, the most exalted object which we are capable of conceiving, namely, the production of the higher animals, directly follows. There is grandeur in this view of life, with its several powers, having been originally breathed into a few forms or into one and that, while this planet has gone cycling on according to the fixed law of gravity, from so simple a beginning endless forms most beautiful and most wonderful have been, and are being, evolved.

## Content Questions

1. According to Darwin, what are the two main reasons that most naturalists tended to believe that species were immutable? (57–58)

2. In Darwin's view, why are so many experienced naturalists likely to resist the theory of evolution? Why are younger naturalists likely to embrace it? (58)

3. What reasons does Darwin give for considering false the distinction between "real" (separately created) and "not real" species? (58–59)

4. What is the only distinction between species and well-marked varieties, according to Darwin? (60)

5. What are "the laws acting around us" that have produced life on Earth, in Darwin's account? (63)

## Application Questions

1. As evidence that "all animals and plants have descended from some one prototype," Darwin asserts that "all living things have much in common, in their chemical composition, their germinal vesicles, their cellular structure, and their laws of growth and reproduction." (59) What are some specific examples of these similarities, especially ones that have been discovered since 1859?

2. What does Darwin mean when he states that "natural selection works solely by and for the good of each being" and that "all corporeal and mental endowments will tend to progress toward perfection"? (63) Would you modify this claim, based on your knowledge of evolutionary process?

## Discussion Questions

1. Why does evolution, as Darwin puts it, make the study of natural history "far more interesting"? (60–61)

2. Darwin concludes that "from the war of nature, from famine and death, the most exalted object which we are capable of conceiving, namely, the production of the higher animals, directly follows." What point about the origins of humanity is he making here? What does he mean when he says that "there is grandeur in this view of life"? (63)

# Struggle for Existence

Before entering on the subject of this chapter, I must make a few preliminary remarks to show how the struggle for existence bears on natural selection. It has been seen in the last chapter that amongst organic beings in a state of nature there is some individual variability: indeed I am not aware that this has ever been disputed. It is immaterial for us whether a multitude of doubtful forms be called species or subspecies or varieties—what rank, for instance, the two or three hundred doubtful forms of British plants are entitled to hold, if the existence of any well-marked varieties be admitted. But the mere existence of individual variability and of some few well-marked varieties, though necessary as the foundation for the work, helps us but little in understanding how species arise in nature. How have all those exquisite adaptations of one part of the organization to another part, and to the conditions of life, and of one organic being to another being, been perfected? We see these beautiful coadaptations most plainly in the woodpecker and the mistletoe, and only a little less plainly in the humblest parasite which clings to the hairs of a quadruped or feathers of a bird, in the structure of the beetle which dives through the water, in the plumed seed which is wafted by the gentlest

*This selection is taken from* The Origin of Species by Means of Natural Selection, or The Preservation of Favored Races in the Struggle for Life, *Sixth Edition (1872), chapter 3, "Struggle for Existence."*

breeze; in short, we see beautiful adaptations everywhere and in every part of the organic world.

Again, it may be asked, how is it that varieties, which I have called incipient species, become ultimately converted into good and distinct species which in most cases obviously differ from each other far more than do the varieties of the same species? How do those groups of species, which constitute what are called distinct genera and which differ from each other more than do the species of the same genus, arise? All these results, as we shall more fully see in the next chapter, follow from the struggle for life. Owing to this struggle, variations, however slight and from whatever cause proceeding, if they are in any degree profitable to the individuals of a species in their infinitely complex relations to other organic beings and to their physical conditions of life, will tend to the preservation of such individuals and will generally be inherited by the offspring. The offspring, also, will thus have a better chance of surviving, for, of the many individuals of any species which are periodically born, but a small number can survive. I have called this principle, by which each slight variation, if useful, is preserved, by the term *natural selection* in order to mark its relation to man's power of selection. But the expression often used by Mr. Herbert Spencer of the *survival of the fittest* is more accurate and is sometimes equally convenient. We have seen that man by selection can certainly produce great results and can adapt organic beings to his own uses through the accumulation of slight but useful variations given to him by the hand of nature. But natural selection, as we shall hereafter see, is a power incessantly ready for action and is as immeasurably superior to man's feeble efforts as the works of nature are to those of art.

## Content Questions

1. What are *coadaptations,* and why does Darwin consider them so important to the theory of natural selection? (65)

2. How does Darwin answer the question of how, over time, varieties of plants and animals become distinct species? (66)

3. Based on this selection, how would you define the terms *natural selection* and *survival of the fittest?*

## Application Questions

Darwin writes that "owing to this struggle, variations, however slight and from whatever cause proceeding, if they are in any degree profitable to the individuals of a species . . . will tend to the preservation of such individuals and will generally be inherited by the offspring." (66)

1. Darwin was unaware of the sources of the variations to which he refers. What are the sources of genetic variation known to us today?

2. In general, from what we know today, what kinds of variations can be inherited as Darwin suggests? What kinds of variations cannot be inherited? Give examples of each.

## Discussion Question

What does Darwin mean when he says that "natural selection . . . is a power incessantly ready for action and is as immeasurably superior to man's feeble efforts as the works of nature are to those of art"? (66)

# The Descent of Man

*(selection)*

## Introduction

In consequence of the views now adopted by most naturalists and which will ultimately, as in every other case, be followed by others who are not scientific, I have been led to put together my notes, so as to see how far the general conclusions arrived at in my former works were applicable to man. This seemed all the more desirable, as I had never deliberately applied these views to a species taken singly. When we confine our attention to any one form, we are deprived of the weighty arguments derived from the nature of the affinities which connect together whole groups of organisms—their geographical distribution in past and present times, and their geological succession. The homological structure, embryological development, and rudimentary organs of a species remain to be considered, whether it be man or any other animal to which our attention may be directed; but these great classes of facts afford, as it appears to me, ample and conclusive evidence in favor of the principle of gradual evolution. The strong support derived from the other arguments should, however, always be kept before the mind.

The sole object of this work is to consider, firstly, whether man, like every other species, is descended from some preexisting form; secondly, the manner of his development; and thirdly, the value of the differences between the so-called races of man. . . .

This work contains hardly any original facts in regard to man, but as the conclusions at which I arrived, after drawing up a rough draft, appeared to

*This selection is taken from the introduction and chapter 1, "The Evidence of the Descent of Man from Some Lower Form."*

me interesting, I thought that they might interest others. It has often and confidently been asserted that man's origin can never be known, but ignorance more frequently begets confidence than does knowledge: it is those who know little, and not those who know much, who so positively assert that this or that problem will never be solved by science. The conclusion that man is the codescendant with other species of some ancient, lower, and extinct form is not in any degree new. Lamarck long ago came to this conclusion, which has lately been maintained by several eminent naturalists and philosophers. . . .

He who wishes to decide whether man is the modified descendant of some preexisting form would probably first inquire whether man varies, however slightly, in bodily structure and in mental faculties and, if so, whether the variations are transmitted to his offspring in accordance with the laws which prevail with the lower animals. Again, are the variations the result, as far as our ignorance permits us to judge, of the same general causes, and are they governed by the same general laws, as in the case of other organisms, for instance, by correlation, the inherited effects of use and disuse, etc.? Is man subject to similar malconformations, the result of arrested development, of reduplication of parts, etc., and does he display in any of his anomalies reversion to some former and ancient type of structure? It might also naturally be inquired whether man, like so many other animals, has given rise to varieties and subraces, differing but slightly from each other, or to races differing so much that they must be classed as doubtful species? How are such races distributed over the world, and how, when crossed, do they react on each other in the first and succeeding generations? And so with many other points.

The inquirer would next come to the important point, whether man tends to increase at so rapid a rate as to lead to occasional severe struggles for existence and consequently to beneficial variations, whether in body or mind, being preserved, and injurious ones eliminated. Do the races or species of men, whichever term may be applied, encroach on and replace one another so that some finally become extinct? We shall see that all these questions, as indeed is obvious in respect to most of them, must be answered in the affirmative, in the same manner as with the lower animals.

But the several considerations just referred to may be conveniently deferred for a time, and we will first see how far the bodily structure of man shows traces, more or less plain, of his descent from some lower form. . . .

## The Bodily Structure of Man

It is notorious that man is constructed on the same general type or model as other mammals. All the bones in his skeleton can be compared with corresponding bones in a monkey, bat, or seal. So it is with his muscles, nerves, blood vessels, and internal viscera. The brain, the most important of all the organs, follows the same law, as shown by Huxley and other anatomists. Bischoff, who is a hostile witness, admits that every chief fissure and fold in the brain of man has its analogy in that of the orang, but he adds that at no period of development do their brains perfectly agree; nor could perfect agreement be expected, for otherwise their mental powers would have been the same. . . . But it would be superfluous here to give further details on the correspondence between man and the higher mammals in the structure of the brain and all other parts of the body.

It may, however, be worthwhile to specify a few points, not directly or obviously connected with structure, by which this correspondence or relationship is well shown.

Man is liable to receive from the lower animals, and to communicate to them, certain diseases, as hydrophobia, variola, the glanders, syphilis, cholera, herpes, etc., and this fact proves the close similarity[1] of their tissues and blood, both in minute structure and composition, far more plainly than does their comparison under the best microscope or by the aid of the best chemical analysis. Monkeys are liable to many of the same noncontagious diseases as we are; thus Rengger, who carefully observed for a long time the *Cebus azarae* in its native land, found it liable to catarrh, with the usual symptoms, and which, when often recurrent, led to consumption. These monkeys suffered also from apoplexy, inflammation of the bowels,

---

1. A reviewer has criticized ("British Quarterly Review," Oct. 1, 1871, p. 472) what I have here said with much severity and contempt, but as I do not use the term *identity*, I cannot see that I am greatly in error. There appears to me a strong analogy between the same infection or contagion producing the same result, or one closely similar, in two distinct animals, and the testing of two distinct fluids by the same chemical reagent.

and cataract in the eye. The younger ones when shedding their milk teeth often died from fever. Medicines produced the same effect on them as on us. Many kinds of monkeys have a strong taste for tea, coffee, and spirituous liquors; they will also, as I have myself seen, smoke tobacco with pleasure.[2] Brehm asserts that the natives of northeastern Africa catch the wild baboons by exposing vessels with strong beer, by which they are made drunk. He has seen some of these animals, which he kept in confinement, in this state, and he gives a laughable account of their behavior and strange grimaces. On the following morning they were very cross and dismal; they held their aching heads with both hands and wore a most pitiable expression; when beer or wine was offered them, they turned away with disgust, but relished the juices of lemons. An American monkey, an Ateles, after getting drunk on brandy, would never touch it again and, thus, was wiser than many men. These trifling facts prove how similar the nerves of taste must be in monkeys and man, and how similarly their whole nervous system is affected.

Man is infested with internal parasites, sometimes causing fatal effects, and is plagued by external parasites, all of which belong to the same genera or families as those infesting other mammals, and in the case of scabies to the same species. Man is subject, like other mammals, birds, and even insects, to that mysterious law which causes certain normal processes, such as gestation as well as the maturation and duration of various diseases, to follow lunar periods. His wounds are repaired by the same process of healing, and the stumps left after the amputation of his limbs, especially during an embryonic period, occasionally possess some power of regeneration, as in the lowest animals.

The whole process of that most important function, the reproduction of the species, is strikingly the same in all mammals, from the first act of courtship by the male to the birth and nurturing of the young. Monkeys are born in almost as helpless a condition as our own infants, and in certain genera the young differ fully as much in appearance from the adults as do our children from their full-grown parents. It has been urged by some

2. The same tastes are common to some animals much lower in the scale. Mr. A. Nicols informs me that he kept in Queensland, in Australia, three individuals of the *Phaseolarctus cinereus* and that, without having been taught in any way, they acquired a strong taste for rum and for smoking tobacco.

writers as an important distinction that with man the young arrive at maturity at a much later age than with any other animal; but if we look to the races of mankind which inhabit tropical countries, the difference is not great, for the orang is believed not to be adult till the age of from ten to fifteen years. Man differs from woman in size, bodily strength, hairiness, etc., as well as in mind, in the same manner as do the two sexes of many mammals. So that the correspondence in general structure, in the minute structure of the tissues, in chemical composition and in constitution, between man and the higher animals, especially the anthropomorphous apes, is extremely close.

## Embryonic Development

Man is developed from an ovule, about a 125th of an inch in diameter, which differs in no respect from the ovules of other animals. The embryo itself at a very early period can hardly be distinguished from that of other members of the vertebrate kingdom. At this period the arteries run in arch-like branches, as if to carry the blood to branchiae which are not present in the higher vertebrate, though the slits on the sides of the neck still remain . . . marking their former position. At a somewhat later period, when the extremities are developed, "the feet of lizards and mammals," as the illustrious Von Baer remarks, "the wings and feet of birds, no less than the hands and feet of man, all arise from the same fundamental form." It is, says Prof. Huxley, quite in the later stages of development that the young human being presents marked differences from the young ape, while the latter departs as much from the dog in its developments as the man does. Startling as this last assertion may appear to be, it is demonstrably true. . . .

After the foregoing statements made by such high authorities, it would be superfluous on my part to give a number of borrowed details, showing that the embryo of man closely resembles that of other mammals. It may, however, be added, that the human embryo likewise resembles certain low forms when adult in various points of structure. For instance, the heart at first exists as a simple pulsating vessel, the excreta are voided through a cloacal passage, and the os coccyx projects like a true tail, "extending considerably beyond the rudimentary legs." In the embryos of all air-breathing vertebrates, certain glands, called the corpora Wolffiana, correspond with, and act like the kidneys of mature fishes. Even at a later embryonic period, some striking resemblances between man and the lower animals may be observed. Bischoff says "that the convolutions of the brain in a human fetus at the end of the seventh month reach about the same stage of development as in a baboon when adult." The great toe, as Professor Owen remarks, "which forms the fulcrum when standing or walking, is perhaps the most characteristic peculiarity in the human structure," but in an embryo, about an inch in length, Prof. Wyman found "that the great toe was shorter than the others and, instead of being parallel to them, projected at an angle from the side of the foot, thus corresponding with the permanent condition of this part in the quadrumana." I will conclude with a quotation from Huxley, who after asking, Does man originate in a different way from a dog, bird, frog, or fish? says, "The reply is not doubtful for a moment, without question, the mode of origin and the early stages of the development of man are identical with those of the animals immediately below him in the scale: without a doubt in these respects, he is far nearer to apes than the apes are to the dog."

## Rudiments

This subject, though not intrinsically more important than the two last, will for several reasons be treated here more fully. Not one of the higher animals can be named which does not bear some part in a rudimentary condition, and man forms no exception to the rule. . . .

Rudiments of various muscles have been observed in many parts of the human body, and not a few muscles which are regularly present in some of the lower animals can occasionally be detected in man in a greatly reduced condition. Everyone must have noticed the power which many animals, especially horses, possess of moving or twitching their skin, and this is effected by the *panniculus carnosus*. Remnants of this muscle in an efficient state are found in various parts of our bodies; for instance, the muscle on the forehead, by which the eyebrows are raised. . . .

Some few persons have the power of contracting the superficial muscles on their scalps, and these muscles are in a variable and partially rudimentary condition. M. A. de Candolle has communicated to me a curious instance of the long-continued persistence or inheritance of this power as well as of its unusual development. He knows a family in which one member, the present head of the family, could, when a youth, pitch several heavy books from his head by the movement of the scalp alone, and he won wagers by performing this feat. His father, uncle, grandfather, and his three children possess the same power to the same unusual degree. . . .

The extrinsic muscles which serve to move the external ear and the intrinsic muscles which move the different parts are in a rudimentary condition in man, and they all belong to the system of the *panniculus;* they are also variable in development, or at least in function. I have seen one man who could draw the whole ear forward; other men can draw it upward; another who could draw it backward, and from what one of these persons told me, it is probable that most of us, by often touching our ears, and thus directing our attention toward them, could recover some power of movement by repeated trials. The power of erecting and directing the shell of the ears to the various points of the compass is no doubt of the highest service to many animals as they thus perceive the direction of danger; but I have never heard, on sufficient evidence, of a man who possessed this power, the one which might be of use to him. . . .

The sense of smell is of the highest importance to the greater number of mammals—to some, as the ruminants, in warning them of danger; to others, as the carnivora, in finding their prey; to others again, as the wild boar, for both purposes combined. But the sense of smell is of extremely slight service, if any, even to the dark-colored races of men, in whom it is much more highly developed than in the white and civilized races.[3] Nevertheless it does not warn them of danger nor guide them to their food, nor does it prevent the Eskimos from sleeping in the most fetid atmosphere nor many savages from eating half-putrid meat. In Europeans the power differs greatly in different individuals as I am assured by an eminent naturalist who possesses this sense highly developed and who has attended to the subject. Those who believe in the principle of gradual evolution will not readily admit that the sense of smell in its present state was originally

3. The account given by Humboldt of the power of smell possessed by the natives of South America is well known and has been confirmed by others. M. Houzeau ("Études sur les Facultés Mentales," etc., tom. i., 1872, p. 91) asserts that he repeatedly made experiments and proved that Negroes and Indians could recognize persons in the dark by their odor. Dr. W. Ogle has made some curious observations on the connection between the power of smell and the coloring matter of the membrane of the olfactory region as well as of the skin of the body. I have, therefore, spoken in the text of the dark-colored races having a finer sense of smell than the white races. . . .

acquired by man as he now exists. He inherits the power in an enfeebled and so far rudimentary condition from some early progenitor to whom it was highly serviceable and by whom it was continually used. In those animals which have this sense highly developed, such as dogs and horses, the recollection of persons and of places is strongly associated with their odor, and we can thus perhaps understand how it is, as Dr. Maudsley has truly remarked, that the sense of smell in man "is singularly effective in recalling vividly the ideas and images of forgotten scenes and places."

Man differs conspicuously from all the other Primates in being almost naked. But a few short straggling hairs are found over the greater part of the body in the man, and fine down on that of a woman. The different races differ much in hairiness, and in the individuals of the same race the hairs are highly variable, not only in abundance, but likewise in position: thus in some Europeans the shoulders are quite naked, while in others they bear thick tufts of hair. There can be little doubt that the hairs thus scattered over the body are the rudiments of the uniform hairy coat of the lower animals. . . .

It appears as if the posterior molar, or wisdom teeth, were tending to become rudimentary in the more civilized races of man. These teeth are rather smaller than the other molars, as is likewise the case with the corresponding teeth in the chimpanzee and orang, and they have only two separate fangs. They do not cut through the gums till about the seventeenth year, and I have been assured that they are much more liable to decay and are earlier lost than the other teeth; but this is denied by some eminent dentists. They are also much more liable to vary, both in structure and in the period of their development, than the other teeth. . . .

With respect to the alimentary canal, I have met with an account of only a single rudiment, namely the vermiform appendage[4] of the cecum. The cecum is a branch, or diverticulum, of the intestine, ending in a cul-de-sac, and is extremely long in many of the lower vegetable-feeding mammals. In the marsupial koala it is actually more than thrice as long as the whole body. It is sometimes produced into a long, gradually tapering point and is sometimes constricted in parts. It appears as if, in consequence of changed diet or habits, the cecum had become much shortened in various animals, the vermiform appendage being left as a rudiment of the shortened part.

4. [*vermiform appendage:* appendix.]

That this appendage is a rudiment we may infer from its small size and from the evidence which Prof. Canestrini has collected of its variability in man. It is occasionally quite absent, or again is largely developed. The passage is sometimes completely closed for half or two-thirds of its length, with the terminal part consisting of a flattened solid expansion. In the orang this appendage is long and convoluted; in man it arises from the end of the short cecum, and is commonly from four to five inches in length, being only about a third of an inch in diameter. Not only is it useless, but it is sometimes the cause of death, of which fact I have lately heard two instances; this is due to small hard bodies, such as seeds, entering the passage and causing inflammation. . . .

In man, the os coccyx, together with certain other vertebrae hereafter to be described, though functionless as a tail, plainly represents this part in other vertebrate animals. At an early embryonic period it is free, and projects beyond the lower extremities; as may be seen in the drawing . . . of a human embryo. Even after birth it has been known, in certain rare and anomalous cases, to form a small external rudiment of a tail. . . .

The bearing of the three great classes of facts now given is unmistakable. But it would be superfluous fully to recapitulate the line of argument given in detail in my *Origin of Species*. The homological construction of the whole frame in the members of the same class is intelligible if we admit their descent from a common progenitor, together with their subsequent adaptation to diversified conditions. On any other view, the similarity of pattern between the hand of a man or monkey, the foot of a horse, the flipper of a seal, the wing of a bat, etc., is utterly inexplicable. It is no scientific explanation to assert that they have all been formed on the same ideal plan. With respect to development, we can clearly understand, on the principle of variation supervening at a rather late embryonic period and being inherited at a corresponding period, how it is that the embryos of wonderfully different forms should still retain, more or less perfectly, the structure of their common progenitor. No other explanation has ever been given of the marvelous fact that the embryos of a man, dog, seal, bat, reptile, etc., can at first hardly be distinguished from each other. In order to understand the existence of rudimentary organs, we have only to suppose that a former progenitor possessed the parts in question in a perfect state and that under changed habits of life they became greatly reduced, either from simple disuse or through the natural selection of those individuals which were least encumbered with a superfluous part, aided by the other means previously indicated.

Thus we can understand how it has come to pass that man and all other vertebrate animals have been constructed on the same general model, why they pass through the same early stages of development, and why they retain certain rudiments in common. Consequently we ought frankly to admit their community of descent; to take any other view is to admit that our own structure, and that of all the animals around us, is a mere snare laid to entrap our judgment. This conclusion is greatly strengthened if we look to the members of the whole animal series and consider the evidence derived from their affinities or classification, their geographical distribution, and geological succession. It is only our natural prejudice and that arrogance which made our forefathers declare that they were descended from demigods which leads us to demur to this conclusion. But the time will before long come when it will be thought wonderful that naturalists who were well acquainted with the comparative structure and development of man and other mammals should have believed that each was the work of a separate act of creation.

## Content Questions

1. What three types of evidence does Darwin emphasize, and what does he assert they will prove? (68)

2. How does Darwin answer the question of whether human races differ only slightly from each other or are so distinct as to be "doubtful species"? (69–70)

3. According to Darwin, what do the similarities between illnesses and reactions to liquor in monkeys and humans prove? (71)

4. What point is Darwin making when he discusses the ability of the members of a particular family to contract their scalp muscles? Why is this point important to his argument? (73–74)

5. Why does Darwin believe that that the human sense of smell has been inherited in "an enfeebled . . . condition"? (75)

6. According to Darwin, what does the uselessness of the wisdom teeth and appendix illustrate about humankind's descent from a lower form? (75–76)

## Application Questions

1. Darwin provides many examples of homologous similarities between humans and other animals. What is the definition of a homologous similarity? Explain the difference between homologous and analogous similarities. What are the potential problems that arise for the evolutionary biologist if this distinction is not made correctly?

2. Since the publication of *The Descent of Man,* additional evidence has been collected to support the idea that humans have evolved from an apelike ancestor. Describe some of this evidence.

## Discussion Questions

1. In Darwin's view, why is evolution the only tenable scientific explanation for the facts he presents? (76–77)

2. Darwin states that ignorance is more likely than knowledge to make someone assert that humankind's origin will never be known. (69) Why might this be so?

3. Analyze the conclusion of this excerpt, in which Darwin asserts that evolution is the only intellectually satisfying way to explain the similarities between humans and other animals. How convincing is Darwin's case for this conclusion?

# Natural Selection

We have now seen that man is variable in body and mind, and that the variations are induced, either directly or indirectly, by the same general causes and obey the same general laws as with the lower animals. Man has spread widely over the face of the earth and must have been exposed during his incessant migration to the most diversified conditions. The inhabitants of Tierra del Fuego, the Cape of Good Hope, and Tasmania in the one hemisphere and of the Arctic regions in the other must have passed through many climates and changed their habits many times before they reached their present homes. The early progenitors of man must also have tended, like all other animals, to have increased beyond their means of subsistence; they must, therefore, occasionally have been exposed to a struggle for existence and consequently to the rigid law of natural selection. Beneficial variations of all kinds will thus, either occasionally or habitually, have been preserved and injurious ones eliminated. I do not refer to strongly marked deviations of structure, which occur only at long intervals of time, but to mere individual differences. We know, for instance, that the muscles of our hands and feet, which determine our powers of movement, are liable, like those of the lower animals, to

*This selection is taken from* The Descent of Man, *chapter 2, "On the Manner of Development of Man from Some Lower Form."*

incessant variability. If then the progenitors of man inhabiting any district, especially one undergoing some change in its conditions, were divided into two equal bodies, the one half which included all the individuals best adapted by their powers of movement for gaining subsistence or for defending themselves would on an average survive in greater numbers and procreate more offspring than the other and less well endowed half.

Man in the rudest state in which he now exists is the most dominant animal that has ever appeared on this earth. He has spread more widely than any other highly organized form, and all others have yielded before him. He manifestly owes this immense superiority to his intellectual faculties, to his social habits, which lead him to aid and defend his fellows, and to his corporeal structure. The supreme importance of these characters has been proved by the final arbitrament of the battle for life. Through his powers of intellect, articulate language has been evolved, and on this his wonderful advancement has mainly depended. As Mr. Chauncey Wright remarks, "A psychological analysis of the faculty of language shows that even the smallest proficiency in it might require more brainpower than the greatest proficiency in any other direction." He has invented and is able to use various weapons, tools, traps, etc., with which he defends himself, kills or catches prey, and otherwise obtains food. He has made rafts or canoes for fishing or crossing over to neighboring fertile islands. He has discovered the art of making fire, by which hard and stringy roots can be rendered digestible, and poisonous roots or herbs innocuous. This discovery of fire, probably the greatest ever made by man, excepting language, dates from before the dawn of history. These several inventions by which man in the rudest state has become so preeminent are the direct results of the development of his powers of observation, memory, curiosity, imagination, and reason. I cannot, therefore, understand how it is that Mr. Wallace maintains that "natural selection could only have endowed the savage with a brain a little superior to that of an ape."

Although the intellectual powers and social habits of man are of paramount importance to him, we must not underrate the importance of his bodily structure, to which subject the remainder of this chapter will be devoted. . . .

Even to hammer with precision is no easy matter, as everyone who has tried to learn carpentry will admit. To throw a stone with as true an aim as a Fuegian in defending himself or in killing birds requires the most consummate perfection in the correlated action of the muscles of the hand, arm, and shoulder, and, further, a fine sense of touch. In throwing a stone or spear, and in many other actions, a man must stand firmly on his feet, and this again demands the perfect coadaptation of numerous muscles. To chip a flint into the rudest tool or to form a barbed spear or hook from a bone demands the use of a perfect hand, for, as a most capable judge, Mr. Schoolcraft, remarks, the shaping fragments of stone into knives, lances, or arrowheads, shows "extraordinary ability and long practice." This is to a great extent proved by the fact that primeval men practiced a division of labor; each man did not manufacture his own flint tools or rude pottery, but certain individuals appear to have devoted themselves to such work, no doubt receiving in exchange the produce of the chase. Archeologists are con-vinced that an enormous interval of time elapsed before our ancestors thought of grinding chipped flints into smooth tools. One can hardly doubt that a manlike animal who possessed a hand and arm sufficiently perfect to throw a stone with precision or to form a flint into a rude tool could, with sufficient practice, as far as mechanical skill alone is concerned, make almost anything which a civilized man can make. The structure of the hand in this respect may be compared with that of the vocal organs, which in the apes are used for uttering various signal cries, as in one genus, musical cadences; but in man the closely similar vocal organs have become adapted through the inherited effects of use for the utterance of articulate language.

Turning now to the nearest allies of man, and therefore to the best rep-resentatives of our early progenitors, we find that the hands of the quadru-mana are constructed on the same general pattern as our own, but are far less perfectly adapted for diversified uses. Their hands do not serve for locomo-tion so well as the feet of a dog, as may be seen in such monkeys as the chim-panzee and orang, which walk on the outer margins of the palms, or on the knuckles. Their hands, however, are admirably adapted for climbing trees. Monkeys seize thin branches or ropes with the thumb on one side and the fingers and palm on the other, in the same manner as we do. They can thus also lift rather large objects, such as the neck of a bottle, to their mouths. Baboons turn over stones and scratch up roots with their hands. They seize nuts, insects, or other small objects with the thumb in opposition to the fin-gers, and no doubt they thus extract eggs and young from the nests of birds. American monkeys beat the wild oranges on the branches until the rind is cracked and then tear it off with the fingers of the two hands. In a wild state they break open hard fruits with stones. Other monkeys open mussel shells with the two thumbs. With their fingers they pull out thorns and burs, and hunt for each other's parasites. They roll down stones or throw them at their enemies; nevertheless, they are clumsy in these various actions and, as I have myself seen, are quite unable to throw a stone with precision.

It seems to me far from true that because "objects are grasped clumsily" by monkeys, "a much less specialized organ of prehension" would have served them equally well with their present hands. On the contrary, I see no reason to doubt that more perfectly constructed hands would have been an advantage to them, provided that they were not thus rendered less fitted for climbing trees. We may suspect that a hand as perfect as that of man would have been disadvantageous for climbing, for the most arboreal monkeys in the world, namely, *Ateles* in America, *Colobus* in Africa, and *Hylobates* in Asia, are either thumbless or their toes partially cohere, so that their limbs are converted into mere grasping hooks.[1]

As soon as some ancient member in the great series of the Primates came to be less arboreal, owing to a change in its manner of procuring subsistence or to some change in the surrounding conditions, its habitual manner of progression would have been modified, and thus it would have been rendered more strictly quadrupedal or bipedal. Baboons frequent hilly and rocky districts, and only from necessity climb high trees, and they have acquired almost the gait of a dog. Man alone has become a biped, and we can, I think, partly see how he has come to assume his erect attitude, which forms one of his most conspicuous characters. Man could not have attained his present dominant position in the world without the use of his hands, which are so admirably adapted to act in obedience to his will. Sir C. Bell insists that "the hand supplies all instruments and by its correspondence with the intellect gives him universal dominion." But the hands and arms could hardly have become perfect enough to have manufactured weapons or to have hurled stones and spears with a true aim as long as they were habitually used for locomotion and for supporting the whole weight of the body or, as before remarked, so long as they were especially fitted for

---

1. In *Hylobates syndactylus,* as the name expresses, two of the toes regularly cohere; and this, as Mr. Blyth informs me, is occasionally the case with the toes of *H. agilis, lar,* and *leuciscus. Colobus* is strictly arboreal and extraordinarily active (Brehm, "Thierleben," B. i. s. 50), but whether a better climber than the species of the allied genera, I do not know. It deserves notice that the feet of the sloths, the most arboreal animals in the world, are wonderfully hooklike.

climbing trees. Such rough treatment would also have blunted the sense of touch, on which their delicate use largely depends. From these causes alone it would have been an advantage to man to become a biped; but for many actions it is indispensable that the arms and whole upper part of the body should be free, and he must for this end stand firmly on his feet. To gain this great advantage, the feet have been rendered flat, and the great toe has been peculiarly modified, though this has entailed the almost complete loss of its power of prehension. It accords with the principle of the division of physiological labor, prevailing throughout the animal kingdom, that as the hands became perfected for prehension, the feet should have become perfected for support and locomotion. With some savages, however, the foot has not altogether lost its prehensile power, as shown by their manner of climbing trees and of using them in other ways.

If it be an advantage to man to stand firmly on his feet and to have his hands and arms free, of which, from his preeminent success in the battle of life, there can be no doubt, then I can see no reason why it should not have been advantageous to the progenitors of man to have become more and more erect or bipedal. They would thus have been better able to defend themselves with stones or clubs, to attack their prey, or otherwise to obtain food. The best-built individuals would in the long run have succeeded best and have survived in large numbers. If the gorilla and a few allied forms had become extinct, it might have been argued, with great force and apparent truth, that an animal could not have been gradually converted from a quadruped into a biped, as all the individuals in an intermediate condition would have been miserably ill fitted for progression. But we know (and this is well worthy of reflection) that the anthropomorphous apes are now actually in an intermediate condition, and no one doubts that they are on the whole well adapted for their conditions of life. Thus the gorilla runs with a sidelong shambling gait, but more commonly progresses by resting on its bent hands. The long-armed apes occasionally use their arms like crutches, swinging their bodies forward between them, and some kinds of *Hylobates*, without having been taught, can walk or run upright with tolerable quickness, yet they move awkwardly and much less securely than man. We see, in short, in existing monkeys a manner of progression intermediate between that of a quadruped and a biped, but as an unprejudiced judge insists, the anthropomorphous apes approach in structure more nearly to the bipedal than to the quadrupedal type.

As the progenitors of man became more and more erect, with their hands and arms more and more modified for prehension and other purposes, with their feet and legs at the same time transformed for firm support and progression, endless other changes of structure would have become necessary. The pelvis would have to be broadened, the spine peculiarly curved, and the head fixed in an altered position, all which changes have been attained by man. Prof. Schaaffhausen maintains that "the powerful mastoid processes of the human skull are the result of his erect position," and these processes are absent in the orang, chimpanzee, etc., and are smaller in the gorilla than in man. Various other structures, which appear connected with man's erect position, might here have been added. It is very difficult to decide how far these correlated modifications are the result of natural selection and how far of the inherited effects of the increased use of certain parts or of the action of one part on another. No doubt these means of change often cooperate: thus when certain muscles and the crests of bone to which they are attached become enlarged by habitual use, this shows that certain actions are habitually performed and must be serviceable. Hence the individuals which performed them best would tend to survive in greater numbers.

The free use of the arms and hands, partly the cause and partly the result of man's erect position, appears to have led to an indirect manner to other modifications of structure. The early male forefathers of man were, as previously stated, probably furnished with great canine teeth, but as they gradually acquired the habit of using stones, clubs, or other weapons for fighting with their enemies or rivals, they would use their jaws and teeth less and less. In this case, the jaws, together with the teeth, would become reduced in size, as we may feel almost sure from innumerable analogous cases. . . .

In the adult male anthropomorphous apes, as Rütimeyer and others have insisted, it is the effect on the skull of the great development of the jaw muscles that causes it to differ so greatly in many respects from that of man and has given to these animals "a truly frightful physiognomy." Therefore, as the jaws and teeth in man's progenitors gradually become reduced in size, the adult skull would have come to resemble more and more that of existing man. As we shall hereafter see, a great reduction of the canine teeth in the males would almost certainly affect the teeth of the females through inheritance.

As the various mental faculties gradually developed themselves the brain would almost certainly become larger. No one, I presume, doubts that the large proportion which the size of man's brain bears to his body, compared to the same proportion in the gorilla or orang, is closely connected with his higher mental powers. We meet with closely analogous facts with insects, for in ants the cerebral ganglia are of extraordinary dimensions, and in all the Hymenoptera these ganglia are many times larger than in the less intelligent orders, such as beetles. On the other hand, no one supposes that the intellect of any two animals or of any two men can be accurately gauged by the cubic contents of their skulls. It is certain that there may be extraordinary mental activity with an extremely small absolute mass of nervous matter; thus the wonderfully diversified instincts, mental powers, and affections of ants are notorious, yet their cerebral ganglia are not so large as the quarter of a small pin's head. Under this point of view, the brain of an ant is one of the most marvelous atoms of matter in the world, perhaps more so than the brain of a man.

The belief that there exists in man some close relation between the size of the brain and the development of the intellectual faculties is supported by the comparison of the skulls of savage and civilized races, of ancient and modern people, and by the analogy of the whole vertebrate series. Dr. J. Bernard Davis has proved by many careful measurements that the mean internal capacity of the skull in Europeans is 92.3 cubic inches; in Americans, 87.5; in Asiatics, 87.1; and in Australians, only 81.9 cubic inches. Professor Broca found that the nineteenth-century skulls from graves in Paris were larger than those from vaults of the twelfth century, in the proportion of 1484 to 1426, and that the increased size, as ascertained by measurements, was exclusively in the frontal part of the skull—the seat of the intellectual faculties. Prichard is persuaded that the present inhabitants of Britain have "much more capacious brain cases" than the ancient inhabitants. Nevertheless, it must be admitted that some skulls of very high antiquity, such as the famous one of Neanderthal, are well developed and capacious.[2]

---

2. In the interesting article just referred to, Prof. Broca has well remarked that in civilized nations, the average capacity of the skull must be lowered by the preservation of a considerable number of individuals, weak in mind and body, who would have been promptly eliminated in the savage state. On the other hand, with savages, the average includes only the more capable individuals, who have been able to survive under extremely hard conditions of life. Broca thus explains the otherwise inexplicable fact that the mean capacity of the skull of the ancient Troglodytes of Lozère is greater than that of modern Frenchmen.

With respect to the lower animals, M. E. Lartet, by comparing the crania of tertiary and recent mammals belonging to the same groups, has come to the remarkable conclusion that the brain is generally larger and the convolutions are more complex in the more recent forms. On the other hand, I have shown that the brains of domestic rabbits are considerably reduced in bulk in comparison with those of the wild rabbit or hare, and this may be attributed to their having been closely confined during many generations so that they have exerted their intellect, instincts, senses, and voluntary movements but little.

The gradually increasing weight of the brain and skull in man must have influenced the development of the supporting spinal column, more especially while he was becoming erect. As this change of position was being brought about, the internal pressure of the brain will also have influenced the form of the skull, for many facts show how easily the skull is thus affected. Ethnologists believe that it is modified by the kind of cradle in which infants sleep. Habitual spasms of the muscles and a cicatrix from a severe burn have permanently modified the facial bones. In young persons whose heads have become fixed either sideways or backward owing to disease, one of the two eyes has changed its position, and the shape of the skull has been altered apparently by the pressure of the brain in a new direction.[3] I have shown that with long-eared rabbits even so trifling a cause as the lopping forward of one ear drags forward almost every bone of the skull on that side so that the bones on the opposite side no longer strictly correspond. Lastly, if any animal were to increase or diminish much in general size without any change in its mental powers or if the mental powers were to be much increased or diminished without any great change in the size of the body, the shape of the skull would almost certainly be altered. I infer this from my observations on domestic rabbits, some kinds of which have become very much larger than the wild animal, while others have retained nearly the same size, but in both cases the brain has been much reduced

3. Schaaffhausen gives from Blumenbach and Busch the cases of the spasms and cicatrix, in "Anthropolog. Review," Oct. 1868, p. 420. Dr. Jarrold ("Anthropologia," 1808, pp. 115, 116) adduces from Camper and from his own observations cases of the modification of the skull from the head being fixed in an unnatural position. He believes that in certain trades, such as that of a shoemaker, where the head is habitually held forward, the forehead becomes more rounded and prominent.

relatively to the size of the body. Now I was at first much surprised on finding that in all these rabbits the skull had become elongated or dolichocephalic; for instance, of two skulls of nearly equal breadth, the one from a wild rabbit and the other from a large domestic kind, the former was 3.15 and the latter 4.3 inches in length. One of the most marked distinctions in different races of men is that the skull in some is elongated, and in others rounded; and here the explanation suggested by the case of the rabbits may hold good, for Welcker finds that short "men incline more to brachycephaly, and tall men to dolichocephaly," and tall men may be compared with the larger and longer-bodied rabbits, all of which have elongated skulls, or are dolichocephalic.

From these several facts we can understand, to a certain extent, the means by which the great size and more or less rounded form of the skull have been acquired by man, and these are characters eminently distinctive of him in comparison with the lower animals.

Another most conspicuous difference between man and the lower animals is the nakedness of his skin. Whales and porpoises (Cetacea), dugongs (Sirenia), and the hippopotamus are naked; and this may be advantageous to them for gliding through the water, nor would it be injurious to them from the loss of warmth, as the species which inhabit the colder regions are protected by a thick layer of blubber, serving the same purpose as the fur of seals and others. Elephants and rhinoceroses are almost hairless, and as certain extinct species which formerly lived under an Arctic climate were covered with long wool or hair, it would almost appear as if the existing species of both genera had lost their hairy covering from exposure to heat. This appears the most probable, as the elephants in India which live on elevated and cool districts are more hairy than those on the lowlands. May we then infer that man became divested of hair from having aboriginally inhabited some tropical land? That the hair is chiefly retained in the male sex on the chest and face, and in both sexes at the junction of all four limbs with the trunk, favors this inference—on the assumption that the hair was lost before man became erect, for the parts which now retain most hair would then have been most protected from the heat of the sun. The crown of the head, however, offers a curious exception, for at all times it must have been one of the most exposed parts, yet it is thickly clothed with hair. The fact, however, that the other members of the order of Primates, to which man belongs, although inhabiting various hot regions, are well clothed with hair, generally thickest on the upper surface,[4] is opposed to the supposition that man became naked through the action of the sun. Mr. Belt believes that within the tropics it is an advantage to man to be destitute of hair, as he is thus enabled to free himself of the multitude of ticks (acari) and other parasites with which he is often infested and which sometimes cause ulceration. But whether this evil is of sufficient magnitude to have led to the denudation of his body through natural selection may be doubted, since none of the many quadrupeds inhabiting the tropics have, as far as I know, acquired any specialized means of relief. The view which seems to me the most probable is that man, or rather primarily woman, became divested of hair for ornamental purposes, as we shall see under Sexual Selection, and according to this belief, it is not surprising that man should differ so greatly in hairiness from all other Primates, for characters gained through sexual selection often differ to an extraordinary degree in closely related forms.

According to a popular impression, the absence of a tail is eminently distinctive of man, but as those apes which come nearest to him are destitute of this organ, its disappearance does not relate exclusively to man. The tail often differs remarkably in length within the same genus; thus in some species of *Macacus* it is longer than the whole body and is formed of twenty-four vertebrae; in others it consists of a scarcely visible stump, containing only three or four vertebrae. In some kinds of baboons there are twenty-five, while in the mandrill there are ten very small stunted caudal vertebrae, or, according to Cuvier, sometimes only five. The tail, whether it be long or short, almost always tapers toward the end, and this, I presume, results from the atrophy of the terminal muscles, together with their arteries and nerves, through disuse, leading to the atrophy of the terminal bones. But no explanation can at present be given of the great diversity which often occurs in its length. Here, however, we are more specially concerned with the complete external disappearance of the tail. Professor Broca has recently shown that the tail in all quadrupeds consists of two portions, generally separated abruptly from each other; the basal portion consists of vertebrae, more or

4. Isidore Geoffroy Saint-Hilaire remarks ("Hist. Nat. Générale," tom. ii., 1859, pp. 215–217) on the head of a man being covered with long hair; also on the upper surfaces of monkeys and of other mammals being more thickly clothed than the lower surfaces. This has likewise been observed by various authors. Prof. P. Gervais ("Hist. Nat. des Mammifères," tom. i., 1854, p. 28), however, states that in the gorilla the hair is thinner on the back, where it is partly rubbed off, than on the lower surface.

less perfectly channeled and furnished with apophyses like ordinary verte-brae, whereas those of the terminal portion are not channeled, are almost smooth, and scarcely resemble true vertebrae. A tail, though not externally visible, is really present in man and the anthropomorphous apes and is constructed on exactly the same pattern in both. In the terminal portion the vertebrae constituting the os coccyx are quite rudimentary, being much reduced in size and number. In the basal portion, the vertebrae are likewise few, are united firmly together, and are arrested in development, but they have been rendered much broader and flatter than the corresponding vertebrae in the tails of other animals: they constitute what Broca calls the accessory sacral vertebrae. These are of functional importance by sup-porting certain internal parts and in other ways, and their modification is directly connected with the erect or semierect attitude of man and the anthropomorphous apes. This conclusion is the more trustworthy, as Broca formerly held a different view, which he has now abandoned. The modifi-cation, therefore, of the basal caudal vertebrae in man and the higher apes may have been effected, directly or indirectly, through natural selection.

But what are we to say about the rudimentary and variable vertebrae of the terminal portion of the tail, forming the os coccyx? A notion which has often been and will no doubt again be ridiculed, namely, that friction has had something to do with the disappearance of the external portion of the tail, is not so ridiculous as it at first appears. Dr. Anderson states that the extremely short tail of *Macacus brunneus* is formed of eleven vertebrae, including the imbedded basal ones. The extremity is tendonous and con-tains no vertebrae; this is succeeded by five rudimentary ones, so minute that together they are only one line and a half in length, and these are per-manently bent to one side in the shape of a hook. The free part of the tail, only a little above an inch in length, includes only four more small verte-brae. This short tail is carried erect, but about a quarter of its total length is doubled onto itself to the left, and this terminal part, which includes the hooklike portion, serves "to fill up the interspace between the upper diver-gent portion of the callosities," so that the animal sits on it and thus renders it rough and callous. Dr. Anderson thus sums up his observations: "These facts seem to me to have only one explanation: this tail, from its short size, is in the monkey's way when it sits down and frequently becomes placed under the animal while it is in this attitude, and from the circumstance that it does not extend beyond the extremity of the ischial tuberosities, it seems as if the tail originally had been bent round by the will of the animal, into the interspace between the callosities, to escape being pressed between them and the ground, and that in time the curvature became permanent, fitting in of itself when the organ happens to be sat upon." Under these circumstances it is not surprising that the surface of the tail should have been roughened and rendered callous, and Dr. Murie, who carefully observed this species in the zoological gardens as well as three other closely allied forms with slightly longer tails, says that when the animal sits down, the tail "is necessarily thrust to one side of the buttocks, and whether long or short its root is consequently liable to be rubbed or chafed." As we now have evidence that mutilations occasionally produce an inherited effect,[5] it is not very improbable that in short-tailed monkeys, the projecting part of the tail, being functionally useless, should after many generations have become rudimentary and distorted from being continually rubbed and chafed. We see the projecting part in this condition in the *Macacus brunneus* and absolutely aborted in the *M. ecaudatus* and in several of the higher apes. Finally, then, as far as we can judge, the tail has disappeared in man and the anthropomorphous apes, owing to the terminal portion having been injured by friction during a long lapse of time, the basal and embedded portion having been reduced and modified so as to become suitable to the erect or semierect position.

I have now endeavored to show that some of the most distinctive characters of man have in all probability been acquired, either directly or more commonly indirectly, through natural selection. We should bear in mind that modifications in structure or constitution which do not serve to adapt an organism to its habits of life, to the food which it consumes, or passively to the surrounding conditions cannot have been thus acquired. We must not, however, be too confident in deciding what modifications are of service to each being; we should remember how little we know about the use of many parts or what changes in the blood tissues may serve to fit an

5. I allude to Dr. Brown-Séquard's observations on the transmitted effect of an operation causing epilepsy in guinea pigs and likewise more recently on the analogous effects of cutting the sympathetic nerve in the neck. I shall hereafter have occasion to refer to Mr. Salvin's interesting case of the apparently inherited effects of motmots biting off the barbs of their own tail feathers. See also on the general subject "Variation of Animals and Plants Under Domestication," vol. ii., pp. 22–24.

organism for a new climate or new kinds of food. Nor must we forget the principle of correlation, by which, as Isidore Geoffroy has shown in the case of man, many strange deviations of structure are tied together. Independently of correlation, a change in one part often leads, through the increased or decreased use of other parts, to other changes of a quite unexpected nature. It is also well to reflect on such facts, as the wonderful growth of galls on plants caused by the poison of an insect, and on the remarkable changes of color in the plumage of parrots when fed on certain fishes or inoculated with the poison of toads, for we can thus see that the fluids of the system, if altered for some special purpose, might induce other changes. We should especially bear in mind that modifications acquired and continually used during past ages for some useful purpose would probably become firmly fixed and might be long inherited.

Thus a large yet undefined extension may safely be given to the direct and indirect results of natural selection, but I now admit, after reading the essay by Nägeli on plants and the remarks by various authors with respect to animals, more especially those recently made by Professor Broca, that in the earlier editions of my *Origins of Species* I perhaps attributed too much to the action of natural selection or the survival of the fittest. I have altered the fifth edition of the *Origin* so as to confine my remarks to adaptive changes of structure, but I am convinced, from the light gained during even the last few years, that very many structures which now appear to us useless will hereafter be proved to be useful and will therefore come within the range of natural selection. Nevertheless, I did not formerly consider sufficiently the existence of structures which, as far as we can at present judge, are neither beneficial nor injurious, and this I believe to be one of the greatest oversights as yet detected in my work. I may be permitted to say, as some excuse, that I had two distinct objects in view: firstly, to show that species had not been separately created, and secondly, that natural selection had been the chief agent of change, though largely aided by the inherited effects of habit and slightly by the direct action of the surrounding conditions. I was not, however, able to annul the influence of my former belief, then almost universal, that each species had been purposely created, and this led to my tacit assumption that every detail of structure, excepting rudiments, was of some special, though unrecognized, service. Anyone with this assumption in his mind would naturally extend too far the action of natural selection, either during past or present times. Some of those who admit the principle of evolution, but reject natural selection, seem to forget, when criticizing my book, that I had the above two objects in view; hence if I have erred in giving to natural selection great power, which I am very far from admitting, or in having exaggerated its power, which is in itself probable, I have at least, as I hope, done good service in aiding to overthrow the dogma of separate creations.

It is, as I can now see, probable that all organic beings, including man, possess peculiarities of structure which neither are now nor were formerly of any service to them and which, therefore, are of no physiological importance. We know not what produces the numberless slight differences between the individuals of each species, for reversion only carries the problem a few steps backward, but each peculiarity must have had its efficient cause. If these causes, whatever they may be, were to act more uniformly and energetically during a lengthened period (and against this no reason can be assigned), the result would probably be not a mere slight individual difference, but a well-marked and constant modification, though one of no physiological importance. Changed structures which are in no way beneficial cannot be kept uniform through natural selection, though the injurious will be thus eliminated. Uniformity of character would, however, naturally follow from the assumed uniformity of the exciting causes and likewise from the free intercrossing of many individuals. During successive periods, the same organism might in this manner acquire successive modifications, which would be transmitted in a nearly uniform state as long as the exciting causes remained the same and there was free intercrossing. With respect to the exciting causes we can only say, as when speaking of so-called spontaneous variations, that they relate much more closely to the constitution of the varying organism than to the nature of the conditions to which it has been subjected.

## Content Questions

1. Based on this selection, what does Darwin mean by the term *natural selection?*

2. Why is the "intermediate condition" of the anthropomorphous apes important to Darwin's argument about human evolution? (84)

3. How does Darwin relate the present structure of human hands to the process by which humans became bipedal? (83–85)

4. In discussing the changes in body structure related to an erect posture, Darwin offers both "natural selection" and "the inherited effects of the increased use of certain parts or . . . the action of one part on another" as possible causes. (85) How are we to understand the difference between these causes?

5. What other "modifications of structure" does Darwin say would naturally have followed from early humans' free use of their arms and hands? (85–86)

6. How does Darwin explain the relative hairlessness of humans, as compared to other primates? (88–89)

7. What reasons does Darwin give for having, in the past, "perhaps attributed too much to the action of natural selection or the survival of the fittest"? (92) What modifications does Darwin suggest to his previous remarks about natural selection?

## Application Questions

1. Applying the principles of the theory of natural selection, summarize Darwin's argument for the process by which humans became bipeds. Is his argument with regard to this particular process consistent with the general theory? Why or why not?

2. In explaining human evolutionary changes in body structure due to erect posture and the loss of a tail, Darwin offers the principle of use and disuse as a possible contributing mechanism. What does this imply about the traditional distinction between Darwin and Lamarck that is made in many textbooks?

## Discussion Questions

1. Does this selection place greater emphasis on the similarities or the differences Darwin sees between humans and the lower animals?

2. Does Darwin undermine his own theory when he warns that we must not "be too confident in deciding what modifications are of service to each being"? (91)

3. How effectively does this selection demonstrate that species were not "separately created"? (92)

# Gregor Mendel

Gregor Mendel (1822–1884) was a monk in Brünn, Austria (now Brno, Czech Republic), whose experiments with heredity in pea plants were carried out during the height of controversy over Charles Darwin's *On the Origin of Species* (1859). Mendel's work addressed the central evolutionary question of how modifications to species arise over time, but Darwin apparently never learned of it. In fact, Mendel's results went unnoticed until well after his death.

Working alone, Mendel formulated the basic principles of heredity, overturning the old conception of heredity as a process of "blending," in which parental characteristics appear in less pronounced form in their offspring. For eight years, he conducted lengthy experiments with thousands of pea plants, painstakingly collecting and transferring pollen by hand, and wrapping the pea plants after fertilization to prevent accidental cross-pollination. The exactitude of Mendel's experiments and recordkeeping enabled him to determine that precise laws of probability governed the inheritance of characteristics in his plants, thereby establishing the existence of heritable units and the statistical laws that govern them. His discoveries laid the foundation for all further work in genetics.

Mendel's findings met with indifference when they were published in 1866 by the Brünn scientific society. This was partly because his results were published by a relatively obscure local organization and partly because few scientists were ready to grasp the implications of his research. In 1868, Mendel was elected abbot of his monastery, and administrative duties limited his opportunities for scientific research. Not until 1900, when three scientists in three different countries independently verified and rediscovered Mendel's findings, was the significance of his work appreciated.

# Experiments in Plant Hybridization

*(selection)*

## Introductory Remarks

Experience of artificial fertilization, such as is effected with ornamental plants in order to obtain new variations in color, has led to the experiments which will here be discussed. The striking regularity with which the same hybrid forms always reappeared whenever fertilization took place between the same species induced further experiments to be undertaken, the object of which was to follow up the developments of the hybrids in their progeny.

. . . That, so far, no generally applicable law governing the formation and development of hybrids has been successfully formulated can hardly be wondered at by anyone who is acquainted with the extent of the task and can appreciate the difficulties with which experiments of this class have to contend. A final decision can only be arrived at when we shall have before us the results of detailed experiments made on plants belonging to the most diverse orders.

Those who survey the work done in this department will arrive at the conviction that among all the numerous experiments made, not one has been carried out to such an extent and in such a way as to make it possible to determine the number of different forms under which the offspring of hybrids appear, or to arrange these forms with certainty according to their separate generations, or to ascertain definitely their statistical relations.

It requires indeed some courage to undertake a labor of such far-reaching extent; this appears, however, to be the only right way by which we can finally reach the solution of a question the importance of which cannot be over-estimated in connection with the history of the evolution of organic forms.

The paper now presented records the results of such a detailed experiment. This experiment was practically confined to a small plant group and is now, after eight years' pursuit, concluded in all essentials. Whether the plan upon which the separate experiments were conducted and carried out was the best suited to attain the desired end is left to the friendly decision of the reader.

## Selection of the Experimental Plants

. . . The selection of the plant group which shall serve for experiments of this kind must be made with all possible care if it is desired to avoid from the outset every risk of questionable results.

The experimental plants must necessarily—

1. Possess constant differentiating characters.

2. The hybrids of such plants must, during the flowering period, be protected from the influence of all foreign pollen, or be easily capable of such protection.

The hybrids and their offspring should suffer no marked disturbance in their fertility in the successive generations.

Accidental impregnation by foreign pollen, if it occurred during the experiments and was not recognized, would lead to entirely erroneous conclusions. Reduced fertility or entire sterility of certain forms, such as occurs in the offspring of many hybrids, would render the experiments very difficult or entirely frustrate them. In order to discover the relations in which the hybrid forms stand toward each other and also toward their progenitors, it appears to be necessary that all members of the series developed in each successive generation should be, *without exception*, subjected to observation.

At the very outset special attention was devoted to the *Leguminosae* on account of their peculiar floral structure. Experiments which were made with several members of this family led to the result that the genus *Pisum* was found to possess the necessary qualifications.

Some thoroughly distinct forms of this genus possess characters which are constant, and easily and certainly recognizable, and when their hybrids are mutually crossed they yield perfectly fertile progeny. Furthermore, a disturbance through foreign pollen cannot easily occur, since the fertilizing organs are closely packed inside the keel, and the anther bursts within the bud, so that the stigma becomes covered with pollen even before the flower opens. This circumstance is of especial importance. As additional advantages worth mentioning, there may be cited the easy culture of these plants in the open ground and in pots, and also their relatively short period of growth. Artificial fertilization is certainly a somewhat elaborate process, but nearly always succeeds. For this purpose the bud is opened before it is perfectly developed, the keel is removed, and each stamen carefully extracted by means of forceps, after which the stigma can at once be dusted over with the foreign pollen. . . .

## Division and Arrangement of the Experiments

If two plants which differ constantly in one or several characters are crossed, numerous experiments have demonstrated that the common characters are transmitted unchanged to the hybrids and their progeny; but each pair of differentiating characters, on the other hand, unites in the hybrid to form a new character, which in the progeny of the hybrid is usually variable. The object of the experiment was to observe these variations in the case of each pair of differentiating characters and to deduce the law according to which they appear in the successive generations. . . .

The characters which were selected for experiment relate

1.  To the *difference in the form of the ripe seeds.* These are either round or roundish; the depressions, if any, occur on the surface, being always only shallow, or they are irregularly angular and deeply wrinkled *(P. quadratum).*

2.  To the *difference in the color of the seed albumen* (endosperm). The albumen of the ripe seeds is either pale yellow, bright-yellow-and-orange colored, or it possesses a more or less intense green tint. This difference of color is easily seen in the seeds, as their coats are transparent.

3. To the *difference in the color of the seed coat*. This is either white, with which character white flowers are constantly correlated, or it is gray, gray-brown, leather-brown, with or without violet spotting, in which case the color of the standards is violet, that of the wings purple, and the stem in the axils of the leaves is of a reddish tint. The gray seed coats become dark brown in boiling water.

4. To the *difference in the form of the ripe pods*. These are either simply inflated, not contracted in places; or they are deeply constricted between the seeds and more or less wrinkled *(P. saccharatum)*.

5. To the *difference in the color of the unripe pods*. They are either light to dark green, or vividly yellow, in which coloring the stalks, leaf veins, and calyx participate.

6. To the *difference in the position of the flowers*. They are either axial, that is, distributed along the main stem, or they are terminal, that is, bunched at the top of the stem and arranged almost in a false umbel; in this case the upper part of the stem is more or less widened in section *(P. umbellatum)*.

7. To the *difference in the length of the stem*. The length of the stem is very various in some forms; it is, however, a constant character for each, insofar that healthy plants, grown in the same soil, are only subject to unimportant variations in this character.

    In experiments with this character, in order to be able to discriminate with certainty, the long axis of 6 to 7 feet was always crossed with the short one of $3/4$ feet to $1^{1}/2$ feet.

Each two of the differentiating characters enumerated above were united by cross-fertilization. There were made for the

    1st trial 60 fertilizations on 15 plants
    2nd trial 58 fertilizations on 10 plants
    3rd trial 35 fertilizations on 10 plants
    4th trial 40 fertilizations on 10 plants
    5th trial 23 fertilizations on 5 plants
    6th trial 34 fertilizations on 10 plants
    7th trial 37 fertilizations on 10 plants

From a larger number of plants of the same variety only the most vigorous were chosen for fertilization. Weakly plants always afford uncertain results, because even in the first generation of hybrids, and still more so in the subsequent ones, many of the offspring either entirely fail to flower or only form a few and inferior seeds.

Furthermore, in all the experiments reciprocal crossings were effected in such a way that each of the two varieties which in one set of fertilizations served as seed bearer in the other set was used as the pollen plant. . . .

## The Forms of the Hybrids

Experiments which in previous years were made with ornamental plants have already afforded evidence that the hybrids, as a rule, are not exactly intermediate between the parental species. . . . This is . . . the case with the pea hybrids. In the case of each of the seven crosses the hybrid character resembles that of one of the parental forms so closely that the other either escapes observation completely or cannot be detected with certainty. This circumstance is of great importance in the determination and classification of the forms under which the offspring of the hybrids appear. Henceforth in this paper, those characters which are transmitted entirely, or almost unchanged in the hybridization, and therefore in themselves constitute the characters of the hybrid, are termed the *dominant*, and those which become latent in the process *recessive*. The expression "recessive" has been chosen because the characters thereby designated withdraw or entirely disappear in the hybrids, but nevertheless reappear unchanged in their progeny, as will be demonstrated later on.

It was furthermore shown by the whole of the experiments that it is perfectly immaterial whether the dominant character belongs to the seed bearer or to the pollen parent; the form of the hybrid remains identical in both cases. . . .

Of the differentiating characters which were used in the experiments, the following are dominant:

1. The round or roundish form of the seed with or without shallow depressions

2. The yellow color of the seed albumen

3. The gray, gray brown, or leather brown color of the seed coat, in association with violet-red blossoms and reddish spots in the leaf axils

4. The simply inflated form of the pod

5. The green coloring of the unripe pod, in association with the same color in the stems, the leaf veins, and the calyx

6. The distribution of the flowers along the stem

7. The greater length of stem . . .

## The First Generation [Bred] from the Hybrids

In this generation there reappear, together with the dominant characters, also the recessive ones, with their peculiarities fully developed, and this occurs in the definitely expressed average proportion of three to one, so that among four plants of this generation three display the dominant character and one the recessive. This relates without exception to all the characters which were investigated in the experiments. . . . *Transitional forms were not observed in any experiment.*

. . . The relative numbers which were obtained for each pair of differentiating characters are as follows:

Experiment 1. Form of seed—From 253 hybrids, 7,324 seeds were obtained in the second trial year. Among them were 5,474 round or roundish ones and 1,850 angular wrinkled ones. Therefrom the ratio 2.96 to 1 is deduced.

Experiment 2. Color of albumen—258 plants yielded 8,023 seeds, 6,022 yellow and 2,001 green; their ratio, therefore, is as 3.01 to 1. . . .

Experiment 3. Color of the seed coats—Among 929 plants, 705 bore violet-red flowers and gray-brown seed coats, giving the proportion 3.15 to 1.

Experiment 4. Form of pods—Of 1,181 plants, 882 had them simply inflated, and in 299 they were constricted. Resulting ratio: 2.95 to 1.

Experiment 5. Color of the unripe pods—The number of trial plants was 580, of which 428 had green pods and 152 [had] yellow ones. Consequently these stand in the ratio 2.82 to 1.

Experiment 6. Position of flowers—Among 858 cases, 651 had axial inflorescences and 207 [had] terminal. Ratio: 3.14 to 1.

Experiment 7. Length of stem—Out of 1,064 plants, in 787 cases the stem was long, and in 277 short. Hence a mutual ratio of 2.84 to 1. In this experiment the dwarfed plants were carefully lifted and transferred to a special bed. This precaution was necessary, as otherwise they would have perished through being overgrown by their tall relatives. Even in their quite young state they can be easily picked out by their compact growth and thick dark-green foliage.

If now the results of the whole of the experiments are brought together, there is found, as between the number of forms with the dominant and recessive characters, an average ratio of 2.98 to 1, or 3 to 1.

The dominant character can here have a *double signification*—namely, that of a parental character or a hybrid character. In which of the two significations it appears in each separate case can only be determined by the following generation. As a parental character it must pass over unchanged to the whole of the offspring; as a hybrid character, on the other hand, it must maintain the same behavior as in the first generation.

## The Second Generation [Bred] from the Hybrids

Those forms which in the first generation exhibit the recessive character do not further vary in the second generation as regards this character; they remain constant in their offspring.

It is otherwise with those which possess the dominant character in the first generation (bred from the hybrids). Of these, *two*-thirds yield offspring which display the dominant and recessive characters in the proportion of 3 to 1, and thereby show exactly the same ratio as the hybrid forms, while only *one*-third remain with the dominant character constant.

The separate experiments yielded the following results:

Experiment 1. Among 565 plants which were raised from round seeds of the first generation, 193 yielded round seeds only, and remained therefore constant in this character; 372, however, gave both round and wrinkled seeds, in the proportion of 3 to 1. The number of the hybrids, therefore, as compared with the constants is 1.93 to 1.

Experiment 2. Of 519 plants which were raised from seeds whose albumen was of yellow color in the first generation, 166 yielded exclusively yellow, while 353 yielded yellow and green seeds in the proportion of 3 to 1. There resulted, therefore, a division into hybrid and constant forms in the proportion of 2.13 to 1.

For each separate trial in the following experiments, 100 plants were selected which displayed the dominant character in the first generation, and in order to ascertain the significance of this, ten seeds of each were cultivated.

Experiment 3. The offspring of 36 plants yielded exclusively gray-brown seed coats, while of the offspring of 64 plants some had gray brown and some had white.

Experiment 4. The offspring of 29 plants had only simply inflated pods; of the offspring of 71, on the other hand, some had inflated and some had constricted.

Experiment 5. The offspring of 49 plants had only green pods; of the offspring of 60 plants some had green, some yellow ones.

Experiment 6. The offspring of 33 plants had only axial flowers; of the offspring of 67, on the other hand, some had axial and some terminal flowers.

Experiment 7. The offspring of 28 plants inherited the long axis, and of those of 72 plants some [inherited] the long and some the short axis.

In each of these experiments a certain number of the plants came constant with the dominant character. For the determination of the proportion in which the separation of the forms with the constantly persistent character results, the two first experiments are of especial importance, since in these a larger number of plants can be compared. The ratios 1.93 to 1 and 2.13 to 1 gave together almost exactly the average ratio of 2 to 1. The sixth experiment gave a quite concordant result; in the others the ratio varies more or less, as was only to be expected in view of the smaller number of 100 trial plants. Experiment 5, which shows the greatest departure, was repeated, and then, in lieu of the ratio of 60 and 40, that of 65 and 35 resulted. *The average ratio of 2 to 1 appears, therefore, as fixed with certainty*. It is therefore demonstrated that of those forms which possess the dominant character in the first generation, ⅔ have the hybrid character, while ⅓ remain constant with the dominant character.

The ratio of 3 to 1, in accordance with which the distribution of the dominant and recessive characters results in the first generation, resolves itself therefore in all experiments into the ratio of 2 : 1 : 1 if the dominant character is differentiated according to its significance as a hybrid character or as a parental one. Since the members of the first generation spring directly from the seed of the hybrids, *it is now clear that the hybrids form seeds having one or the other of the two differentiating characters, and of these one-half develop again the hybrid form, while the other half yield plants which remain constant and receive the dominant or the recessive characters in equal numbers.*

## The Subsequent Generations [Bred] from the Hybrids

The proportions in which the descendants of the hybrids develop and split up in the first and second generations presumably hold good for all subsequent progeny. Experiments 1 and 2 have already been carried through six generations, 3 and 7 through five, and 4, 5, and 6 through four, these experiments being continued from the third generations with a small number of plants, and no departure from the rule has been perceptible. The offspring of the hybrids separated in each generation in the ratio of 2 : 1 : 1 into hybrids and constant forms.

If $A$ is taken as denoting one of the two constant characters, for instance, the dominant; $a$, the recessive; and $Aa$ the hybrid form in which both are conjoined, the expression

$$A + 2Aa + a$$

shows the terms in the series for the progeny of the hybrids of two differentiating characters. . . .

## The Offspring of Hybrids in Which Several Differentiating Characters Are Associated

In the experiments above described, plants were used which differed only in one essential character. The next task consisted in ascertaining whether the law of development discovered in these applied to each pair of differentiating characters when several diverse characters are united in the hybrid by crossing.

As regards the form of the hybrids in these cases, the experiments showed throughout that this invariably more nearly approaches that one of the two parental plants which possesses the greater number of dominant characters. . . . Should one of the two parental types possess only dominant characters, then the hybrid is scarcely or not at all distinguishable from it.

Two experiments were made with a considerable number of plants. In the first experiment the parental plants differed in the form of the seed and in the color of the albumen; in the second in the form of the seed, in the color of the albumen, and in the color of the seed coats. Experiments with seed characters give the result in the simplest and most certain way. . . .

In addition, further experiments were made with a smaller number of experimental plants in which the remaining characters by twos and threes were united as hybrids; all yielded approximately the same results. There is therefore no doubt that for the whole of the characters involved in the experiments the principle applies that *the offspring of the hybrids in which several essentially different characters are combined exhibit the terms of a series of combinations, in which the developmental series for each pair of differentiating characters are united*. It is demonstrated at the same time that *the relation of each pair of different characters in hybrid union is independent of the other differences in the two original parental stocks.* . . .

All constant combinations which in peas are possible by the combination of the said seven differentiating characters were actually obtained by repeated crossing. . . . Thereby is . . . given the practical proof *that the constant characters which appear in the several varieties of a group of plants may be obtained in all the associations which are possible according to the [mathematical] laws of combination, by means of repeated artificial fertilization.* . . .

If we endeavor to collate in a brief form the results arrived at, we find that those differentiating characters, which admit of easy and certain recognition in the experimental plants, all behave exactly alike in their hybrid associations. The offspring of the hybrids of each pair of differentiating characters are, one-half, hybrid again, while the other half are constant in equal proportions, having the characters of the seed and pollen parents respectively. If several differentiating characters are combined by cross-fertilization in a hybrid, the resulting offspring form the terms of a combination series in which the combination series for each pair of differentiating characters are united.

The uniformity of behavior shown by the whole of the characters submitted to experiment permits, and fully justifies, the acceptance of the principle that a similar relation exists in the other characters which appear less sharply defined in plants and therefore could not be included in the separate experiments. . . .

## The Reproductive Cells of the Hybrids

The results of the previously described experiments led to further experiments, the results of which appear fitted to afford some conclusions as regards the composition of the egg and pollen cells of hybrids. An important clue is afforded in *Pisum* by the circumstance that among the progeny of the hybrids constant forms appear, and that this occurs, too, in respect of all combinations of the associated characters. So far as experience goes, we find it in every case confirmed that constant progeny can only be formed when the egg cells and the fertilizing pollen are of like character, so that both are provided with the material for creating quite similar individuals, as is the case with the normal fertilization of pure species. We must therefore regard it as certain that exactly similar factors must be at work also in the production of the constant forms in the hybrid plants. Since the various constant forms are produced in *one* plant, or even in one flower of a plant, the conclusion appears logical that in the ovaries of the hybrids there are formed as many sorts of egg cells, and in the anthers as many sorts of pollen cells, as there are possible constant combination forms, and that these egg and pollen cells agree in their internal composition with those of the separate forms.

In point of fact it is possible to demonstrate theoretically that this hypothesis would fully suffice to account for the development of the hybrids in the separate generations, if we might at the same time assume that the various kinds of egg and pollen cells were formed in the hybrids on the average in equal numbers.

In order to bring these assumptions to an experimental proof, the following experiments were designed. Two forms which were constantly different in the form of the seed and the color of the albumen were united by fertilization.

If the differentiating characters are again indicated as *A, B, a, b,* we have

|  |  |
|---|---|
| *AB*, seed parent; | *ab*, pollen parent; |
| *A*, form round; | *a*, form wrinkled; |
| *B*, albumen yellow. | *b*, albumen green. |

The artificially fertilized seeds were sown together with several seeds of both original stocks, and the most vigorous examples were chosen for the reciprocal crossing. There were fertilized

1. The hybrids with the pollen of *AB*
2. The hybrids with the pollen of *ab*
3. *AB* with the pollen of the hybrids
4. *ab* with the pollen of the hybrids

For each of these four experiments the whole of the flowers on three plants were fertilized. If the above theory is correct, there must be developed on the hybrids egg and pollen cells of the forms *AB, Ab, aB, ab,* and there would be combined

1. The egg cells *AB, Ab, aB, ab* with the pollen cells *AB*
2. The egg cells *AB, Ab, aB, ab* with the pollen cells *ab*
3. The egg cells *AB* with the pollen cells *AB, Ab, aB, ab*
4. The egg cells *ab* with the pollen cells *AB, Ab, aB, ab*

From each of these experiments there could then result only the following forms:

1. *AB, ABb, AaB, AaBb*
2. *AaBb, Aab, aBb, ab*
3. *AB, ABb, AaB, AaBb*
4. *AaBb, Aab, aBb, ab*

If, furthermore, the several forms of the egg and pollen cells of the hybrids were produced on an average in equal numbers, then in each experiment the said four combinations should stand in the same ratio to each other. A perfect agreement in the numerical relations was, however, not to be expected, since in each fertilization, even in normal cases, some egg cells remain undeveloped or subsequently die, and many even of the well-formed seeds fail to germinate when sown. . . .

The first and second experiments had primarily the object of proving the composition of the hybrid egg cells, while the third and fourth experiments were to decide that of the pollen cells. As is shown by the above demonstration the first and third experiments and the second and fourth should produce precisely the same combinations, and even in the second year the result should be partially visible in the form and color of the artificially fertilized seed. In the first and third experiments the dominant characters of form and color, *A* and *B*, appear in each union, . . . partly constant and partly in hybrid union with the recessive characters *a* and *b*, for which reason they must impress their peculiarity upon the whole of the seeds. All seeds should therefore appear round and yellow, if the theory is justified. In the second and fourth experiments, on the other hand, one union is hybrid in form and in color, and consequently the seeds are round and yellow; another is hybrid in form, but constant in the recessive character of color, whence the seeds are round and green; the third is constant in the recessive character of form but hybrid in color, consequently the seeds are wrinkled and yellow; the fourth is constant in both recessive characters, so that the seeds are wrinkled and green. In both these experiments there were consequently four sorts of seed to be expected—namely, round and yellow, round and green, wrinkled and yellow, wrinkled and green.

The crop fulfilled these expectations perfectly. There were obtained in the 1st experiment, 98 exclusively round yellow seeds; in the 3rd experiment, 94 exclusively round yellow seeds.

In the 2nd experiment, [there were] 31 round and yellow, 26 round and green, 27 wrinkled and yellow, 26 wrinkled and green seeds.

In the 4th experiment, [there were] 24 round and yellow, 25 round and green, 22 wrinkled and yellow, 27 wrinkled and green seeds.

In a further experiment the characters of flower color and length of stem were experimented upon. . . . For the characters of form of pod, color of pod, and position of flowers, experiments were also made on a small scale, and results [were] obtained in perfect agreement. All combinations which were possible through the union of the differentiating characters duly appeared, and in nearly equal numbers.

Experimentally, therefore, the theory is confirmed that *the pea hybrids form pollen and egg cells which, in their constitution, represent in equal numbers all constant forms which result from the combination of the characters united in fertilization.*

The difference of the forms among the progeny of the hybrids, as well as the respective ratios of the numbers in which they are observed, find a sufficient explanation in the principle above deduced. The simplest case is afforded by the developmental series of each pair of differentiating characters. This series is represented by the expression $A + 2Aa + a$, in which $A$ and $a$ signify the forms with constant differentiating characters, and $Aa$ the hybrid form of both. It includes in three different classes four individuals. In the formation of these, pollen and egg cells of the form *A* and *a* take part on the average equally in the fertilization, hence each form occurs twice, since four individuals are formed. There participate consequently in the fertilization

The pollen cells *A+A+a+a*

The egg cells *A+A+a+a*

It remains, therefore, purely a matter of chance which of the two sorts of pollen will become united with each separate cell. According, however, to the law of probability, it will always happen, on the average of many cases, that each pollen form *A* and *a* will unite equally often with each egg cell form *A* and *a*; consequently one of the two pollen cells *A* in the fertilization will meet with the egg cell *A*, and the other with an egg cell *a*, and so likewise one pollen cell will unite with an egg cell *A*, and the other with egg cell *a*.

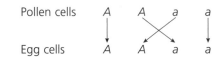

The results of the fertilization may be made clear by putting the signs for the conjoined egg and pollen cells in the form of fractions, those for the pollen cells above and those for the egg cells below the line. We then have

$$\frac{A}{A}+\frac{A}{a}+\frac{a}{A}+\frac{a}{a}.$$

In the first and fourth term the egg and pollen cells are of like kind; consequently the product of their union must be constant, namely, *A* and *a*. In the second and third, on the other hand, there again results a union of the two differentiating characters of the stocks; consequently the forms resulting from these fertilizations are identical to those of the hybrid from which they sprang. *There occurs accordingly a repeated hybridization.* This explains the striking fact that the hybrids are able to produce, besides the two parental forms, offspring that are like themselves; $\frac{A}{a}$ and $\frac{a}{A}$ both give the same union *Aa*, since, as already remarked above, it makes no difference in the result of fertilization to which of the two characters the pollen or egg cells belong. We may write then

$$\frac{A}{A}+\frac{A}{a}+\frac{a}{A}+\frac{a}{a}=A+2Aa+a.$$

This represents the average result of the self-fertilization of the hybrids when two differentiating characters are united in them. In individual flowers and in individual plants, however, the ratios in which the forms of the series are produced may suffer not inconsiderable fluctuations. Apart from the fact that the numbers in which both sorts of egg cells occur in the seed vessels can only be regarded as equal on the average, it remains purely a matter of chance which of the two sorts of pollen may fertilize each separate egg cell. For this reason the separate values must necessarily be subject to fluctuations, and there are even extreme cases possible, as were described earlier in connection with the experiments on the form of the seed and the color of the albumen. The true ratios of the numbers can only be ascertained by an average deduced from the sum of as many single values as possible; the greater the number, the more are merely chance effects eliminated.

The law of combination of different characters which governs the development of the hybrids finds therefore its foundation and explanation in the principle enunciated, that the hybrids produce egg cells and pollen cells which in equal numbers represent all constant forms which result from the combinations of all the characters brought together in fertilization.

## Content Questions

1. In the design of Mendel's experiment, why is it important that "all members of the series developed in each successive generation should be, *without exception,* subjected to observation"? (100)

2. What does Mendel mean by the "statistical relations" of different forms? (99)

3. Why is it important for Mendel to confirm that "the pea hybrids form pollen and egg cells which, in their constitution, represent in equal numbers all constant forms which result from the combination of the characters united in fertilization"? (111)

## Application Questions

1. How do the results from the experiment examining the first generation bred from the hybrids help to explain what we know today as Mendel's law of segregation?

2. Today, we often construct Punnett squares to aid in the analysis of patterns of inheritance. Using a Punnett square analysis, explain why the ratio obtained for experiment 1 (dealing with seed shape) for the first generation bred from the hybrids was approximately 3:1. (104) Include in your explanation the following terms: *gene, allele, dominant, recessive, genotype, phenotype, homozygous,* and *heterozygous.*

## Discussion Questions

1. Why does Mendel say that the importance of the solution to the question he is investigating "cannot be overestimated in connection with the history of the evolution of organic forms"? (100)

2. What do Mendel's experiments, and the way in which he recounts them, reveal about his conception of the scientific method?

3. What is the question that Mendel is seeking a solution to?

4. Why is it important that "transitional forms were not observed in any experiment"? (104)

# Claude Bernard

A French scientist who became one of the first and most influential experimental physiologists, Claude Bernard (1813–1878) was a contemporary of Gregor Mendel and Charles Darwin. He made several important physiological discoveries, including how pancreatic juices function in digestion, how the vasomotor nerves regulate blood supply, and how the liver helps regulate glucose levels. He is best known, however, for his crusade to make physiology an exact, experimental science. He was a fierce opponent of vitalism, the belief that life is defined by a nonmaterial vital principle, and earned a reputation as one of the strictest mechanists, who believed that life could be wholly explained on a physical and chemical basis. Bernard argued that biology could advance only when scientists recognized the principle of absolute determinism, which dictated that living beings were governed by scientific laws as rigid as those that obtained in the inorganic world.

Bernard earned a doctorate in science in 1853, and the next year the Sorbonne created a chair of general physiology for him. He had not always planned to pursue a career in science, however; as a young man he had hoped to make a living as a composer and playwright. He wrote a musical farce, which was produced, and a five-act tragedy. He decided to pursue a career in medicine after a Paris literary critic, whom he had consulted about his play, advised him to do so.

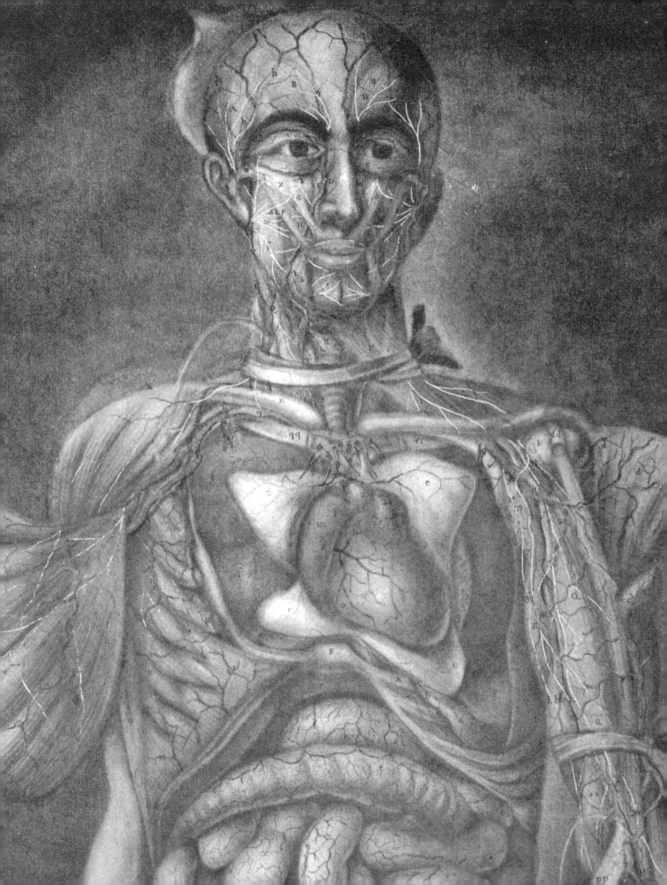

# An Introduction to the Study of Experimental Medicine

*(selection)*

## The Aim of Experimentation Is the Same in Study of Phenomena of Living Bodies As in Study of Phenomena of Inorganic Bodies

If the physicist and the physiologist differ in this, that one busies himself with phenomena taking place in inorganic matter and the other with phenomena occurring in living matter, still they do not differ in the object which they mean to attain. Indeed, they both set themselves a common object, namely, getting back to the immediate cause of the phenomena which they are studying.

Now, what we call the immediate cause of a phenomenon is nothing but the physical and material condition in which it exists or appears. The object of the experimental method or the limit of every scientific research is therefore the same for living bodies as for inorganic bodies; it consists in finding the relations which connect any phenomenon with its immediate cause, or putting it differently, it consists in defining the conditions necessary to the appearance of the phenomenon. Indeed, when an experimenter succeeds in learning the necessary conditions of a phenomenon, he is, in some sense, its master; he can predict its course and its appearance, he can

*This selection is taken from part 2, chapter 1, "Experimental Considerations Common to Living Things and Inorganic Bodies."*

promote or prevent it at will. An experimenter's object, then, is reached; through science, he has extended his power over a natural phenomenon.

We shall therefore define physiology thus: the science whose object it is to study the phenomena of living beings and to *determine* the material conditions in which they appear. Only by the analytic or experimental method can we attain the determination of the conditions of phenomena, in living bodies as well as in inorganic bodies, for we reason in identically the same way in experimenting in all the sciences.

For physiological experimenters, neither spiritualism nor materialism can exist. These words belong to a philosophy which has grown old; they will fall into disuse through the progress of science. We shall never know either spirit or matter, and if this were the proper place I should easily show that on one side, as on the other, we quickly fall into scientific negations. The conclusion is that all such considerations are idle and useless. It is our sole concern to study phenomena, to learn their material conditions and manifestations, and to determine the laws of those manifestations. . . .

To sum up, the object of science is everywhere the same: to learn the material conditions of phenomena. But though this goal is the same in the physicochemical and in biological sciences, it is much harder to reach in the latter because of the mobility and complexity of the phenomena which we meet.

## The Necessary Conditions of Natural Phenomena Are Absolutely Determined in Living Bodies As Well As in Inorganic Bodies

. . . Everything so far said may seem elementary to men cultivating the physicochemical sciences. But among naturalists and especially among physicians, we find men who, in the name of what they call vitalism, express most erroneous ideas on the subject which concerns us. They believe that study of the phenomena of living matter can have no relation to study of the phenomena of inorganic matter. They look on life as a mysterious supernatural influence which acts arbitrarily by freeing itself wholly from determinism, and they brand as materialists all who attempt to reconcile vital phenomena with definite organic and physicochemical conditions. These false ideas are not easy to uproot when once established in the mind; only the progress of science can dispel them. But vitalistic ideas, taken in the sense which we have just indicated, are just a kind of medical superstition—a belief in the supernatural. Now, in medicine, belief in occult causes, whether it is called vitalism or is otherwise named, encourages ignorance and gives birth to a sort of unintentional quackery; that is to say, the belief in an inborn, indefinable science. Confidence in absolute determinism in the phenomena of life leads, on the contrary, to real science and gives the modesty which comes from the consciousness of our little learning and the difficulty of science. This feeling incites us, in turn, to work toward knowledge, and to this feeling alone, science in the end owes all its progress. . . .

## The Limits of Our Knowledge Are the Same in the Phenomena of Living Bodies and in the Phenomena of Inorganic Bodies

The nature of our mind leads us to seek the essence or the why of things. Thus we aim beyond the goal that it is given us to reach, for experience soon teaches us that we cannot get beyond the how, i.e., beyond the immediate cause or the necessary conditions of phenomena. In this respect the limits of our knowledge are the same in biological as in physicochemical sciences.

When, by successive analyses, we find the immediate cause determining the circumstances in which a phenomenon presents itself, we reach a scientific goal beyond which we cannot pass. When we know that water, with all its properties, results from combining oxygen and hydrogen in certain proportions, we know everything we can know about it, and that corresponds to the how and not to the why of things. We know how water can be made, but why does the combination of one volume of oxygen with two volumes of hydrogen produce water? We have no idea. In medicine it is equally absurd to concern oneself with the question why. Yet physicians ask it often. It was probably to make fun of this tendency, which results from lack of the sense of limits to our learning, that Molière put the following answer into the mouth of his candidate for the medical degree. Asked why opium puts people to sleep, he answered: *"Quia est in eo virtus dormitiva, cujus est natura sensus assoupire."*[1] This answer seems ludicrous and absurd,

---

1. ["Because of its sleep-inducing power, the nature of which is to make the senses sleepy."]

119

yet no other answer could be made. In the same way, if we wished to answer the question "Why does hydrogen, in combining with oxygen, produce water?" we should have to answer "Because hydrogen has the quality of being able to beget water." Only the question why, then, is really absurd, because it necessarily involves a naive or ridiculous answer. So we had better recognize that we do not know and that the limits of our knowledge are precisely here.

In physiology, if we prove, for instance, that carbon monoxide is deadly when uniting more firmly than oxygen with the hemoglobin, we know all that we can know about the cause of death. Experience teaches us that a part of the mechanism of life is lacking; oxygen can no longer enter the organism, because it cannot displace the carbon monoxide in its union with the hemoglobin. But why has carbon monoxide more affinity than oxygen for this substance? Why is entrance of oxygen into the organism necessary to life? Here is the limit of our knowledge in our present state of learning; and even assuming that we succeed in further advancing our experimental analysis, we shall reach a blind cause at which we shall be forced to stop, without finding the primal reason for things.

Let us add that, when the relative determinism of a phenomenon is established, our scientific goal is reached. Experimental analysis of the conditions of the phenomenon, when pushed still further, gives us fresh information, but really teaches us nothing about the nature of the phenomenon originally determined. The conditions necessary to a phenomenon teach us nothing about its nature. When we know that physical and chemical contact between the blood and the cerebral nerve cells is necessary to the production of intellectual phenomena, that points to conditions, but it cannot teach us anything about the primary nature of intelligence. Similarly, when we know that friction and that chemical action produce electricity, we are still ignorant of the primary nature of electricity.

We must therefore, in my opinion, stop differentiating the phenomena of living bodies from those of inorganic bodies by a distinction based on our own ability to know the nature of the former and our inability to know that of the latter. The truth is that the nature or very essence of phenomena, whether vital or mineral, will always remain unknown. The essence of the simplest mineral phenomenon is as completely unknown to chemists and physicists today as is the essence of intellectual phenomena or of any other vital phenomenon to physiologists. That, moreover, is easy to apprehend;

knowledge of the inmost nature or the absolute, in the simplest phenomenon, would demand knowledge of the whole universe, for every phenomenon of the universe is evidently a sort of radiation from that universe to whose harmony it contributes. In living bodies absolute truth would be still harder to attain, because, besides implying knowledge of the universe outside a living body, it would also demand complete knowledge of the organism which, as we have long been saying, is a little world (microcosm) in the great universe (macrocosm). Absolute knowledge could, therefore, leave nothing outside itself, and only on condition of knowing everything could man be granted its attainment. Man behaves as if he were destined to reach this absolute knowledge, and the incessant why which he puts to nature proves it. Indeed, this hope, constantly disappointed, constantly reborn, sustains and always will sustain successive generations in the passionate search for truth.

Our feelings lead us at first to believe that absolute truth must lie within our realm, but study takes from us, little by little, these chimerical conceits. Science has just the privilege of teaching us what we do not know by replacing feeling with reason and experience and clearly showing us the present boundaries of our knowledge. But by a marvelous compensation, science, in humbling our pride, proportionately increases our power. Men of science who carry experimental analysis to the point of relatively determining a phenomenon doubtless see clearly their own ignorance of the phenomenon in its primary cause, but they have become its master; the instrument at work is unknown, but they can use it. This is true of all experimental sciences in which we can reach only relative or partial truths and know phenomena only in their necessary conditions. But this knowledge is enough to broaden our power over nature. Though we do not know the essence of phenomena, we can produce or prevent their appearance, because we can regulate their physicochemical conditions. We do not know the essence of fire, of electricity, of light, and still we regulate their phenomena to our own advantage. We know absolutely nothing of the essence even of life, but we shall nevertheless regulate vital phenomena as soon as we know enough of their necessary conditions. Only in living bodies these conditions are much more complex and more difficult to grasp than in inorganic bodies; that is the whole difference.

To sum up, if our feeling constantly puts the question why, our reason shows us that only the question how is within our range; for the moment, then, only the question how concerns men of science and experimenters. If we cannot know why opium and its alkaloids put us to sleep, we can learn the mechanism of sleep and know how opium or its ingredients puts us to sleep, for sleep takes place only because an active substance enters into contact with certain organic substances which it changes. Learning these changes will give us the means of producing or preventing sleep, and we shall be able to act on the phenomenon and regulate it at pleasure.

## Content Questions

1. According to Bernard, how does "getting back to the immediate cause of the phenomena" that a scientist is studying lead to power over those phenomena? (117–118)

2. Why does Bernard think that physiological experimenters must recognize that both spiritualism and materialism are "idle and useless"? (118)

3. What is the scientific experimenter's goal, as Bernard defines it? Why must those studying life use the same experimental method used by physicists and chemists?

4. Why does belief in vitalism pose a threat to the practice of biological science, in Bernard's view? (118–119)

5. According to Bernard, why is it absurd to attempt to answer why questions, as opposed to how questions? Why will the scientist eventually reach a "blind cause" and be "forced to stop, without finding the primal reason for things"? (120)

6. What does Bernard mean when he says that "science, in humbling our pride, proportionately increases our power"? (121)

## Application Questions

At the time Bernard wrote, he and his colleagues were unaware of the biochemical reason that carbon monoxide has a greater affinity for hemoglobin than does oxygen. They were also unaware of the fundamental biochemical reason that oxygen is essential to life.

1. What is our current understanding of the biochemical reason that carbon monoxide has a greater affinity for hemoglobin than does oxygen?

2. What is our current understanding of the fundamental reason that oxygen is essential to life? What is our current understanding of the central role that oxygen plays in the process of energy transfer in living things?

3. Does our current understanding of the biochemical answers to these questions invalidate all or parts of Bernard's argument? Why or why not?

4. How is Bernard's argument affected when we take into account that life has an evolutionary history? For example, if we begin to understand the roles played by hemoglobin and oxygen in terms of their evolutionary history within living systems, does this enable us to answer why questions as well as how questions?

## Discussion Questions

1. Why is power over nature desirable, in Bernard's view? Does he acknowledge any ethical limitations to this power?

2. In Bernard's view, is there any explanation for "the nature of our mind" being such that we "seek the essence or the why of things," thus setting our "aim beyond the goal that it is given us to reach"? (119)

3. Bernard says that "man behaves as if he were destined to reach this absolute knowledge, and the incessant why which he puts to nature proves it. Indeed, this hope, constantly disappointed, constantly reborn, sustains and always will sustain successive generations in the passionate search for truth." (121) Is this a good thing, in Bernard's view? If it is, what does it mean for this behavior to be founded on an illusion?

# Loren Eiseley

By bringing a poetic sensibility to bear on scientific questions, Loren Eiseley (1907–1977) awakened a wide audience to anthropology in the years following World War II. Writing at a time when anxiety about the prospects for humanity's survival was increasing, Eiseley offered his readers a longer perspective on human development, and his often dark meditations on life and its origins struck a national nerve. His 1957 book *The Immense Journey,* from which "The Snout" is taken, became a surprise bestseller. Throughout his writing career, he focused on evolution and the effort to make sense of a Darwinian universe. He went on to write more than a dozen books, which included poetry and autobiography as well as scientific works.

Eiseley was profoundly influenced by his childhood in Lincoln, Nebraska, where he learned that outwardly uninspiring landscapes may reveal unexpected natural wonders. After an academic career that was repeatedly interrupted—once by tuberculosis—Eiseley earned a Ph.D. from the University of Pennsylvania, where he became a professor of anthropology and pursued research into early postglacial man, Pleistocene fossils, and Ice Age plants. He also served as the curator of early man at the university's museum for thirty years.

# The Snout

Ihave long been an admirer of the octopus. The cephalopods are very old, and they have slipped, protean, through many shapes. They are the wisest of the mollusks, and I have always felt it to be just as well for us that they never came ashore, but—there are other things that have.

There is no need to be frightened. It is true some of the creatures are odd, but I find the situation rather heartening than otherwise. It gives one a feeling of confidence to see nature still busy with experiments, still dynamic, and not through nor satisfied because a Devonian fish managed to end as a two-legged character with a straw hat. There are other things brewing and growing in the oceanic vat. It pays to know this. It pays to know there is just as much future as there is past. The only thing that doesn't pay is to be sure of man's own part in it.

There are things down there still coming ashore. Never make the mistake of thinking life is now adjusted for eternity. It gets into your head—the certainty, I mean—the human certainty, and then you miss it all: the things on the tide flats and what they mean, and why, as my wife says, "they ought to be watched."

The trouble is we don't know what to watch for. I have a friend, one of these Explorers Club people, who drops in now and then between trips to tell me about the size of crocodile jaws in Uganda or what happened on some back beach in Arnhem Land.

"They fell out of the trees," he said. "Like rain. And into the boat."

"Uh?" I said, noncommittally.

"They did *so*," he protested, "and they were hard to catch."

"Really—," I said.

"We were pushing a dugout up one of the tidal creeks in northern Australia and going fast when *smacko* we jam this mangrove bush and the things come tumbling down.

"What were they doing sitting up there in bunches? I ask you. It's no place for a fish. Besides that they had a way of sidling off with those popeyes trained on you. I never liked it. Somebody ought to keep an eye on them."

"Why?" I asked.

"I don't know why," he said impatiently, running a rough, square hand through his hair and wrinkling his forehead. "I just mean they make you feel that way, is all. A fish belongs in the water. It ought to stay there—just as we live on land in houses. Things ought to know their place and stay in it, but those fish have got a way of sidling off. As though they had mental reservations and weren't keeping any contracts. See what I mean?"

"I see what you mean," I said gravely. "They ought to be watched. My wife thinks so too. About a lot of things."

"She does?" He brightened. "Then that's two of us. I don't know why, but they give you that feeling."

He didn't know why, but I thought that I did.

It began as such things always begin—in the ooze of unnoticed swamps, in the darkness of eclipsed moons. It began with a strangled gasping for air.

The pond was a place of reek and corruption, of fetid smells, and of oxygen-starved fish breathing through laboring gills. At times the slowly contracting circle of the water left little windrows of minnows who skittered desperately to escape the sun, but who died, nevertheless, in the fat, warm mud. It was a place of low life. In it the human brain began.

There were strange snouts in those waters, strange barbels nuzzling the bottom ooze, and there was time—three hundred million years of it—but mostly, I think, it was the ooze. By day the temperature in the world outside the pond rose to a frightful intensity; at night the sun went down in smoking red. Dust storms marched in incessant progression across a wilderness whose plants were the plants of long ago. Leafless and weird and stiff they lingered by the water, while over vast areas of grassless uplands the winds blew until red stones took on the polish of reflecting mirrors. There was nothing to hold the land in place. Winds howled, dust clouds rolled, and brief erratic torrents choked with silt ran down to the sea. It was a time of dizzying contrasts, a time of change.

On the oily surface of the pond, from time to time a snout thrust upward, took in air with a queer grunting inspiration, and swirled back to the bottom. The pond was doomed, the water was foul, and the oxygen almost gone, but the creature would not die. It could breathe air direct through a little accessory lung, and it could walk. In all that weird and lifeless landscape, it was the only thing that could. It walked rarely and under protest, but that was not surprising. The creature was a fish.

In the passage of days the pond became a puddle, but the Snout survived. There was dew one dark night and a coolness in the empty streambed. When the sun rose next morning the pond was an empty place of cracked mud, but the Snout did not lie there. He had gone. Downstream there were other ponds. He breathed air for a few hours and hobbled slowly along on the stumps of heavy fins.

It was an uncanny business if there had been anyone there to see. It was a journey best not observed in daylight, it was something that needed swamps and shadows and the touch of the night dew. It was a monstrous penetration of a forbidden element, and the Snout kept his face from the light. It was just as well, though the face should not be mocked. In three hundred million years it would be our own.

There was something fermenting in the brain of the Snout. He was no longer entirely a fish. The ooze had marked him. It takes a swamp-and-tide-flat zoologist to tell you about life; it is in this domain that the living suffer great extremes, it is here that the water failures, driven to desperation, make starts in a new element. It is here that strange compromises are made and new senses are born. The Snout was no exception. Though he breathed and walked primarily in order to stay in the water, he was coming ashore.

He was not really a successful fish except that he was managing to stay alive in a noisome, uncomfortable, oxygen-starved environment. In fact the time was coming when the last of his kind, harried by more ferocious and speedier fishes, would slip off the edge of the continental shelf, to seek safety in the sunless abysses of the deep sea. But the Snout was a freshwater crossopterygian, to give him his true name, and cumbersome and plodding though he was, something had happened back of his eyes. The ooze had gotten in its work.

It is interesting to consider what sort of creatures we, the remote descendants of the Snout, might be, except for that green quagmire out of which he came. Mammalian insects perhaps we should have been—solid-brained, our neurons wired for mechanical responses, our lives running out with the perfection of beautiful, intricate, and mindless clocks. More likely we should never have existed at all. It was the Snout and the ooze that did it. Perhaps there also, among rotting fish heads and blue, night-burning bog lights, moved the eternal mystery, the careful finger of God. The increase was not much. It was two bubbles, two thin-walled little balloons at the end of the Snout's small brain. The cerebral hemispheres had appeared.

Among all the experiments in that dripping, ooze-filled world, one was vital: the brain had to be fed. The nerve tissues are insatiable devourers of oxygen. If they do not get it, life is gone. In stagnant swamp waters, only the development of a highly efficient blood supply to the brain can prevent disaster. And among those gasping, dying creatures, whose small brains winked out forever in the long Silurian drought, the Snout and his brethren survived.

Over the exterior surface of the Snout's tiny brain ran the myriad blood vessels that served it; through the greatly enlarged choroid plexuses, other vessels pumped oxygen into the spinal fluid. The brain was a thin-walled tube fed from both surfaces. It could only exist as a thing of thin walls permeated with oxygen. To thicken, to lay down solid masses of nervous tissue such as exist among the fishes in oxygenated waters was to invite disaster. The Snout lived on a bubble, two bubbles in his brain.

It was not that his thinking was deep; it was only that it had to be thin. The little bubbles of the hemispheres helped to spread the area upon which higher correlation centers could be built, and yet preserve those areas from the disastrous thickenings which meant oxygen death to the swamp dweller. There is a mystery about those thickenings which culminate in the so-called solid brain. It is the brain of insects, of the modern fishes, of some reptiles and all birds. Always it marks the appearance of elaborate patterns of instinct and the end of thought. A road has been taken which, anatomically, is well-nigh irretraceable; it does not lead in the direction of a high order of consciousness.

Wherever, instead, the thin sheets of gray matter expand upward into the enormous hemispheres of the human brain, laughter, or it may be sorrow, enters in. Out of the choked Devonian waters emerged sight and sound and the music that rolls invisible through the composer's brain. They are there still in the ooze along the tideline, though no one notices. The world is fixed, we say: fish in the sea, birds in the air. But in the mangrove swamps by the Niger, fish climb trees and ogle uneasy naturalists who try unsuccessfully to chase them back to the water. There are things still coming ashore.

The door to the past is a strange door. It swings open and things pass through it, but they pass in one direction only. No man can return across that threshold, though he can look down still and see the green light waver in the water weeds.

There are two ways to seek the doorway: in the swamps of the inland waterways and along the tide flats of the estuaries where rivers come to the sea. By those two pathways life came ashore. It was not the magnificent march through the breakers and up the cliffs that we fondly imagine. It was a stealthy advance made in suffocation and terror, amid the leaching bite of chemical discomfort. It was made by the failures of the sea.

Some creatures have slipped through the invisible chemical barrier between salt and fresh water into the tidal rivers, and later come ashore; some have crept upward from the salt. In all cases, however, the first adventure into the dreaded atmosphere seems to have been largely determined by the inexorable crowding of enemies and by the retreat further and further into marginal situations where the oxygen supply was depleted. Finally, in the ruthless selection of the swamp margins or in the scramble for food on the tide flats, the land becomes home.

Not the least interesting feature of some of the tide-flat emergents is their definite antipathy for the full tide. It obstructs their food-collecting on the mud banks and brings their enemies. Only extremes of fright will drive them into the water for any period.

I think it was the great nineteenth-century paleontologist Cope who first clearly enunciated what he called the "law of the unspecialized," the contention that it was not from the most highly organized and dominant forms of a given geological era that the master type of a succeeding period evolved, but that instead the dominant forms tended to arise from more lowly and generalized animals which were capable of making new adaptations and which were not narrowly restricted to a given environment.

There is considerable truth to this observation, but, for all that, the idea is not simple. Who is to say without foreknowledge of the future which animal is specialized and which is not? We have only to consider our remote ancestor, the Snout, to see the intricacies into which the law of the unspecialized may lead us.

If we had been making zoological observations in the Paleozoic age, with no knowledge of the strange realms life was to penetrate in the future, we would probably have regarded the Snout as specialized. We would have seen his air-bladder lung, his stubby, sluggish fins, and his odd ability to wriggle overland as specialized adaptations to a peculiarly restricted environmental niche in stagnant continental waters. We would have thought in water terms, and we would have dismissed the Snout as an interesting failure off the main line of progressive evolution, escaping from his enemies and surviving successfully only in the dreary and marginal surroundings scorned by the swift-finned teleost fishes who were destined to dominate the seas and all quick waters.

Yet it was this poor specialization—this bog-trapped failure—whose descendants, in three great movements, were to dominate the earth. It is only now, looking backward, that we dare to regard him as "generalized." The Snout was the first vertebrate to pop completely through the water membrane into a new dimension. His very specializations and failures, in a water sense, had preadapted him for a world he scarcely knew existed.

The day of the Snout was over three hundred million years ago. Not long since, I read a book in which a prominent scientist spoke cheerfully of some ten billion years of future time remaining to us. He pointed out happily the things that man might do throughout that period. Fish in the sea, I thought again, birds in the air. The climb all far behind us, the species fixed and sure. No wonder my explorer friend had had a momentary qualm when he met the mudskippers with their mental reservations and lack of promises. There is something wrong with our worldview. It is still Ptolemaic, though the sun is no longer believed to revolve around the earth.

We teach the past, we see farther backward into time than any race before us, but we stop at the present, or at best, we project far into the future idealized versions of ourselves. All that long way behind us we see, perhaps inevitably, through human eyes alone. We see ourselves as the culmination and the end, and if we do indeed consider our passing, we think that sunlight will go with us and the earth be dark. We are the end. For us continents rose and fell, for us the waters and the air were mastered, for us the great living web has pulsated and grown more intricate.

To deny this, a man once told me, is to deny God. This puzzled me. I went back along the pathway to the marsh. I went, not in the past, not by the bones of dead things, not down the lost roadway of the Snout. I went instead in daylight, in the Now, to see if the door was still there and to see what things passed through.

## Content Questions

1. What is "the law of the unspecialized"? (131) According to Eiseley, why is it difficult to determine which animals are "specialized"? (132)

2. Why does Eiseley characterize our view of the world as "still Ptolemaic, though the sun is no longer believed to revolve around the earth"? (132) What characterizes the Ptolemaic view he describes, and what does he imply is a more accurate way of looking at the world?

## Application Questions

1. According to Eiseley, the Snout possessed a "little accessory lung" that allowed it to take oxygen from the air, thus giving it an adaptive advantage over other fish that were attempting to take a limited supply of oxygen from the water through their gills. What are the underlying structural reasons why lungs are more efficient than gills in removing oxygen from the air? (129)

2. Eiseley states that the brain of the Snout "could only exist as a thing of thin walls permeated with oxygen. To thicken, to lay down solid masses of nervous tissue such as exist among the fishes in oxygenated waters was to invite disaster." (130) Taking into account the relation between surface area and volume, explain the underlying biological reason that solid masses of nervous tissue would be so disastrous.

3. Making reference to "The Snout," show how Darwin's theory of natural selection explains the evolutionary movement of vertebrates onto land. Identify the key anatomical and physiological variations in our vertebrate ancestors and important features of the environment that probably played a role in the process.

## Discussion Questions

1. What does Eiseley mean when he says that "the only thing that doesn't pay is to be sure of man's own part in it [the future]"? (127)

2. Why does Eiseley name the air-breathing, walking fish "the Snout"? Why does he give the essay this title?

3. Why does Eiseley say that evolution was an advance "made by the failures of the sea"? (131) How was the Snout a failure?

4. What does Eiseley mean when he says that "wherever . . . the thin sheets of gray matter expand upward into the enormous hemispheres of the human brain, laughter, or it may be sorrow, enters in"? (131) Why is he uncertain of whether it's laughter or sorrow that enters in?

5. How can denying that the earth was made for human beings be to "deny God," as a man once told Eiseley? (133)

6. In "The Snout," what major point is Eiseley making about human evolution? About the typical human view of the past and the future?

# Rachel Carson

Rachel Carson (1907–1964) galvanized public opinion as few science writers have when she tackled the subject of ecological damage caused by the extensive and poorly regulated use of synthetic pesticides. In her book *Silent Spring* (1962), Carson alerted the American people to the hazards of the more than two hundred chemicals for killing insects and weeds that had been synthesized and sold since the 1940s. She also emphasized the ongoing nature of the danger: the long-term effects of these chemicals were unknown and laboratories were developing approximately five hundred new chemicals a year. Carson's clear prose and compelling evidence so influenced public opinion that DDT, one of the most dangerous pesticides at the time, was banned in the United States except in extreme health emergencies. From a scientific standpoint, Carson's work placed an important new stress on how humankind's alteration of the environment could affect natural selection.

*Silent Spring* grew out of Carson's lifelong concern with nature and the environment. After graduating from college, Carson studied at Woods Hole Marine Biological Laboratory and earned an M.A. in zoology from Johns Hopkins University. Her writing career began during the Great Depression, when she was hired to write radio spots by what is now the U.S. Fish and Wildlife Service. In 1949, Carson became the service's editor in chief, researching and writing about natural resources and conservation. In 1952, the year after her prize-winning book *The Sea Around Us* was published, she resigned from her job to become a full-time writer.

# Silent Spring

*(selection)*

For the first time in the history of the world, every human being is now subjected to contact with dangerous chemicals, from the moment of conception until death. In the less than two decades of their use, the synthetic pesticides have been so thoroughly distributed throughout the animate and inanimate world that they occur virtually everywhere. They have been recovered from most of the major river systems and even from streams of groundwater flowing unseen through the earth. Residues of these chemicals linger in soil to which they may have been applied a dozen years before. They have entered and lodged in the bodies of fish, birds, reptiles, and domestic and wild animals so universally that scientists carrying on animal experiments find it almost impossible to locate subjects free from such contamination. They have been found in fish in remote mountain lakes, in earthworms burrowing in soil, in the eggs of birds—and in man himself. For these chemicals are now stored in the bodies of the vast majority of human beings, regardless of age. They occur in the mother's milk and probably in the tissues of the unborn child.

All this has come about because of the sudden rise and prodigious growth of an industry for the production of man-made, or synthetic, chemicals with insecticidal properties. This industry is a child of the Second

*This selection is taken from chapter 3, "Elixirs of Death," and chapter 17, "The Other Road."*

World War. In the course of developing agents of chemical warfare, some of the chemicals created in the laboratory were found to be lethal to insects. The discovery did not come by chance: insects were widely used to test chemicals as agents of death for man.

The result has been a seemingly endless stream of synthetic insecticides. In being man-made—by ingenious laboratory manipulation of the molecules, substituting atoms, altering their arrangement—they differ sharply from the simpler insecticides of prewar days. These were derived from naturally occurring minerals and plant products—compounds of arsenic, copper, lead, manganese, zinc, and other minerals; pyrethrum from the dried flowers of chrysanthemums; nicotine sulphate from some of the relatives of tobacco; and rotenone from leguminous plants of the East Indies.

What sets the new synthetic insecticides apart is their enormous biological potency. They have immense power not merely to poison but to enter into the most vital processes of the body and change them in sinister and often deadly ways. Thus, as we shall see, they destroy the very enzymes whose function is to protect the body from harm, they block the oxidation processes from which the body receives its energy, they prevent the normal functioning of various organs, and they may initiate in certain cells the slow and irreversible change that leads to malignancy.

Yet new and more deadly chemicals are added to the list each year and new uses are devised, so that contact with these materials has become practically worldwide. The production of synthetic pesticides in the United States soared from 124,259,000 pounds in 1947 to 637,666,000 pounds in 1960—more than a fivefold increase. The wholesale value of these products was well over a quarter of a billion dollars. But in the plans and hopes of the industry this enormous production is only a beginning.

A Who's Who of pesticides is therefore of concern to us all. If we are going to live so intimately with these chemicals—eating and drinking them, taking them into the very marrow of our bones—we had better know something about their nature and their power. . . .

The vast majority [of modern insecticides] fall into one of two large groups of chemicals. One, represented by DDT, is known as the "chlorinated hydrocarbons." The other group consists of the organic phosphorus insecticides and is represented by the reasonably familiar Malathion and parathion.

All have one thing in common. As mentioned above, they are built on a basis of carbon atoms, which are also the indispensable building blocks of the living world, and thus classed as "organic." To understand them, we must see of what they are made and how, although linked with the basic chemistry of all life, they lend themselves to the modifications which make them agents of death.

The basic element, carbon, is one whose atoms have an almost infinite capacity for uniting with each other in chains and rings and various other configurations and for becoming linked with atoms of other substances. Indeed, the incredible diversity of living creatures from bacteria to the great blue whale is largely due to this capacity of carbon. The complex protein molecule has the carbon atom as its basis, as have molecules of fat, carbohydrates, enzymes, and vitamins. So, too, have enormous numbers of non-living things, for carbon is not necessarily a symbol of life.

Some organic compounds are simply combinations of carbon and hydrogen. The simplest of these is methane, or marsh gas, formed in nature by the bacterial decomposition of organic matter under water. Mixed with air in proper proportions, methane becomes the dreaded "fire damp" of coal mines. Its structure is beautifully simple, consisting of one carbon atom to which four hydrogen atoms have become attached:

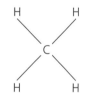

Chemists have discovered that it is possible to detach one or all of the hydrogen atoms and substitute other elements. For example, by substituting one atom of chlorine for one of hydrogen we produce methyl chloride:

Take away three hydrogen atoms and substitute chlorine and we have the anesthetic chloroform:

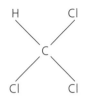

Substitute chlorine atoms for all of the hydrogen atoms and the result is carbon tetrachloride, the familiar cleaning fluid:

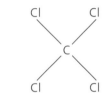

In the simplest possible terms, these changes rung upon the basic molecule of methane illustrate what a chlorinated hydrocarbon is. But this illustration gives little hint of the true complexity of the chemical world of the hydrocarbons, or of the manipulations by which the organic chemist creates his infinitely varied materials. For instead of the simple methane molecule with its single carbon atom, he may work with hydrocarbon molecules consisting of many carbon atoms, arranged in rings or chains, with side chains or branches, holding to themselves with chemical bonds not merely simple atoms of hydrogen or chlorine but also a wide variety of chemical groups. By seemingly slight changes the whole character of the substance is changed; for example, not only what is attached but the place of attachment to the carbon atom is highly important. Such ingenious manipulations have produced a battery of poisons of truly extraordinary power.

DDT (short for dichloro-diphenyl-trichloroethane) was first synthesized by a German chemist in 1874, but its properties as an insecticide were not discovered until 1939. Almost immediately DDT was hailed as a means of stamping out insect-borne disease and winning the farmers' war against crop destroyers overnight. The discoverer, Paul Müller of Switzerland, won the Nobel Prize.

DDT is now so universally used that in most minds the product takes on the harmless aspect of the familiar. Perhaps the myth of the harmlessness of DDT rests on the fact that one of its first uses was the wartime dusting of many thousands of soldiers, refugees, and prisoners, to combat lice. It is widely believed that since so many people came into extremely intimate contact with DDT and suffered no immediate ill effects the chemical must certainly be innocent of harm. This understandable misconception arises from the fact that—unlike other chlorinated hydrocarbons—DDT *in powder form* is not readily absorbed through the skin. Dissolved in oil, as it usually is, DDT is definitely toxic. If swallowed, it is absorbed slowly through the digestive tract; it may also be absorbed through the lungs. Once it has entered the body it is stored largely in organs rich in fatty substances (because DDT itself is fat soluble), such as the adrenals, testes, or thyroid. Relatively large amounts are deposited in the liver, kidneys, and the fat of the large, protective mesenteries that enfold the intestines.

This storage of DDT begins with the smallest conceivable intake of the chemical (which is present as residues on most foodstuffs) and continues until quite high levels are reached. The fatty storage depots act as biological magnifiers, so that an intake of as little as $1/10$ of 1 part per million in the diet results in storage of about 10 to 15 parts per million, an increase of one hundredfold or more. These terms of reference, so commonplace to the chemist or the pharmacologist, are unfamiliar to most of us. One part in a million sounds like a very small amount—and so it is. But such substances are so potent that a minute quantity can bring about vast changes in the body. In animal experiments, 3 parts per million has been found to inhibit an essential enzyme in heart muscle; only 5 parts per million has brought about necrosis or disintegration of liver cells; only 2.5 parts per million of the closely related chemicals dieldrin and chlordane did the same.

This is really not surprising. In the normal chemistry of the human body there is just such a disparity between cause and effect. For example, a quantity of iodine as small as $2/10,000$ of a gram spells the difference between health and disease. Because these small amounts of pesticides are cumulatively stored and only slowly excreted, the threat of chronic poisoning and degenerative changes of the liver and other organs is very real.

Scientists do not agree upon how much DDT can be stored in the human body. Dr. Arnold Lehman, who is the chief pharmacologist of the Food and Drug Administration,[1] says there is neither a floor below which DDT is not absorbed nor a ceiling beyond which absorption and storage cease. On the other hand, Dr. Wayland Hayes of the United States Public Health Service contends that in every individual a point of equilibrium is reached and that DDT in excess of this amount is excreted. For practical purposes it is not particularly important which of these men is right. Storage in human beings has been well investigated, and we know that the average person is storing potentially harmful amounts. According to various studies, individuals with no known exposure (except the inevitable dietary one) store an average of 5.3 parts per million to 7.4 parts per million; agricultural workers 17.1 parts per million; and workers in insecticide plants as high as 648 parts per million! So the range of proven storage is quite wide, and what is even more to the point, the minimum figures are above the level at which damage to the liver and other organs or tissues may begin.

One of the most sinister features of DDT and related chemicals is the way they are passed on from one organism to another through all the links of the food chains. For example, fields of alfalfa are dusted with DDT; meal is later prepared from the alfalfa and fed to hens; the hens lay eggs which contain DDT. Or the hay, containing residues of 7 to 8 parts per million, may be fed to cows. The DDT will turn up in the milk in the amount of about 3 parts per million, but in butter made from this milk the concentration may run to 65 parts per million. Through such a process of transfer, what started out as a very small amount of DDT may end as a heavy concentration. Farmers nowadays find it difficult to obtain uncontaminated fodder for their milk cows, though the Food and Drug Administration forbids the presence of insecticide residues in milk shipped in interstate commerce.

The poison may also be passed on from mother to offspring. Insecticide residues have been recovered from human milk in samples tested by Food and Drug Administration scientists. This means that the breast-fed human infant is receiving small but regular additions to the load of toxic chemicals building up in his body. It is by no means his first exposure, however: there is good reason to believe this begins while he is still in the womb.

1. [In 1962, when *Silent Spring* was first published.]

144

In experimental animals the chlorinated hydrocarbon insecticides freely cross the barrier of the placenta, the traditional protective shield between the embryo and harmful substances in the mother's body. While the quantities so received by human infants would normally be small, they are not unimportant, because children are more susceptible to poisoning than adults. This situation also means that today the average individual almost certainly starts life with the first deposit of the growing load of chemicals his body will be required to carry thenceforth.

All these facts—storage at even low levels, subsequent accumulation, and occurrence of liver damage at levels that may easily occur in normal diets caused Food and Drug Administration scientists to declare as early as 1950 that it is "extremely likely the potential hazard of DDT has been underestimated." There has been no parallel situation in medical history. No one yet knows what the ultimate consequences may be.

Chlordane, another chlorinated hydrocarbon, has all these unpleasant attributes of DDT plus a few that are peculiarly its own. Its residues are long persistent in soil, on foodstuffs, or on surfaces to which it may be applied. Chlordane makes use of all available portals to enter the body. It may be absorbed through the skin, may be breathed in as a spray or dust, and of course is absorbed from the digestive tract if residues are swallowed. Like all other chlorinated hydrocarbons, its deposits build up in the body in cumulative fashion. A diet containing such a small amount of chlordane as 2.5 parts per million may eventually lead to storage of 75 parts per million in the fat of experimental animals.

So experienced a pharmacologist as Dr. Lehman described chlordane in 1950 as "one of the most toxic of insecticides—anyone handling it could be poisoned." Judging by the carefree liberality with which dusts for lawn treatments by suburbanites are laced with chlordane, this warning has not been taken to heart. The fact that the suburbanite is not instantly stricken has little meaning, for the toxins may sleep long in his body, to become manifest months or years later in an obscure disorder almost impossible to trace to its origins. On the other hand, death may strike quickly. One victim who accidentally spilled a 25 percent industrial solution on the skin developed symptoms of poisoning within 40 minutes and died before medical help could be obtained. No reliance can be placed on receiving advance warning which might allow treatment to be had in time.

Heptachlor, one of the constituents of chlordane, is marketed as a separate formulation. It has a particularly high capacity for storage in fat. If the diet contains as little as $1/10$ of 1 part per million, there will be measurable amounts of heptachlor in the body. It also has the curious ability to undergo change into a chemically distinct substance known as heptachlor epoxide. It does this in soil and in the tissues of both plants and animals. Tests on birds indicate that the epoxide that results from this change is more toxic than the original chemical, which in turn is four times as toxic as chlordane.

As long ago as the mid-1930s a special group of hydrocarbons, the chlorinated naphthalenes, was found to cause hepatitis and also a rare and almost invariably fatal liver disease in persons subjected to occupational exposure. They have led to illness in and death of workers in electrical industries; and more recently, in agriculture, they have been considered a cause of a mysterious and usually fatal disease of cattle. In view of these antecedents, it is not surprising that three of the insecticides that are related to this group are among the most violently poisonous of all the hydrocarbons. These are dieldrin, aldrin, and endrin.

Dieldrin, named for a German chemist Diels, is about 5 times as toxic as DDT when swallowed but 40 times as toxic when absorbed through the skin in solution. It is notorious for striking quickly and with terrible effect at the nervous system, sending the victims into convulsions. Persons thus poisoned recover so slowly as to indicate chronic effects. As with other chlorinated hydrocarbons, these long-term effects include severe damage to the liver. The long duration of its residues and the effective insecticidal action make dieldrin one of the most used insecticides today, despite the appalling destruction of wildlife that has followed its use. As tested on quail and pheasants, it has proved to be about 40 to 50 times as toxic as DDT.

There are vast gaps in our knowledge of how dieldrin is stored or distributed in the body, or excreted, for the chemists' ingenuity in devising insecticides has long ago outrun biological knowledge of the way these poisons affect the living organism. However, there is every indication of long storage in the human body, where deposits may lie dormant like a slumbering volcano, only to flare up in periods of physiological stress when the body draws upon its fat reserves. Much of what we do know has been learned through hard experience in the antimalarial campaigns carried out by the World Health Organization. As soon as dieldrin was substituted for DDT in malaria-control work (because the malaria mosquitoes had become resistant to DDT), cases of poisoning among the spraymen began to occur. The seizures were severe—from half to all (varying in the different programs) of the men affected went into convulsions and several died. Some had convulsions as long as *four months* after the last exposure.

Aldrin is a somewhat mysterious substance, for although it exists as a separate entity it bears the relation of alter ego to dieldrin. When carrots are taken from a bed treated with aldrin they are found to contain residues of dieldrin. This change occurs in living tissues and also in soil. Such alchemistic transformations have led to many erroneous reports, for if a chemist, knowing aldrin has been applied, tests for it he will be deceived into thinking all residues have been dissipated. The residues are there, but they are dieldrin and this requires a different test.

Like dieldrin, aldrin is extremely toxic. It produces degenerative changes in the liver and kidneys. A quantity the size of an aspirin tablet is enough to kill more than 400 quail. Many cases of human poisonings are on record, most of them in connection with industrial handling.

Aldrin, like most of this group of insecticides, projects a menacing shadow into the future, the shadow of sterility. Pheasants fed quantities too small to kill them nevertheless laid few eggs, and the chicks that hatched soon died. The effect is not confined to birds. Rats exposed to aldrin had fewer pregnancies and their young were sickly and short-lived. Puppies born of treated mothers died within three days. By one means or another, the new generations suffer for the poisoning of their parents. No one knows whether the same effect will be seen in human beings, yet this chemical has been sprayed from airplanes over suburban areas and farmlands.

Endrin is the most toxic of all the chlorinated hydrocarbons. Although chemically rather closely related to dieldrin, a little twist in its molecular structure makes it 5 times as poisonous. It makes the progenitor of all this group of insecticides, DDT, seem by comparison almost harmless. It is 15 times as poisonous as DDT to mammals, 30 times as poisonous to fish, and about 300 times as poisonous to some birds.

In the decade of its use, endrin has killed enormous numbers of fish, has fatally poisoned cattle that have wandered into sprayed orchards, has poisoned wells, and has drawn a sharp warning from at least one state health department that its careless use is endangering human lives.

In one of the most tragic cases of endrin poisoning there was no apparent carelessness; efforts had been made to take precautions apparently considered adequate. A year-old child had been taken by his American parents to live in Venezuela. There were cockroaches in the house to which they moved, and after a few days a spray containing endrin was used. The baby and the small family dog were taken out of the house before the spraying was done, about nine o'clock one morning. After the spraying the floors were washed. The baby and dog were returned to the house in midafternoon. An hour or so later the dog vomited, went into convulsions, and died. At ten o'clock on the evening of the same day, the baby also vomited, went into convulsions, and lost consciousness. After that fateful contact with endrin, this normal, healthy child became little more than a vegetable—unable to see or hear, subject to frequent muscular spasms, apparently completely cut off from contact with his surroundings. Several months of treatment in a New York hospital failed to change his condition or bring hope of change. "It is extremely doubtful," reported the attending physicians, "that any useful degree of recovery will occur."

The second major group of insecticides, the alkyl, or organic, phosphates, are among the most poisonous chemicals in the world. The chief and most obvious hazard attending their use is that of acute poisoning of people applying the sprays or accidentally coming in contact with drifting spray, with vegetation coated by it, or with a discarded container. In Florida, two children found an empty bag and used it to repair a swing. Shortly thereafter both of them died and three of their playmates became ill. The bag had once contained an insecticide called parathion, one of the organic phosphates; tests established death by parathion poisoning. On another occasion two small boys in Wisconsin, cousins, died on the same night. One had been playing in his yard when spray drifted in from an adjoining field where his father was spraying potatoes with parathion; the other had run playfully into the barn after his father and had put his hand on the nozzle of the spray equipment.

The origin of these insecticides has a certain ironic significance. Although some of the chemicals themselves—organic esters of phosphoric acid—had been known for many years, their insecticidal properties remained to be discovered by a German chemist, Gerhard Schrader, in the late 1930s. Almost immediately the German government recognized the value of these same chemicals as new and devastating weapons in man's war against his own kind, and the work on them was declared secret. Some became the deadly nerve gases. Others, of closely allied structure, became insecticides.

The organic phosphorus insecticides act on the living organism in a peculiar way. They have the ability to destroy enzymes—enzymes that perform necessary functions in the body. Their target is the nervous system, whether the victim is an insect or a warm-blooded animal. Under normal conditions, an impulse passes from nerve to nerve with the aid of a "chemical transmittor" called acetylcholine, a substance that performs an essential function and then disappears. Indeed, its existence is so ephemeral that medical researchers are unable, without special procedures, to sample it before the body has destroyed it. This transient nature of the transmitting chemical is necessary to the normal functioning of the body. If the acetylcholine is not destroyed as soon as a nerve impulse has passed, impulses continue to flash across the bridge from nerve to nerve, as the chemical exerts its effects in an ever more intensified manner. The movements of the whole body become uncoordinated: tremors, muscular spasms, convulsions, and death quickly result.

This contingency has been provided for by the body. A protective enzyme called cholinesterase is at hand to destroy the transmitting chemical once it is no longer needed. By this means a precise balance is struck and the body never builds up a dangerous amount of acetylcholine. But on contact with the organic phosphorus insecticides, the protective enzyme is destroyed, and as the quantity of the enzyme is reduced that of the transmitting chemical builds up. In this effect, the organic phosphorus compounds resemble the alkaloid poison muscarine, found in a poisonous mushroom, the fly amanita.

Repeated exposures may lower the cholinesterase level until an individual reaches the brink of acute poisoning, a brink over which he may be pushed by a very small additional exposure. For this reason it is considered important to make periodic examinations of the blood of spray operators and others regularly exposed.

Parathion is one of the most widely used of the organic phosphates. It is also one of the most powerful and dangerous. Honeybees become "wildly agitated and bellicose" on contact with it, perform frantic cleaning movements, and are near death within half an hour. A chemist, thinking to learn by the most direct possible means the dose acutely toxic to human beings, swallowed a minute amount, equivalent to about 0.00424 ounce. Paralysis followed so instantaneously that he could not reach the antidotes he had prepared at hand, and so he died. Parathion is now said to be a favorite instrument of suicide in Finland. In recent years the State of California has reported an average of more than 200 cases of accidental parathion poisoning annually. In many parts of the world the fatality rate from parathion is startling: 100 fatal cases in India and 67 in Syria in 1958, and an average of 336 deaths per year in Japan.

Yet some 7 million pounds of parathion are now applied to fields and orchards of the United States—by hand sprayers, motorized blowers and dusters, and airplane. The amount used on California farms alone could, according to one medical authority, "provide a lethal dose for 5 to 10 times the whole world's population."

One of the few circumstances that save us from extinction by this means is the fact that parathion and other chemicals of this group are decomposed rather rapidly. Their residues on the crops to which they are applied are therefore relatively short-lived compared with that of the chlorinated hydrocarbons. However, they last long enough to create hazards and produce consequences that range from the merely serious to the fatal. In Riverside, California, 11 out of 30 men picking oranges became violently ill and all but 1 had to be hospitalized. Their symptoms were typical of parathion poisoning. The grove had been sprayed with parathion some two and a half weeks earlier; the residues that reduced them to retching, half-blind, semiconscious misery were 16 to 19 days old. And this is not by any means a record for persistence. Similar mishaps have occurred in groves sprayed a month earlier, and residues have been found in the peel of oranges six months after treatment with standard dosages.

The danger to all workers applying the organic phosphorus insecticides in fields, orchards, and vineyards is so extreme that some states using these chemicals have established laboratories where physicians may obtain aid in diagnosis and treatment. Even the physicians themselves may be in some danger, unless they wear rubber gloves in handling the victims of poisoning. So may a laundress washing the clothing of such victims, which may have absorbed enough parathion to affect her.

Malathion, another of the organic phosphates, is almost as familiar to the public as DDT, being widely used by gardeners, in household insecticides, in mosquito spraying, and in such blanket attacks on insects as the spraying of nearly a million acres of Florida communities for the Mediterranean fruit fly. It is considered the least toxic of this group of chemicals and many people assume they may use it freely and without fear of harm. Commercial advertising encourages this comfortable attitude.

The alleged "safety" of malathion rests on rather precarious ground, although—as often happens—this was not discovered until the chemical had been in use for several years. Malathion is "safe" only because the mammalian liver, an organ with extraordinary protective powers, renders it relatively harmless. The detoxification is accomplished by one of the enzymes of the liver. If, however, something destroys this enzyme or interferes with its action, the person exposed to malathion receives the full force of the poison.

Unfortunately for all of us, opportunities for this sort of thing to happen are legion. A few years ago a team of Food and Drug Administration scientists discovered that when malathion and certain other organic phosphates are administered simultaneously a massive poisoning results—up to 50 times as severe as would be predicted on the basis of adding together the toxicities of the two. In other words, $1/100$ of the lethal dose of each compound may be fatal when the two are combined.

This discovery led to the testing of other combinations. It is now known that many pairs of organic phosphate insecticides are highly dangerous, the toxicity being stepped up or "potentiated" through the combined action. Potentiation seems to take place when one compound destroys the liver enzyme responsible for detoxifying the other. The two need not be given simultaneously. The hazard exists not only for the man who may spray this week with one insecticide and next week with another; it exists also for the consumer of sprayed products. The common salad bowl may easily present a combination of organic phosphate insecticides. Residues well within the legally permissible limits may interact.

The full scope of the dangerous interaction of chemicals is as yet little known, but disturbing findings now come regularly from scientific laboratories. Among these is the discovery that the toxicity of an organic phosphate can be increased by a second agent that is not necessarily an insecticide. For example, one of the plasticizing agents may act even more strongly than another insecticide to make malathion more dangerous. Again, this is because it inhibits the liver enzyme that normally would "draw the teeth" of the poisonous insecticide.

What of other chemicals in the normal human environment? What, in particular, of drugs? A bare beginning has been made on this subject, but already it is known that sonic organic phosphates (parathion and malathion) increase the toxicity of some drugs used as muscle relaxants and that several others (again including malathion) markedly increase the sleeping time of barbiturates.

In Greek mythology the sorceress Medea, enraged at being supplanted by a rival for the affections of her husband, Jason, presented the new bride with a robe possessing magic properties. The wearer of the robe immediately suffered a violent death. This death-by-indirection now finds its counterpart in what are known as "systemic insecticides." These are chemicals with extraordinary properties which are used to convert plants or animals into a sort of Medea's robe by making them actually poisonous. This is done with the purpose of killing insects that may come in contact with them, especially by sucking their juices or blood.

The world of systemic insecticides is a weird world, surpassing the imaginings of the brothers Grimm—perhaps most closely akin to the cartoon world of Charles Addams. It is a world where the enchanted forest of the fairy tales has become the poisonous forest in which an insect that chews a leaf or sucks the sap of a plant is doomed. It is a world where a flea bites a dog and dies because the dog's blood has been made poisonous, where an insect may die from vapors emanating from a plant it has never touched, where a bee may carry poisonous nectar back to its hive and presently produce poisonous honey.

The entomologists' dream of the built-in insecticide was born when workers in the field of applied entomology realized they could take a hint from nature: they found that wheat growing in soil containing sodium selenate was immune to attack by aphids or spider mites. Selenium, a naturally occurring element found sparingly in rocks and soils of many parts of the world, thus became the first systemic insecticide.

What makes an insecticide a systemic is the ability to permeate all the tissues of a plant or animal and make them toxic. This quality is possessed by some chemicals of the chlorinated hydrocarbon group and by others of the organophosphorus group, all synthetically produced, as well as by certain naturally occurring substances. In practice, however, most systemics are drawn from the organophosphorus group because the problem of residues is somewhat less acute.

Systemics act in other devious ways. Applied to seeds, either by soaking or in a coating combined with carbon, they extend their effects into the following plant generation and produce seedlings poisonous to aphids and other sucking insects. Vegetables such as peas, beans, and sugar beets are sometimes thus protected. Cotton seeds coated with a systemic insecticide have been in use for some time in California, where 25 farm laborers planting cotton in the San Joaquin Valley in 1959 were seized with sudden illness, caused by handling the bags of treated seeds.

In England someone wondered what happened when bees made use of nectar from plants treated with systemics. This was investigated in areas treated with a chemical called schradan. Although the plants had been sprayed before the flowers were formed, the nectar later produced contained the poison. The result, as might have been predicted, was that the honey made by the bees also was contaminated with schradan.

Use of animal systemics has concentrated chiefly on control of the cattle grub, a damaging parasite of livestock. Extreme care must be used in order to create an insecticidal effect in the blood and tissues of the host without setting up a fatal poisoning. The balance is delicate, and government veterinarians have found that repeated small doses can gradually deplete an animal's supply of the protective enzyme cholinesterase, so that without warning, a minute additional dose will cause poisoning.

There are strong indications that fields closer to our daily lives are being opened up. You may now give your dog a pill which, it is claimed, will rid him of fleas by making his blood poisonous to them. The hazards discovered in treating cattle would presumably apply to the dog. As yet no one seems to have proposed a human systemic that would make us lethal to a mosquito. Perhaps this is the next step.

~ ~ ~

We stand now where two roads diverge. But unlike the roads in Robert Frost's familiar poem, they are not equally fair. The road we have long been traveling is deceptively easy, a smooth superhighway on which we progress with great speed, but at its end lies disaster. The other fork of the road—the one "less traveled by"—offers our last, our only chance to reach a destination that assures the preservation of our earth.

The choice, after all, is ours to make. If, having endured much, we have at last asserted our "right to know," and if, knowing, we have concluded that we are being asked to take senseless and frightening risks, then we should no longer accept the counsel of those who tell us that we must fill our world with poisonous chemicals; we should look about and see what other course is open to us.

A truly extraordinary variety of alternatives to the chemical control of insects is available. Some are already in use and have achieved brilliant success. Others are in the stage of laboratory testing. Still others are little more than ideas in the minds of imaginative scientists waiting for the opportunity to put them to the test. All have this in common: they are *biological* solutions, based on understanding of the living organisms they seek to control and of the whole fabric of life to which these organisms belong. Specialists representing various areas of the vast field of biology are contributing— entomologists, pathologists, geneticists, physiologists, biochemists, ecologists—all pouring their knowledge and their creative inspirations into the formation of a new science of biotic controls.

"Any science may be likened to a river," says a Johns Hopkins biologist, Professor Carl P. Swanson. "It has its obscure and unpretentious beginning; its quiet stretches as well as its rapids; its periods of drought as well as of fullness. It gathers momentum with the work of many investigators and as it is fed by other streams of thought; it is deepened and broadened by the concepts and generalizations that are gradually evolved."

So it is with the science of biological control in its modern sense. In America it had its obscure beginnings a century ago with the first attempts to introduce natural enemies of insects that were proving troublesome to farmers, an effort that sometimes moved slowly or not at all, but now and again gathered speed and momentum under the impetus of an outstanding success. It had its period of drought when workers in applied entomology, dazzled by the spectacular new insecticides of the 1940s, turned their backs on all biological methods and set foot on "the treadmill of chemical control." But the goal of an insect-free world continued to recede. Now at last, as it has become apparent that the heedless and unrestrained use of chemicals is a greater menace to ourselves than to the targets, the river which is the science of biotic control flows again, fed by new streams of thought.

## Content Questions

1. How does Carson classify modern insecticides? What are the differences between the two largest groups? (140–141)

2. Why is it both ingenious and threatening when insecticides "are built on a basis of carbon atoms"? (141)

3. What characteristics of the carbon atom allow it to serve as the basis of both a huge number of naturally occurring molecules and a wide variety of synthetic pesticides? (141–142)

4. How is the ingestion and accumulation of DDT and other insecticides possible even when foods directly treated with these chemicals are avoided? (143–145)

5. How do the organic phosphorous insecticides attack the nervous system? (149)

6. Why is malathion considered the "least toxic" of the organic phosphates? (151)

7. What is *potentiation* and how does it pose a threat to living organisms? (151)

8. How are systemic insecticides different from other kinds of insecticides? (152)

9. Why is the storage of minute amounts of insecticides in fatty tissues potentially dangerous for humans?

10. Why does Carson compare the proliferation of synthetic chemical pesticides to a "smooth superhighway on which we progress with great speed"? (153)

## Application Questions

1. Applying your knowledge of nervous control and the information presented by Carson, summarize the effects of organic phosphorous insecticides on the neuro-muscular system. Include in your explanation the terms *presynaptic membrane, postsynaptic membrane, synaptic cleft, acetylcholine, acetylcholine receptor,* and *cholinesterase.*

2. *Biological magnification* is a term used to describe the process whereby a persistent chemical (a biologically stable compound, like DDT) when ingested is retained rather than excreted, and is then passed up the food chain in increasing concentrations. Describe the results of research performed since the early 1960s on the effects of DDT on predatory birds such as the bald eagle, peregrine falcon, and osprey. What specific effects did DDT have on these predatory bird populations, and in what way was biological magnification responsible for these effects? What steps have been taken to reverse these effects? How successful are these efforts? Why?

3. What effects can heavy pesticide use have on the genetic makeup of target insect populations? Why can these effects be counterproductive to long-term insect population control?

4. Describe some specific examples of "biological control" methods that have been attempted since the publication of *Silent Spring*. How effective are these methods? Why?

5. Determine the kind of pesticides that are routinely used at your school or in your community. What are the biological benefits and risks involved in their use, and what steps are being taken (or not taken) to safeguard public health?

## Discussion Questions

1. *Silent Spring* helped lead to a ban on the use of DDT in the United States. Based on the excerpt you have read, what makes Carson's book so persuasive?

2. What responsibility does Carson believe scientists have to the public?

3. According to Carson, who is to blame for the proliferation of pesticides that are unsafe or potentially unsafe?

4. In Carson's view, what is the only reasonable alternative to chemical pesticides?

5. Why does Carson use biologist Carl P. Swanson's metaphor of science as a river to explain the science of "biological control" in America? (154)

# Konrad Lorenz

Konrad Lorenz (1903–1989) was the founder of ethology, the comparative study of animal behavior. His emphasis on the continuities between the way animals and people act, particularly in groups, helped change scientific understanding of instincts and adaptation. His most famous work is *On Aggression* (1963). This book's investigation of a "killer instinct" in animals and humankind that prompts members of the same species to fight each other resonated strongly with the public during the Cold War era, as concerns about war and urban violence mounted. By combining riveting accounts of his animal experiments with an overall argument that human aggression could be redirected, though not eliminated, Lorenz both built a strong case for the existence of a "killer instinct" and held out hope that it could be controlled.

From his childhood in Vienna, Lorenz was fascinated with animal behavior. He carefully observed his pet fish, birds, monkeys, dogs, cats, and rabbits and kept detailed records of their actions. Lorenz earned a medical degree in 1928, and a doctorate in zoology in 1933. His initial scientific studies concerned only animals, and he was the first to describe imprinting, an interactive process by which ducklings and goslings learn at a particular age to follow and imitate their parents. For two years during World War II he served in the German army as a physician; after the war he eventually went on to found a comparative ethology department at the Max Planck Institute of Behavioral Physiology, in Seewiesen. He served as director of the institute from 1961 to 1973, the same year he was a cowinner of the Nobel Prize in physiology or medicine.

# Ecce Homo!

It is a curious paradox that the greatest gifts of man, the unique faculties of conceptual thought and verbal speech which have raised him to a level high above all other creatures and given him mastery over the globe, are not altogether blessings, or at least are blessings that have to be paid for very dearly indeed. All the great dangers threatening humanity with extinction are direct consequences of conceptual thought and verbal speech. They drove man out of the paradise in which he could follow his instincts with impunity and do or not do whatever he pleased. There is much truth in the parable of the tree of knowledge and its fruit, though I want to make an addition to it to make it fit into my own picture of Adam: that apple was thoroughly unripe! Knowledge springing from conceptual thought robbed man of the security provided by his well-adapted instincts long, long before it was sufficient to provide him with an equally safe adaptation. Man is, as Arnold Gehlen has so truly said, by nature a jeopardized creature.

Conceptual thought and speech changed all man's evolution by achieving something which is equivalent to the inheritance of acquired characters. We have forgotten that the verb *inherit* had a juridic connotation long before it acquired a biological one. When a man invents, let us say, bow and arrow, not

*This selection is taken from chapter 13, "Ecce Homo!" of* On Aggression.

only his progeny but his entire community will inherit the knowledge and the use of these tools and possess them just as surely as organs grown on the body. Nor is their loss any more likely than the rudimentation of an organ of equal survival value. Thus, within one or two generations a process of ecological adaptation can be achieved which, in normal phylogeny and without the interference of conceptual thought, would have taken a time of an altogether different, much greater order of magnitude. Small wonder, indeed, if the evolution of social instincts and, what is even more important, social inhibitions could not keep pace with the rapid development forced on human society by the growth of traditional culture, particularly material culture.

Obviously, instinctive behavior mechanisms failed to cope with the new circumstances which culture unavoidably produced even at its very dawn. There is evidence that the first inventors of pebble tools, the African australopithecines, promptly used their new weapon to kill not only game, but fellow members of their species as well. Peking man, the Prometheus who learned to preserve fire, used it to roast his brothers: beside the first traces of the regular use of fire lie the mutilated and roasted bones of *Sinanthropus pekinensis* himself.

One is tempted to believe that every gift bestowed on man by his power of conceptual thought has to be paid for with a dangerous evil as the direct consequence of it. Fortunately for us, this is not so. Besides the faculty of conceptual thought, another constituent characteristic of man played an important role in gaining a deeper understanding of his environment, and this is curiosity. Insatiable curiosity is the root of exploration and experimentation, and these activities, even in their most primitive form, imply a function akin to asking questions. Explorative experimentation is a sort of dialogue with surrounding nature. Asking a question and recording the answer leads to anticipating the latter and, given conceptual thought, to the linking of cause and effect. From hence it is but a step to consciously foreseeing the consequences of one's actions. Thus, the same human faculties which supplied man with tools and with power dangerous to himself also gave him the means to prevent their misuse: rational responsibility. I shall now proceed to discuss, one by one, the dangers which humanity incurs by rising above the other animals by virtue of its great, specific gifts. Subsequently I shall try to show in what way the greatest gift of all—rational, responsible morality—functions in banning these dangers. Most important of all, I shall have to expound the functional limitation of morality.

In the chapter on behavior mechanisms functionally analogous to morality, I have spoken of the inhibitions controlling aggression in various social animals, preventing them from injuring or killing fellow members of the species. As I explained, these inhibitions are most important and consequently most highly differentiated in those animals which are capable of killing living creatures of about their own size. A raven can peck out the eye of another with one thrust of its beak; a wolf can rip the jugular vein of another with a single bite. There would be no more ravens and no more wolves if reliable inhibitions did not prevent such actions. Neither a dove nor a hare nor even a chimpanzee is able to kill its own kind with a single peck or bite; in addition, animals with relatively poor defense weapons have a correspondingly great ability to escape quickly, even from specially armed predators which are more efficient in chasing, catching, and killing than even the strongest of their own species. Since there rarely is, in nature, the possibility of such an animal seriously injuring one of its own kind, there is no selection pressure at work here to breed in killing inhibitions. The absence of such inhibitions is apparent to the animal keeper, to his own and to his animals' disadvantage, if he does not take seriously the intraspecific fights of completely "harmless" animals. Under the unnatural conditions of captivity, where a defeated animal cannot escape from its victor, it may be killed slowly and cruelly. In my book *King Solomon's Ring*, I have described in the chapter "Morals and Weapons" how the symbol of peace, the dove, can torture one of its own kind to death, without the arousal of any inhibition.

Anthropologists concerned with the habits of *Australopithecus* have repeatedly stressed that these hunting progenitors of man have left humanity with the dangerous heritage of what they term "carnivorous mentality." This statement confuses the concepts of the carnivore and the cannibal, which are, to a large extent, mutually exclusive. One can only deplore the fact that man has definitely not got a carnivorous mentality! All his trouble arises from his being a basically harmless, omnivorous creature, lacking in natural weapons with which to kill big prey and, therefore, also devoid of the built-in safety devices which prevent "professional" carnivores from abusing their killing power to destroy fellow members of their own species. A lion or a wolf may, on extremely rare occasions, kill another [of its own species] by one angry stroke, but . . . all heavily armed carnivores possess sufficiently reliable inhibitions which prevent the self-destruction of the species.

In human evolution, no inhibitory mechanisms preventing sudden manslaughter were necessary, because quick killing was impossible anyhow; the potential victim had plenty of opportunity to elicit the pity of the aggressor by submissive gestures and appeasing attitudes. No selection pressure arose in the prehistory of mankind to breed inhibitory mechanisms preventing the killing of conspecifics until, all of a sudden, the invention of artificial weapons upset the equilibrium of killing potential and social inhibitions. When it did, man's position was very nearly that of a dove which, by some unnatural trick of nature, has suddenly acquired the beak of a raven. One shudders at the thought of a creature as irascible as all prehuman primates are, swinging a well-sharpened hand ax. Humanity would indeed have destroyed itself by its first inventions were it not for the very wonderful fact that inventions and responsibility are both the achievements of the same specifically human faculty of asking questions.

Not that our prehuman ancestor, even at a stage as yet devoid of moral responsibility, was a fiend incarnate; he was by no means poorer in social instincts and inhibitions than a chimpanzee, which, after all, is—his irascibility not withstanding—a social and friendly creature. But whatever his innate norms of social behavior may have been, they were bound to be thrown out of gear by the invention of weapons. If humanity survived as, after all, it did, it never achieved security from the danger of self-destruction. If moral responsibility and unwillingness to kill have indubitably increased, the ease and emotional impunity of killing have increased at the same rate. The distance at which all shooting weapons takes effect screens the killer against the stimulus situation which would otherwise activate his killing inhibitions. The deep, emotional layers of our personality simply do not register the fact that the crooking of the forefinger to release a shot tears the entrails of another man. No sane man would even go rabbit hunting for pleasure if the necessity of killing his prey with his natural weapons brought home to him the full, emotional realization of what he is actually doing.

The same principle applies, to an even greater degree, to the use of modern remote-control weapons. The man who presses the releasing button is so completely screened against seeing, hearing, or otherwise emotionally realizing the consequences of his action that he can commit it with impunity—even if he is burdened with the power of imagination. Only thus can it be explained that perfectly good-natured men, who would not even smack a naughty child, proved to be perfectly able to release rockets or to lay carpets of incendiary bombs on sleeping cities, thereby committing hundreds and thousands of children to a horrible death in the flames. The fact that it is good, normal men who did this is as eerie as any fiendish atrocity of war!

As an indirect consequence, the invention of artificial weapons has brought about a most undesirable predominance of intraspecific selection within mankind. In the third chapter, in which I discussed the survival value of aggression, and also in the tenth, dealing with the structure of society in rats, I have already spoken of the manner in which competition between the fellow members of one species can produce unadaptive results when it exerts a selection pressure totally unrelated to extraspecific environment.

When man, by virtue of his weapons and other tools, of his clothing, and of fire, had more or less mastered the inimical forces of his extraspecific environment, a state of affairs must have prevailed in which the counterpressures of the hostile neighboring hordes had become the chief selecting factor determining the next steps of human evolution. Small wonder indeed if it produced a dangerous excess of what has been termed the "warrior virtues" of man.

In 1955 I wrote a paper, "On the Killing of Members of the Same Species": "I believe—and human psychologists, particularly psychoanalysts, should test this—that present-day civilized man suffers from insufficient discharge of his aggressive drive. It is more than probable that the evil effects of the human aggressive drives, explained by Sigmund Freud as the results of a special death wish, simply derive from the fact that in prehistoric times intraspecific selection bred into man a measure of aggression drive for which in the social order of today he finds no adequate outlet." If these words contain an element of reproach against psychoanalysis, I must here withdraw them. At the time of writing, there were already some psychoanalysts who did not believe in the death wish and rightly explained the self-destroying effects of aggression as misfunctions of an instinct that was essentially life preserving. Later, I came to know one psychiatrist and psychoanalyst who, even at that time, was examining the problem of the hypertrophy of aggression owing to intraspecific selection.

Sydney Margolin, in Denver, Colorado, made very exact psychoanalytical and psychosociological studies on Prairie Indians, particularly the Utes, and showed that these people suffer greatly from an excess of aggression drive which, under the ordered conditions of present-day North American Indian reservations, they are unable to discharge. It is Margolin's opinion that during the comparatively few centuries when Prairie Indians led a wild life consisting almost entirely of war and raids, there must have been an extreme selection pressure at work, breeding extreme aggressiveness. That this produced changes in the hereditary pattern in such a short time is quite possible. Domestic animals can be changed just as quickly by purposeful selection. Margolin's assumption is supported by the fact that Ute Indians now growing up under completely different educational influences suffer in exactly the same way as the older members of their tribe who grew up under the educational system of their own culture; moreover, the pathological symptoms under discussion are seen only in those Prairie Indians whose tribes were subjected to the selection process described.

Ute Indians suffer more frequently from neurosis than any other human group, and again and again Margolin found that the cause of the trouble was undischarged aggression. Many of these Indians feel and describe themselves as ill, and when asked what is the matter with them they can only say, "I am a Ute!" Violence toward people not of their tribe, and even manslaughter, belong to the order of the day, but attacks on members of the tribe are extremely rare, for they are prevented by a taboo, the severity of which is easy to understand considering the early history of the Utes: a tribe constantly at war with neighboring Indians and, later on, with the white man must avoid at all costs fights between its own members. Anyone killing a member of the tribe is compelled by strict tradition to commit suicide. This commandment was obeyed even by a Ute policeman who had shot a member of his tribe in self-defense while trying to arrest him. The offender, while under the influence of drink, had stabbed his father in the femoral artery, causing him to bleed to death. When the policeman was ordered by his sergeant to arrest the man for manslaughter—it was obviously not murder—he protested, saying that the man would want to die, since he was bound by tradition to commit suicide and would do so by resisting arrest and forcing the policeman to shoot him. He, the policeman, would then have to commit suicide himself. The more-than-shortsighted sergeant stuck to his order, and the tragedy took place exactly as predicted. This and other of Margolin's records read like Greek tragedies: an inexorable fate forces crime upon people and then compels them to expiate voluntarily their involuntarily acquired guilt.

It is objectively convincing, indeed it is proof of the correctness of Margolin's interpretation of the behavior of Ute Indians, that these people are particularly susceptible to accidents. It has been proved that accident proneness may result from repressed aggression, and in these Utes the rate of motor accidents exceeds that of any other car-driving human group. Anybody who has ever driven a fast car when really angry knows—insofar as he is capable of self-observation in this condition—what strong inclination there is to self-destructive behavior in a situation like this. Here even the expression "death wish" seems apt.

It is self-evident that intraspecific selection is still working today in an undesirable direction. There is a high positive selection premium on the instinctive foundations conducive to such traits as the amassing of property, self-assertion, etc., and there is an almost equally high negative premium on simple goodness. Commercial competition today might threaten to fix heredetarily in us hypertrophies of these traits as horrible as the intraspecific aggression evolved by competition between warfaring tribes of Stone Age man. It is fortunate that the accumulation of riches and power does not necessarily lead to large families—rather the opposite—or else the future of mankind would look even darker than it does.

Aggressive behavior and killing inhibitions represent only one special case among many in which phylogenetically adapted behavior mechanisms are thrown out of balance by the rapid change wrought in human ecology and sociology by cultural development. In order to explain the function of responsible morality in reestablishing a tolerable equilibrium between man's instincts and the requirements of a culturally evolved social order, a few words must first be said about social instincts in general. It is a widely held opinion, shared by some contemporary philosophers, that all human behavior patterns which serve the welfare of the community, as opposed to that of the individual, are dictated by specifically human rational thought. Not only is this opinion erroneous, but the very opposite is true. If it were not for a rich endowment of social instincts, man could never have risen above the animal world. All specifically human faculties—the power of speech, cultural tradition, moral responsibility—could have evolved only in a being which, before the very dawn of conceptual thinking, lived in well-organized communities. Our prehuman ancestor was indubitably as true a friend to his friend as a chimpanzee or even a dog, as tender and solicitous to the young of his community and as self-sacrificing in its defense, eons before he developed conceptual thought and became aware of the consequences of his actions. . . .

Our Cro-Magnon warrior had plenty of hostile neighbors against whom to discharge his aggressive drive, and he had just the right number of reliable friends to love. His moral responsibility was not overtaxed by an exercise of function which prevented him from striking, in sudden anger, at his companions with his sharpened hand ax. The increase in number of individuals belonging to the same community is in itself sufficient to upset the balance between the personal bonds and the aggressive drive. It is definitely detrimental to the bond of friendship if a person has too many friends. It is proverbial that one can have only a few really close friends. To have a large number of "acquaintances," many of whom may be faithful allies with a legitimate claim to be regarded as real friends, overtaxes a man's capacity for personal love and dilutes the intensity of his emotional attachment. The close crowding of many individuals in a small space brings about a fatigue of all social reactions. Every inhabitant of a modern city is familiar with the surfeit of social relationships and responsibilities and knows the disturbing feeling of not being as pleased as he ought to be at the visit of a friend, even if he is genuinely fond of him and has not seen him for a long time. A tendency to bad temper is experienced when the telephone rings after dinner. That crowding increases the propensity to aggressive behavior has long been known and demonstrated experimentally by sociological research.

On the other hand, there is, in the modern community, no legitimate outlet for aggressive behavior. To keep the peace is the first of civic duties, and the hostile neighboring tribe, once the target at which to discharge phylogenetically programmed aggression, has now withdrawn to an ideal distance, hidden behind a curtain, if possible of iron. Among the many phylogenetically adapted norms of human social behavior, there is hardly one that does not need to be controlled and kept on a leash by responsible morality. This indeed is the deep truth contained in all sermons preaching asceticism. Most of the vices and mortal sins condemned today correspond to inclinations that were purely adaptive or at least harmless in primitive man. Paleolithic people hardly ever had enough to eat, and if, for once, they had trapped a mammoth, it was biologically correct and moral for every member of the horde to gorge to his utmost capacity; gluttony was not a vice. When, for once, they were fully fed, primitive human beings rested from their strenuous life and were as absolutely lazy as possible, but there was nothing reprehensible in their sloth. Their life was so hard that there was no danger of healthy sensuality degenerating into debauch. A man sorely needed to keep his few possessions, weapons, and tools, and a few nuts for tomorrow's meal; there was no danger of his hoarding instinct turning into avarice. Alcohol was not invented, and there are no indications that man had discovered the reinforcing properties of alkaloids, the only real vices known of present-day primitive tribes. In short, man's endowment with phylogenetically adapted patterns of behavior met the requirements well enough to make the task of responsible morality very easy indeed. Its only commandment at the time was Thou shalt not strike thy neighbor with a hand ax even if he angers thee.

Clearly, the task of compensation devolving on responsible morality increases at the same rate as the ecological and sociological conditions created by culture deviate from those to which human instinctive behavior is phylogenetically adapted. Not only does this deviation continue to increase, but it does so with an acceleration that is truly frightening.

The fate of humanity hangs on the question [of] whether or not responsible morality will be able to cope with its rapidly growing burden. We shall not lighten this burden by overestimating the strength of morality, still less by attributing omnipotence to it. We have better chances of supporting moral responsibility in its ever-increasing task if we humbly realize and acknowledge that it is "only" a compensatory mechanism of very limited strength and that, as I have already explained, it derives what power it has from the same kind of motivational sources as those which it has been created to control. I have already said that the dynamics of instinctive drives, of phyletically and culturally ritualized behavior patterns, together with the controlling force of responsible morality form a very complicated systemic whole which is not easy to analyze. However, the recognition of the mutual functional interdependence of its parts, even at the present incomplete stage of our knowledge, helps us to understand a number of phenomena which otherwise would remain completely unintelligible.

We all suffer to some extent from the necessity to control our natural inclinations by the exercise of moral responsibility. Some of us, lavishly endowed with social inclinations, suffer hardly at all; other less lucky ones need all the strength of their sense of moral responsibility to keep from getting into trouble with the strict requirements of modern society. According to a useful old psychiatric definition, a psychopath is a man who either suffers himself from the demands of society or else makes society suffer. Thus in one sense we are all psychopaths, for each of us suffers from the necessity of self-imposed control for the good of the community. The above-mentioned definition, however, was meant to apply particularly to those people who do not just suffer in secret, but overtly break down under the stress imposed upon them, becoming either neurotic or delinquent. Even according to this much narrower interpretation of our definition, the "normal" human being differs from the psychopath, the good man from the criminal, much less sharply than the healthy differs from the pathological. This difference is analogous to that between a man with a compensated valvular deficiency of the heart and one with a decompensated heart disease. In the first case, an increase of the work performed by the heart muscles is sufficient to compensate for the mechanical defect of the valve, so that the overall pumping performance of the heart is adapted to the requirements of the body, at least for the time being. When the muscle finally breaks down under the prolonged strain, the heart becomes "decompensated." This analogy also goes to show that the compensatory function uses up energy. . . .

The stress under which morally responsible behavior breaks down can be of varying kinds. It is not so much the sudden, one-time great temptation that makes human morality break down but the effect of any prolonged situation that exerts an increasing drain on the compensatory power of morality. Hunger, anxiety, the necessity to make difficult decisions, overwork, hopelessness, and the like all have the effect of sapping moral energy and, in the long run, making it break down. Anyone who has had the opportunity to observe men under this kind of strain, for example in war or in prisoner-of-war camps, knows how unpredictably and suddenly moral decompensation sets in. Men in whose strength one trusted unconditionally suddenly break down, and others of whom one would never have expected it prove to be sources of inexhaustible energy, keeping up the morale of others by their example. Anyone who has experienced such things knows that the fervor of good intention and its power of endurance are two independent variables. Once you have realized this, you cease to feel superior to the man who breaks down a little sooner than you do yourself. Even the best and noblest reaches a point where his resistance is at an end: *"Eloi, Eloi, lama sabachthani?"*

As already mentioned, norms of social behavior developed by cultural ritualization play at least as important a part in the context of human society as instinctive motivation and the control exerted by responsible morality. Even at the earliest dawn of culture, when the invention of tools was just beginning to upset the equilibrium of phylogenetically evolved patterns, of social behavior, man's newborn responsibility must have found a strong aid in cultural ritualization. Evidence of cultural rites reaches back almost as far as that of the use of tools and of fire. Of course, we can expect prehistorical evidence of culturally ritualized behavior only when ritualization has reached comparatively high levels of differentiation, as in burial ceremonies or in the arts of painting and sculpture. These make their first appearance simultaneously with our own species, and the marvelous proficiency of the first known painters and sculptors suggests that even by their time, art had quite a long history behind it. Considering all this, it is quite possible that a cultural tradition of behavioral norms originated as early as the use of tools or even earlier. The beginnings of both have been found in the chimpanzee.

. . . Customs and taboos may acquire the power to motivate behavior in a way comparable to that of autonomous instincts. Not only highly developed rites or ceremonies but also simpler and less conspicuous norms of social behavior may attain, after a number of generations, the character of sacred customs which are loved and considered as values whose infringement is severely frowned upon by public opinion. . . . Sacred custom owes its motivating force to phylogenetically evolved behavior patterns, of which two are of particular importance. One is response of militant enthusiasm, by which any group defends its own social norms and rites against another group not possessing them; the other is the group's cruel taunting of any of its members who fail to conform with the accepted "good form" of behavior. Without the phylogenetically programmed love for traditional custom, human society would lack the supporting apparatus to which it owes its indispensable structure. Yet, like any phylogenetically programmed behavior mechanism, the one under discussion can miscarry. School classes or companies of soldiers, both of which can be regarded as models of primitive group structure, can be very cruel indeed in their ganging up against an outsider. The purely instinctive response to a physically abnormal individual, for instance the jeering at a fat boy, is, as far as overt behavior is concerned, absolutely identical to discrimination against a person who differs from the group in culturally developed social norms—for instance, a child who speaks a different dialect.

The ganging up on an individual diverging from the social norms characteristic of a group and the group's enthusiastic readiness to defend these social norms and rites are both good illustrations of the way in which culturally determined conditioned-stimulus situations release activities which are fundamentally instinctive. They are also excellent examples of typical compound behavior patterns whose primary survival value is as obvious as the danger of their misfiring under the conditions of the modern social order. I shall have to come back to the different ways in which the function of militant enthusiasm can miscarry and to possible means of preventing this eventuality. . . .

Militant enthusiasm is particularly suited for the paradigmatic illustration of the manner in which a phylogenetically evolved pattern of behavior interacts with culturally ritualized social norms and rites, and in which, though absolutely indispensable to the function of the compound system, it is prone to miscarry most tragically if not strictly controlled by rational responsibility based on causal insight. The Greek word *enthousiasmos* implies that a person is possessed by a god; the German *Begeisterung* means that he is controlled by a spirit, a *Geist,* more or less holy.

In reality, militant enthusiasm is a specialized form of communal aggression, clearly distinct from and yet functionally related to the more primitive forms of petty individual aggression. Every man of normally strong emotions knows, from his own experience, the subjective phenomena that go hand in hand with the response of militant enthusiasm. A shiver runs down the back and, as more exact observation shows, along the outside of both arms. One soars elated, above all the ties of everyday life; one is ready to abandon all for the call of what, in the moment of this specific emotion, seems to be a sacred duty. All obstacles in its path become unimportant; the instinctive inhibitions against hurting or killing one's fellows lose, unfortunately, much of their power. Rational considerations, criticism, and all reasonable arguments against the behavior dictated by militant enthusiasm are silenced by an amazing reversal of all values, making them appear not only untenable but base and dishonorable. Men may enjoy the feeling of absolute righteousness even while they commit atrocities. Conceptual thought and moral responsibility are at their lowest ebb. As a Ukrainian proverb says: "When the banner is unfurled, all reason is in the trumpet."

The subjective experiences just described are correlated with the following objectively demonstrable phenomena. The tone of the entire striated musculature is raised, the carriage is stiffened, the arms are raised from the sides and slightly rotated inward so that the elbows point outward. The head is proudly raised, the chin stuck out, and the facial muscles mime the "hero face," familiar from the films. On the back and along the outer surface of the arms the hair stands on end. This is the objectively observed aspect of the shiver!

Anybody who has ever seen the corresponding behavior of the male chimpanzee defending his band or family with self-sacrificing courage will doubt the purely spiritual character of human enthusiasm. The chimp, too, sticks out his chin, stiffens his body, and raises his elbows; his hair stands on end, producing a terrifying magnification of his body contours as seen from the front. The inward rotation of his arms obviously has the purpose of turning the longest-haired side outward to enhance the effect. The whole combination of body attitude and hair raising constitutes a bluff. This is also seen when a cat humps its back, and is calculated to make the animal appear bigger and more dangerous than it really is. Our shiver, which in German poetry is called a *"heiliger Schauer,"* a "holy" shiver, turns out to be the vestige of a prehuman vegetative response of making a fur bristle which we no longer have.

To the humble seeker of biological truth there cannot be the slightest doubt that human militant enthusiasm evolved out of a communal defense response of our prehuman ancestors. The unthinking single-mindedness of the response must have been of high survival value even in a tribe of fully evolved human beings. It was necessary for the individual male to forget all his other allegiances in order to be able to dedicate himself, body and soul, to the cause of the communal battle. *"Was schert mich Weib, was schert mich Kind"*—"What do I care for wife or child," says the Napoleonic soldier in a famous poem by Heinrich Heine, and it is highly characteristic of the reaction that this poet, otherwise a caustic critic of emotional romanticism, was so unreservedly enraptured by his enthusiasm for the "great" conqueror as to find this supremely apt expression.

The object which militant enthusiasm tends to defend has changed with cultural development. Originally it was certainly the community of concrete, individually known members of a group, held together by the bond of personal love and friendship. With the growth of the social unit, the social norms and rites held in common by all its members became the main factor holding it together as an entity, and therewith they became automatically the symbol of the unit. By a process of true Pavlovian conditioning plus a certain amount of irreversible imprinting, these rather abstract values have in every human culture been substituted for the primal, concrete object of the communal defense reaction.

This traditionally conditioned substitution of object has important consequences for the function of militant enthusiasm. On the one hand, the abstract nature of its object can give it a definitely inhuman aspect and make it positively dangerous—what do I care for wife or child; on the other hand it makes it possible to recruit militant enthusiasm in the service of really ethical values. Without the concentrated dedication of militant enthusiasm neither art, nor science, nor indeed any of the great endeavors of humanity would ever have come into being. Whether enthusiasm is made to serve these endeavors or whether man's most powerfully motivating instinct makes him go to war in some abjectly silly cause depends almost entirely on the conditioning and/or imprinting he has undergone during certain susceptible periods of his life. There is reasonable hope that our moral responsibility may gain control over the primeval drive, but our only hope of its ever doing so rests on the humble recognition of the fact that militant enthusiasm is an instinctive response with a phylogenetically determined releasing mechanism and that the only point at which intelligent and responsible supervision can get control is in the conditioning of the response to an object which proves to be a genuine value under the scrutiny of the categorical question.

Like the triumph ceremony of the graylag goose, militant enthusiasm in man is a true autonomous instinct: it has its own appetitive behavior, its own releasing mechanisms, and like the sexual urge or any other strong instinct, it engenders a specific feeling of intense satisfaction. The strength of its seductive lure explains why intelligent men may behave as irrationally and immorally in their political as in their sexual lives. Like the triumph ceremony, it has an essential influence on the social structure of the species. Humanity is not enthusiastically combative because it is split into political parties, but it is divided into opposing camps because this is the adequate stimulus situation to arouse militant enthusiasm in a satisfying manner. "If ever a doctrine of universal salvation should gain ascendancy over the whole earth to the exclusion of all others," writes Erich von Holst, "it would at once divide into two strongly opposing factions (one's own true one and the other heretical one) and hostility and war would thrive as before, mankind being—unfortunately—what it is!"

The first prerequisite for rational control of an instinctive behavior pattern is the knowledge of the stimulus situation which releases it. Militant enthusiasm can be elicited with the predictability of a reflex when the following environmental situations arise. First of all, a social unit with which the subject identifies himself must appear to be threatened by some danger from outside. That which is threatened may be a concrete group of people, the family or a little community of close friends, or else it may be a larger social unit held together and symbolized by its own specific social norms and rites. As the latter assume the character of autonomous values, . . . they can, quite by themselves, represent the object in whose defense militant enthusiasm can be elicited. From all this it follows that this response can be brought into play in the service of extremely different objects, ranging from the sports club to the nation, or from the most obsolete mannerisms or cere- monials to the ideal of scientific truth or of the incorruptibility of justice.

A second key stimulus which contributes enormously to the releasing of intense militant enthusiasm is the presence of a hated enemy from whom the threat to the above "values" emanates. This enemy, too, can be of a concrete or of an abstract nature. It can be "the" Jews, Huns, Boches, tyrants, etc., or abstract concepts like world capitalism, Bolshevism, fascism, and any other kind of ism; it can be heresy, dogmatism, scientific fallacy, or whatnot. Just as in the case of the object to be defended, the enemy against whom to defend it is extremely variable, and demagogues are well versed in the dangerous art of producing supranormal dummies to release a very dan- gerous form of militant enthusiasm.

A third factor contributing to the environmental situation eliciting the response is an inspiring leader figure. Even the most emphatically antifascistic ideologies apparently cannot do without it, as the giant pic- tures of leaders displayed by all kinds of political parties prove clearly enough. Again the unselectivity of the phylogenetically programmed response allows for a wide variation in the conditioning to a leader figure. Napoleon, about whom so critical a man as Heinrich Heine became so enthusiastic, does not inspire me in the least; Charles Darwin does.

A fourth, and perhaps the most important, prerequisite for the full elic- iting of militant enthusiasm is the presence of many other individuals, all agitated by the same emotion. Their absolute number has a certain influ- ence on the quality of the response. Smaller numbers at issue with a large majority tend to obstinate defense with the emotional value of "making a last stand," while very large numbers inspired by the same enthusiasm feel the urge to conquer the whole world in the name of their sacred cause. Here the laws of mass enthusiasm are strictly analogous to those of flock formation . . . ; here, too, the excitation grows in proportion, perhaps even in geometrical progression, with the increasing number of individuals. This is exactly what makes militant mass enthusiasm so dangerous.

I have tried to describe, with as little emotional bias as possible, the human response of enthusiasm, its phylogenetic origin, its instinctive as well as its traditionally handed-down components and prerequisites. I hope I have made the reader realize, without actually saying so, what a jumble our philosophy of values is. What is a culture? A system of historically developed social norms and rites which are passed on from generation to generation because emotionally they are felt to be values. What is a value? Obviously, normal and healthy people are able to appreciate something as a high value for which to live and, if necessary, to die, for no other reason than that it was evolved in cultural ritualization and handed down to them by a revered elder. Is, then, a value only defined as the object on which our instinctive urge to preserve and defend traditional social norms has become fixated? Primarily and in the early stages of cultural development this indubitably was the case. The obvious advantages of loyal adherence to tradition must have exerted a considerable selection pressure. However, the greatest loyalty and obedience to culturally ritualized norms of behavior must not be mistaken for responsible morality. Even at their best, they are only functionally analogous to behavior controlled by rational responsibility. In this respect, they are no whit different from the instinctive patterns of social behavior discussed in [an earlier chapter]. Also they are just as prone to miscarry under circumstances for which they have not been "programmed" by the great constructor, natural selection.

In other words, the need to control, by wise rational responsibility, all our emotional allegiances to cultural values is as great as, if not greater than, the necessity to keep in check our other instincts. None of them can ever have such devastating effects as unbridled militant enthusiasm when it infects great masses and overrides all other considerations by its single-mindedness and its specious nobility. It is not enthusiasm in itself that is in any way noble, but humanity's great goals which it can be called upon to defend. That indeed is the Janus head of man: The only being capable of dedicating himself to the very highest moral and ethical values requires for this purpose a phylogenetically adapted mechanism of behavior whose animal properties bring with them the danger that he will kill his brother, convinced that he is doing so in the interests of these very same high values. *Ecce homo!*

# Content Questions

1. According to Lorenz, how has the human capacity for conceptual thought and speech altered our evolution? What dangers does Lorenz associate with this alteration? (159–160)

2. How does human curiosity result in rational responsibility, in Lorenz's account? (160)

3. What does Lorenz mean when he asserts that humans do not have a "carnivorous mentality"? (161)

4. How did the invention of weapons upset the balance between humans' ability to kill each other and their inhibitions against doing so? (162–163)

5. What point is Lorenz making in his discussion of studies involving Ute Indians? How do the examples he gives support this point? (163–164)

6. What argument does Lorenz make for considering altruistic human behavior part of our instincts, rather than the result of rational thought? (165)

7. What two factors does Lorenz emphasize in his explanation of why the aggressive drive is thwarted in modern society? (166)

8. According to Lorenz, what is the most accurate way of understanding the difference between a psychopath and a "normal" person? (167–168)

9. In Lorenz's account, what are the two most important "phylogenetically evolved behavior patterns" that underlie human ritual? How do the examples he gives support this contention? (169)

10. What does Lorenz believe is proved by the similarity between human and chimpanzee behavior when threatened? (170–171)

11. What four prerequisites does Lorenz list for the "full eliciting of militant enthusiasm"? Which does he consider most important? (172–173)

## Application Questions

Lorenz refers to "militant enthusiasm" as an "instinctive behavior pattern," and he asserts that "the first prerequisite for rational control of an instinctive behavior pattern is the knowledge of the stimulus situation which releases it." (172)

1. Describe the research of Lorenz and other ethologists that led to the construction of the concept of a *sign stimulus* (also known as a *releaser*), defined as any signal that elicits a specific behavioral response.

2. Is Lorenz's analysis of human militant enthusiasm within the conceptual framework of an instinctive behavior pattern elicited by sign stimuli reasonable? Why or why not?

## Discussion Questions

1. What does Lorenz mean when he says that asking questions is at the core of the human capacity for both invention and responsibility? Do you agree?

2. If our capacity for invention and responsibility derive from the same source, why shouldn't they evolve at the same pace?

3. When Lorenz claims that "most of the vices and mortal sins condemned today correspond to inclinations that were purely adaptive or at least harmless in primitive man," is he implying that no behavior is inherently moral or immoral? (166)

4. Do you believe that a "genuine value" can be distinguished from one that does not deserve to be defended by militant enthusiasm? (172) If so, how would you tell the difference?

5. Does Lorenz offer any answer to the paradox he describes at the end of the selection, in which the mechanisms that allow humans to kill each other are the same as those that allow us to formulate reasons why killing is wrong? (174)

# Rats

Serious fights between members of the same big family [of rats] occur in one situation only, which in many respects is significant and interesting: such fights take place when a strange rat is present and has aroused intraspecific, interfamily aggression. What rats do when a member of a strange rat clan enters their territory or is put in there by a human experimenter is one of the most horrible and repulsive things which can be observed in animals. The strange rat may run around for minutes on end without having any idea of the terrible fate awaiting it, and the resident rats may continue for an equally long time with their ordinary affairs till finally the stranger comes close enough to one of them for it to get wind of the intruder. The information is transmitted like an electric shock through the resident rat, and at once the whole colony is alarmed by a process of mood transmission which is communicated in the brown rat by expression movements but in the house rat by a sharp, shrill, satanic cry which is taken up by all members of the tribe within earshot.

With their eyes bulging from their sockets, their hair standing on end, the rats set out on the rat hunt. They are so angry that if two of them meet they bite each other. "So they fight for three to five seconds," reports Steiniger, "then with necks outstretched they sniff each other thoroughly

*This selection is taken from chapter 10, "Rats," of* On Aggression.

and afterward part peacefully. On the day of persecution of the strange rat all the members of the clan are irritable and suspicious." Evidently the members of a rat clan do not know each other personally, as jackdaws, geese, and monkeys do, but they recognize each other by the clan smell, as bees and other insects do. A member of the clan can be branded as a hated stranger, or vice versa, if its smell has been influenced one way or the other. Eibl removed a rat from a colony and put it in another terrarium specially prepared for the purpose. On its return to the clan enclosure a few days later, it was treated as a stranger, but if the rat was put, together with some soil, nest, etc., from this clan enclosure, into a clean, empty battery jar so that it took with it a dowry of objects impregnated with a clan smell, it would be recognized afterward, even after an absence of weeks.

Heartbreaking was the fate of a house rat which Eibl had treated in the first way, and which in my presence he put back into the clan enclosure. This animal had obviously not forgotten the smell of the clan, but it did not know that its own smell was changed. So it felt perfectly safe and at home, and the cruel bites of its former friends came as a complete surprise to it. Even after several nasty wounds, it did not react with fear and desperate flight attempts, as really strange rats do at the first meeting with an aggressive member of the resident clan. To softhearted readers I give the assurance, to biologists I admit hesitatingly, that in this case we did not await the bitter end but put the experimental animal into a protective cage which we then placed in the clan enclosure for repatriation.

Without such sentimental interference, the fate of the strange rat would be sealed. The best thing that can happen to it is, as S. A. Barnett has observed in individual cases, that it should die of shock. Otherwise it is slowly torn to pieces by its fellows. Only rarely does one see an animal in such desperation and panic, so conscious of the inevitability of a terrible death, as a rat which is about to be slain by rats. It ceases to defend itself. One cannot help comparing this behavior with what happens when a rat faces a large predator that has driven it into a corner whence there is no more escape than from the rats of a strange clan. In the face of death, it meets the eating enemy with attack, the best method of defense, and springs at it with the shrill war cry of its species.

What is the purpose of group hate between rat clans? What species-preserving function has caused its evolution? The disturbing thought for the human race is that this good old Darwinian train of thought can only be applied where the causes which induce selection derive from the extraspecific environment. Only then does selection bring about adaptation. But wherever competition between members of a species effects sexual selection, there is, as we already know, grave danger that members of a species may in demented competition drive each other into the most stupid blind alley of evolution. . . . We have read of the wings of the Argus pheasant and the working pace of Western civilized man as examples of such efforts of evolution. It is thus quite possible that the group hate between rat clans is really a diabolical invention which serves no purpose. On the other hand it is not impossible that as-yet unknown external selection factors are still at work; we can, however, maintain with certainty that those indispensable species-preserving functions of intraspecific aggression . . . are not served by clan fights. These serve neither spatial distribution nor the selection of strong family defenders—for among rats these are seldom the fathers of the descendants. . . .

It can readily be seen that the constant warfare between large neighboring families of rats must exert a huge selection pressure in the direction of an ever increasing ability to fight, and that a rat clan which cannot keep up in this respect must soon fall victim to extermination. Probably natural selection has put a premium on the most highly populated families, since the members of a clan evidently assist each other in fights against strangers, and thus a smaller clan is at a disadvantage in fights against a larger one. On the small North Sea island of Norderoog, Steiniger found that the ground was divided between a small number of rat clans separated by a strip of about fifty yards of no rat's land where fights were constantly taking place. The front is relatively larger for a small clan than for a big one, and the small one is therefore at a disadvantage.

## Content Questions

1. What arouses "intraspecific, interfamily aggression" in rats? (177)

2. How do the members of a rat clan recognize each other? How does this enable experimenters to make members of a rat clan seem strange to each other? (178)

3. How does a rat's behavior differ when it is attacked by members of its own clan, as opposed to a creature it recognizes as a predator? (178)

4. According to Lorenz, why might natural selection favor "an ever increasing ability to fight"? (179)

## Application Question

How did the series of experiments on European blackbirds performed by ethologist Eberhard Curio shed light on the behavioral programming that underlies enemy recognition? How does classical conditioning play a role in this programming?

## Discussion Questions

1. When describing his experiments with rats, Lorenz says that "to softhearted readers I give the assurance, to biologists I admit hesitatingly, that in this case we did not await the bitter end" of a rat's destruction by its clan. (178) What is Lorenz implying about the characteristics of biologists? Are his sympathies with the biologists or the "softhearted readers"?

2. If a scientist protects an animal from injury or death during an experiment, is the integrity of scientific research compromised?

3. What are the ethical responsibilities of biologists when conducting research with animals? Do these ethical responsibilities apply to vertebrates only, or do they apply to other animals as well? Do they apply to other living things?

4. In biological research with animals, are there circumstances in which the injury or death of an animal is justified? If so, what are those specific research goals?

# James D. Watson

As a codiscoverer of DNA's molecular structure, James D. Watson (1928– ) transformed scientific understanding of genes and how they reproduced. While Gregor Mendel had concluded in 1865 that living things are shaped by hereditary information and transmit it to their offspring, it was not until the twentieth century that genes, chromosomes, and the process of mutation began to be understood. In 1944, Oswald Avery and his collaborators demonstrated that DNA was the genetic material, but how it reproduced and regulated cell activity remained a mystery. When, in 1953, Watson and Francis Crick discovered the double-helix structure of DNA, they began the era of molecular biology. They went on to investigate many of the discipline's basic concepts, including the processes by which DNA performs its functions.

While Watson and Crick initially publicized their discovery in a brief 1953 article in *Nature,* it was Watson's 1968 book *The Double Helix* that gained him a wide readership. This very popular book generated intense scientific and public debate about Watson's account of the process of discovering DNA's structure, especially his portrayals of other scientists and his sometimes unorthodox use of their research. He was accused of grandstanding, backbiting, and egotism. His characterization of Rosalind Franklin, a researcher at King's College, drew particularly sharp criticism from reviewers and scientific peers.

Watson shared the 1962 Nobel Prize in physiology or medicine with Francis Crick and Maurice Wilkins. In 1968, he became director of the Cold Spring Harbor Laboratory in Long Island, New York, and in 1994, he became its president. He was also involved in the early stages of the Human Genome Project.

# The Double Helix

*(selection)*

The next few days saw Francis [Crick] becoming increasingly agitated by my failure to stick close to the molecular models. It did not matter that before his tenish entrance I was usually in the lab. Almost every afternoon, knowing that I was on the tennis court, he would fretfully twist his head away from his work to see the polynucleotide backbone unattended. Moreover, after tea I would show up for only a few minutes of minor fiddling before dashing away to have sherry with the girls at Pop's. Francis's grumbles did not disturb me, however, because further refining of our latest backbone without a solution to the bases would not represent a real step forward.

I went ahead spending most evenings at the films, vaguely dreaming that any moment the answer would suddenly hit me. Occasionally my wild pursuit of the celluloid backfired, the worst occasion being an evening set aside for *Ecstasy*. Peter [Pauling] and I had both been too young to observe the original showings of Hedy Lamarr's romps in the nude, and so on the long-awaited night we collected Elizabeth and went up to the Rex. However, the only swimming scene left intact by the English censor was an inverted reflection from a pool of water. Before the film was half over we joined the violent booing of the disgusted undergraduates as the dubbed voices uttered words of uncontrolled passion.

*This selection is taken from chapters 25–27.*

Even during good films I found it almost impossible to forget the bases. The fact that we had at last produced a stereochemically reasonable configuration for the backbone was always in the back of my head. Moreover, there was no longer any fear that it would be incompatible with the experimental data. By then it had been checked out with Rosy's precise measurements. Rosy [Rosalind Franklin], of course, did not directly give us her data. For that matter, no one at King's realized they were in our hands. We came upon them because of Max's[1] membership on a committee appointed by the Medical Research Council to look into the research activities of Randall's lab to coordinate biophysics research within its laboratories. Since Randall wished to convince the outside committee that he had a productive research group, he had instructed his people to draw up a comprehensive summary of their accomplishments. In due time this was prepared in mimeograph form and sent routinely to all the committee members. The report was not confidential and so Max saw no reason not to give it to Francis and me. Quickly scanning its contents, Francis sensed with relief that following my return from King's I had correctly reported to him the essential features of the B pattern. Thus only minor modifications were necessary in our backbone configuration.

Generally, it was late in the evening after I got back to my rooms that I tried to puzzle out the mystery of the bases. Their formulas were written out in J. N. Davidson's little book *The Biochemistry of Nucleic Acids*, a copy of which I kept in Clare. So I could be sure that I had the correct structures when I drew tiny pictures of the bases on sheets of Cavendish notepaper. My aim was somehow to arrange the centrally located bases in such a way that the backbones on the outside were completely regular—that is, giving the sugar-phosphate groups of each nucleotide identical three-dimensional configurations. But each time I tried to come up with a solution I ran into the obstacle that the four bases each had a quite different shape. Moreover, there were many reasons to believe that the sequences of the bases of a given polynucleotide chain were very irregular. Thus, unless some very special trick existed, randomly twisting two polynucleotide chains around one another should result in a mess. In some places the bigger bases must touch

1. [Max Perutz, chemist and leader of the unit at Cambridge University's Cavendish Laboratories to which Watson and Crick belonged.]

each other, while in other regions, where the smaller bases would lie opposite each other, there must exist a gap or else their backbone regions must buckle in.

There was also the vexing problem of how the intertwined chains might be held together by hydrogen bonds between the bases. Though for over a year Francis and I had dismissed the possibility that bases formed regular hydrogen bonds, it was now obvious to me that we had done so incorrectly. The observation that one or more hydrogen atoms on each of the bases could move from one location to another (a tautomeric shift) had initially led us to conclude that all the possible tautomeric forms of a given base occurred in equal frequencies. But a recent rereading of J. M. Gulland's and D. O. Jordan's papers on the acid and base titrations of DNA made me finally appreciate the strength of their conclusion that a large fraction, if not all, of the bases formed hydrogen bonds to other bases. Even more important, these hydrogen bonds were present at very low DNA concentrations, strongly hinting that the bonds linked together bases in the same molecule. There was in addition the x-ray crystallographic result that each pure base so far examined formed as many irregular hydrogen bonds as stereochemically possible. Thus, conceivably the crux of the matter was a rule governing hydrogen bonding between bases.

My doodling of the bases on paper at first got nowhere, regardless of whether or not I had been to a film. Even the necessity to expunge *Ecstasy* from my mind did not lead to passable hydrogen bonds, and I fell asleep hoping that an undergraduate party the next afternoon at Downing would be full of pretty girls. But my expectations were dashed as soon as I arrived to spot a group of healthy hockey players and several pallid debutantes. Bertrand also instantly perceived he was out of place, and as we passed a polite interval before scooting out, I explained how I was racing Peter's father for the Nobel Prize.

Not until the middle of the next week, however, did a nontrivial idea emerge. It came while I was drawing the fused rings of adenine on paper. Suddenly I realized the potentially profound implications of a DNA structure in which the adenine residue formed hydrogen bonds similar to those found in crystals of pure adenine. If DNA was like this, each adenine residue would form two hydrogen bonds to an adenine residue related to it by a 180-degree rotation. Most important, two symmetrical hydrogen bonds could also hold together pairs of guanine, cytosine, or thymine.

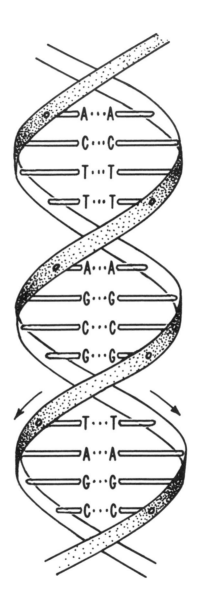

*A schematic view of a DNA molecule built up from like-with-like base pairs.*

I thus started wondering whether each DNA molecule consisted of two chains with identical base sequences held together by hydrogen bonds between pairs of identical bases. There was the complication, however, that such a structure could not have a regular backbone, since the purines (adenine and guanine) and the pyrimidines (thymine and cytosine) have different shapes. The resulting backbone would have to show minor in-and-out buckles depending upon whether pairs of purines or pyrimidines were in the center.

Despite the messy backbone, my pulse began to race. If this was DNA, I should create a bombshell by announcing its discovery. The existence of two intertwined chains with identical base sequences could not be a chance matter. Instead it would strongly suggest that one chain in each molecule had at some earlier stage served as the template for the synthesis of the other chain. Under this scheme, gene replication starts with the separation of its two identical chains. Then two new daughter strands are made on the two parental templates, thereby forming two DNA molecules identical to the original molecule. Thus, the essential trick of gene replication could come from the requirement that each base in the newly synthesized chain always hydrogen-bonds to an identical base. That night, however, I could not see why the common tautomeric form of guanine would not hydrogen-bond to adenine. Likewise, several other pairing mistakes should also occur. But since there was no reason to rule out the participation of specific enzymes, I saw no need to be unduly disturbed. For example, there might exist an enzyme specific for adenine that caused adenine always to be inserted opposite an adenine residue on the template strands.

As the clock went past midnight I was becoming more and more pleased. There had been far too many days when Francis and I worried that the DNA structure might turn out to be superficially very dull, suggesting nothing about either its replication or its function in controlling cell biochemistry. But now, to my delight and amazement, the answer was turning out to be profoundly interesting. For over two hours I happily lay awake with pairs of adenine residues whirling in front of my closed eyes. Only for brief moments did the fear shoot through me that an idea this good could be wrong.

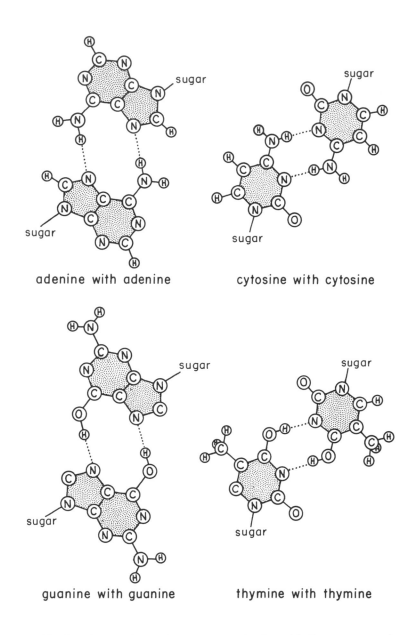

adenine with adenine

cytosine with cytosine

guanine with guanine

thymine with thymine

*The four base pairs used to construct the like-with-like structure (hydrogen bonds are dotted).*

～　～　～

My scheme was torn to shreds by the following noon. Against me was the awkward chemical fact that I had chosen the wrong tautomeric forms of guanine and thymine. Before the disturbing truth came out, I had eaten a hurried breakfast at the Whim, then momentarily gone back to Clare to reply to a letter from Max Delbrück which reported that my manuscript on bacterial genetics looked unsound to the Cal Tech geneticists. Nevertheless, he would accede to my request that he send it to the *Proceedings of the National Academy*. In this way, I would still be young when I committed the folly of publishing a silly idea. Then I could sober up before my career was permanently fixed on a reckless course.

At first this message had its desired unsettling effect. But now, with my spirits soaring on the possibility that I had the self-duplicating structure, I reiterated my faith that I knew what happened when bacteria mated. Moreover, I could not refrain from adding a sentence saying that I had just devised a beautiful DNA structure which was completely different from Pauling's. For a few seconds I considered giving some details of what I was up to, but since I was in a rush I decided not to, quickly dropped the letter in the box, and dashed off to the lab.

The letter was not in the post for more than an hour before I knew that my claim was nonsense. I no sooner got to the office and began explaining my scheme than the American crystallographer Jerry Donohue protested that the idea would not work. The tautomeric forms I had copied out of Davidson's book were, in Jerry's opinion, incorrectly assigned. My immediate retort that several other texts also pictured guanine and thymine in the enol form cut no ice with Jerry. Happily he let out that for years organic chemists had been arbitrarily favoring particular tautomeric forms over their alternatives on only the flimsiest of grounds. In fact, organic-chemistry textbooks were littered with pictures of highly improbable tautomeric forms. The guanine picture I was thrusting toward his face was almost certainly bogus. All his chemical intuition told him that it would occur in the keto form. He was just as sure that thymine was also wrongly assigned an enol configuration. Again he strongly favored the keto alternative.

Jerry, however, did not give a foolproof reason for preferring the keto forms. He admitted that only one crystal structure bore on the problem. This was diketopiperazine, whose three-dimensional configuration had

ENOL                              KETO

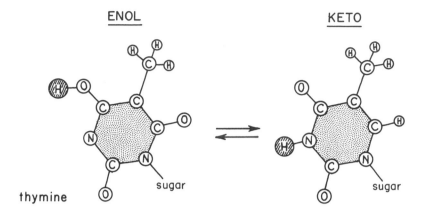

thymine

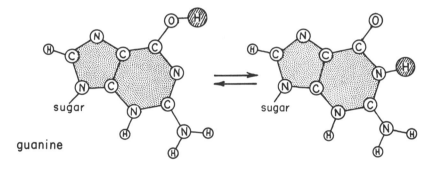

guanine

*The contrasting tautomeric forms of guanine and thymine which
might occur in DNA. The hydrogen atoms that can
undergo the changes in position (a tautomeric shift) are shaded.*

been carefully worked out in Pauling's lab several years before. Here there was no doubt that the keto form, not the enol, was present. Moreover, he felt sure that the quantum-mechanical arguments which showed why diketopiperazine has the keto form should also hold for guanine and thymine. I was thus firmly urged not to waste more time with my hare-brained scheme.

Though my immediate reaction was to hope that Jerry was blowing hot air, I did not dismiss his criticism. Next to Linus himself, Jerry knew more about hydrogen bonds than anyone else in the world. Since for many years he had worked at Cal Tech on the crystal structures of small organic molecules, I couldn't kid myself that he did not grasp our problem. During the six months that he occupied a desk in our office, I had never heard him shooting off his mouth on subjects about which he knew nothing.

Thoroughly worried, I went back to my desk hoping that some gimmick might emerge to salvage the like-with-like idea. But it was obvious that the new assignments were its death blow. Shifting the hydrogen atoms to their keto locations made the size differences between the purines and pyrimidines even more important than would be the case if the enol forms existed. Only by the most special pleading could I imagine the polynucleotide backbone bending enough to accommodate irregular base sequences. Even this possibility vanished when Francis came in. He immediately realized that a like-with-like structure would give a 34 Å crystallographic repeat only if each chain had a complete rotation every 68 Å. But this would mean that the rotation angle between successive bases would be only 18 degrees, a value Francis believed was absolutely ruled out by his recent fiddling with the models. Also Francis did not like the fact that the structure gave no explanation for the Chargaff rules (adenine equals thymine, guanine equals cytosine). I, however, maintained my lukewarm response to Chargaff's data. So I welcomed the arrival of lunchtime, when Francis's cheerful prattle temporarily shifted my thoughts to why undergraduates could not satisfy au pair girls.

After lunch I was not anxious to return to work, for I was afraid that in trying to fit the keto forms into some new scheme I would run into a stone wall and have to face the fact that no regular hydrogen-bonding scheme was compatible with the x-ray evidence. As long as I remained outside, gazing at the crocuses, hope could be maintained that some pretty base arrangement would fall out. Fortunately, when we walked upstairs, I found that I had an

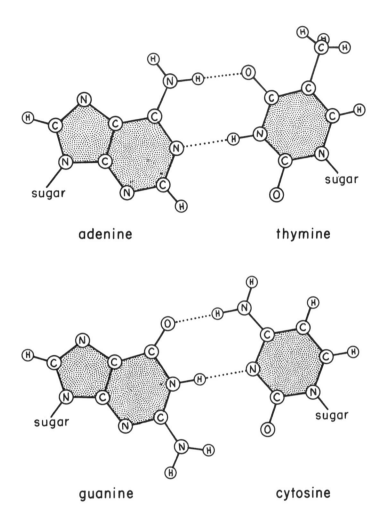

adenine                   thymine

guanine                cytosine

*The adenine-thymine and guanine-cytosine base pairs used to construct the double helix (hydrogen bonds are dotted). The formation of a third hydrogen bond between guanine and cytosine was considered, but rejected because a crystallographic study of guanine hinted that it would be very weak. Now this conjecture is known to be wrong. Three strong hydrogen bonds can be drawn between guanine and cytosine.*

excuse to put off the crucial model-building step for at least several more hours. The metal purine and pyrimidine models, needed for systematically checking all the conceivable hydrogen-bonding possibilities, had not been finished on time. At least two more days were needed before they would be in our hands. This was much too long even for me to remain in limbo, so I spent the rest of the afternoon cutting accurate representations of the bases out of stiff cardboard. But by the time they were ready I realized that the answer must be put off till the next day. After dinner I was to join a group from Pop's at the theater.

When I got to our still-empty office the following morning, I quickly cleared away the papers from my desktop so that I would have a large, flat surface on which to form pairs of bases held together by hydrogen bonds. Though I initially went back to my like-with-like prejudices, I saw all too well that they led nowhere. When Jerry came in I looked up, saw that it was not Francis, and began shifting the bases in and out of various other pairing possibilities. Suddenly I became aware that an adenine-thymine pair held together by two hydrogen bonds was identical in shape to a guanine-cytosine pair held together by at least two hydrogen bonds. All the hydrogen bonds seemed to form naturally; no fudging was required to make the two types of base pairs identical in shape. Quickly I called Jerry over to ask him whether this time he had any objection to my new base pairs.

When he said no, my morale skyrocketed, for I suspected that we now had the answer to the riddle of why the number of purine residues exactly equaled the number of pyrimidine residues. Two irregular sequences of bases could be regularly packed in the center of a helix if a purine always hydrogen-bonded to a pyrimidine. Furthermore, the hydrogen-bonding requirement meant that adenine would always pair with thymine, while guanine could pair only with cytosine. Chargaff's rules then suddenly stood out as a consequence of a double-helical structure for DNA. Even more exciting, this type of double helix suggested a replication scheme much more satisfactory than my briefly considered like-with-like pairing. Always pairing adenine with thymine and guanine with cytosine meant that the base sequences of the two intertwined chains were complementary to each other. Given the base sequence of one chain, that of its partner was automatically determined. Conceptually, it was thus very easy to visualize how a single chain could be the template for the synthesis of a chain with the complementary sequence.

Upon his arrival Francis did not get more than halfway through the door before I let loose that the answer to everything was in our hands. Though as a matter of principle he maintained skepticism for a few moments, the similarly shaped A-T and G-C pairs had their expected impact. His quickly pushing the bases together in a number of different ways did not reveal any other way to satisfy Chargaff's rules. A few minutes later he spotted the fact that the two glycosidic bonds (joining base and sugar) of each base pair were systematically related by a dyad axis perpendicular to the helical axis. Thus, both pairs could be flip-flopped over and still have their glycosidic bonds facing in the same direction. This had the important consequence that a given chain could contain both purines and pyrimidines. At the same time, it strongly suggested that the backbones of the two chains must run in opposite directions.

The question then became whether the A-T and G-C base pairs would easily fit the backbone configuration devised during the previous two weeks. At first glance this looked like a good bet, since I had left free in the center a large vacant area for the bases. However, we both knew that we would not be home until a complete model was built in which all the stereochemical contacts were satisfactory. There was also the obvious fact that the implications of its existence were far too important to risk crying wolf. Thus I felt slightly queasy when at lunch Francis winged into the Eagle to tell everyone within hearing distance that we had found the secret of life.

Francis's preoccupation with DNA quickly became full-time. The first afternoon following the discovery that A-T and G-C base pairs had similar shapes, he went back to his thesis measurements, but his effort was ineffectual. Constantly he would pop up from his chair, worriedly look at the cardboard models, fiddle with other combinations, and then, the period of momentary uncertainty over, look satisfied and tell me how important our work was. I enjoyed Francis's words, even though they lacked the casual sense of understatement known to be the correct way to behave in Cambridge. It seemed almost unbelievable that the DNA structure was solved, that the answer was incredibly exciting, and that our names would be associated with the double helix as Pauling's was with the alpha helix.

When the Eagle opened at six, I went over with Francis to talk about what must be done in the next few days. Francis wanted no time lost in seeing whether a satisfactory three-dimensional model could be built, since the geneticists and nucleic-acid biochemists should not misuse their time and facilities any longer than necessary. They must be told the answer quickly so that they could reorient their research upon our work. Though I was equally anxious to build the complete model, I thought more about Linus and the possibility that he might stumble upon the base pairs before we told him the answer.

That night, however, we could not firmly establish the double helix. Until the metal bases were on hand, any model building would be too sloppy to be convincing. I went back to Pop's to tell Elizabeth and Bertrand that Francis and I had probably beaten Pauling to the gate and that the answer would revolutionize biology. Both were genuinely pleased, Elizabeth with sisterly pride, Bertrand with the idea that he could report back to International Society that he had a friend who would win a Nobel Prize. Peter's reaction was equally enthusiastic and gave no indication that he minded the possibility of his father's first real scientific defeat.

The following morning I felt marvelously alive when I awoke. On my way to the Whim I slowly walked toward the Clare Bridge, staring up at the gothic pinnacles of the King's College Chapel that stood out sharply against the spring sky. I briefly stopped and looked over at the perfect Georgian features of the recently cleaned Gibbs Building, thinking that much of our success was due to the long uneventful periods when we walked among the colleges or unobtrusively read the new books that came into Heffer's Bookstore. After contentedly poring over the *Times*, I wandered into the lab to see Francis, unquestionably early, flipping the cardboard base pairs about an imaginary line. As far as a compass and ruler could tell him, both sets of base pairs neatly fitted into the backbone configuration. As the morning wore on, Max and John successively came by to see if we still thought we had it. Each got a quick, concise lecture from Francis, during the second of which I wandered down to see if the shop could be speeded up to produce the purines and pyrimidines later that afternoon.

Only a little encouragement was needed to get the final soldering accomplished in the next couple of hours. The brightly shining metal plates were then immediately used to make a model in which for the first time all the DNA components were present. In about an hour I had arranged the atoms in positions which satisfied both the x-ray data and the laws of stereo-chemistry. The resulting helix was right-handed with the two chains running in opposite directions. Only one person can easily play with a model, and so Francis did not try to check my work until I backed away and said that I thought everything fitted. While one interatomic contact was slightly shorter than optimal, it was not out of line with several published values, and I was not disturbed. Another fifteen minutes' fiddling by Francis failed to find anything wrong, though for brief intervals my stomach felt uneasy when I saw him frowning. In each case he became satisfied and moved on to verify that another interatomic contact was reasonable. Everything thus looked very good when we went back to have supper with Odile.

Our dinner words fixed on how to let the big news out. Maurice [Wilkins], especially, must soon be told. But remembering the fiasco of sixteen months before,[2] keeping King's in the dark made sense until exact coordinates had been obtained for all the atoms. It was all too easy to fudge a successful series of atomic contacts so that, while each looked almost acceptable, the whole collection was energetically impossible. We suspected that we had not made this error, but our judgment conceivably might be biased by the biological advantages of complementary DNA molecules. Thus the next several days were to be spent using a plumb line and a measuring stick to obtain the relative positions of all atoms in a single nucleotide. Because of the helical symmetry, the locations of the atoms in one nucleotide would automatically generate the other positions.

After coffee Odile wanted to know whether they would still have to go into exile in Brooklyn if our work was as sensational as everyone told her. Perhaps we should stay on in Cambridge to solve other problems of equal importance. I tried to reassure her, emphasizing that not all American men cut all their hair off and that there were scores of American women who did not wear short white socks on the streets. I had less success arguing that the

---

2. [In a face-to-face meeting, Crick and Watson presented an earlier model of DNA to Wilkins, Franklin, and another researcher in the Cavendish Laboratory research group affiliated with King's College at Cambridge. The King's group quickly proved that the model was seriously flawed. Crick and Watson were particularly humiliated because they had based the model in part on Watson's recollection of a talk Franklin had given about her research into the amount of water present in the DNA molecule, and at the meeting it was immediately apparent that Watson had remembered her conclusion inaccurately.]

States' greatest virtue was its wide-open spaces where people never went. Odile looked in horror at the prospect of being long without fashionably dressed people. Moreover, she could not believe that I was serious, since I had just had a tailor cut a tightly fitting blazer, unconnected with the sacks that Americans draped on their shoulders.

The next morning I again found that Francis had beaten me to the lab. He was already at work tightening the model on its support stands so that he could read off the atomic coordinates. While he moved the atoms back and forth, I sat on the top of my desk thinking about the form of the letters that I soon could write, saying that we had found something interesting. Occasionally, Francis would look disgusted when my daydreams kept me from observing that he needed my help to keep the model from collapsing as he rearranged the supporting ring stands.

By then we knew that all my previous fuss about the importance of $Mg^{++}$ ions was misdirected. Most likely Maurice and Rosy were right in insisting that they were looking at the $Na^+$ salt of DNA. But with the sugar-phosphate backbone on the outside, it did not matter which salt was present. Either would fit perfectly well into the double helix.

Bragg had his first look late that morning. For several days he had been home with the flu and was in bed when he heard that Crick and I had thought up an ingenious DNA structure which might be important to biology. During his first free moment back in the Cavendish he slipped away from his office for a direct view. Immediately he caught on to the complementary relation between the two chains and saw how an equivalence of adenine with thymine and guanine with cytosine was a logical consequence of the regular repeating shape of the sugar-phosphate backbone. As he was not aware of Chargaff's rules, I went over the experimental evidence on the relative proportions of the various bases, noticing that he was becoming increasingly excited by its potential implications for gene replication. When the question of the x-ray evidence came up, he saw why we had not yet called up the King's group. He was bothered, however, that we had not yet asked Todd's opinion. Telling Bragg that we had got the organic chemistry straight did not put him completely at ease. The chance that we were using the wrong chemical formula admittedly was small, but since Crick talked so fast, Bragg could never be sure that he would ever slow down long enough to get the right facts. So it was arranged that as soon as we had a set of atomic coordinates, we would have Todd come over.

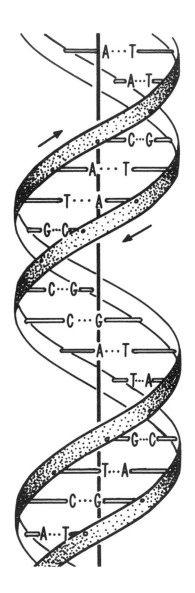

*A schematic illustration of the double helix. The two sugar-phosphate backbones twist about on the outside with the flat hydrogen-bonded base pairs forming the core. Seen this way, the structure resembles a spiral staircase with the base pairs forming the steps.*

The final refinements of the coordinates were finished the following evening. Lacking the exact x-ray evidence, we were not confident that the configuration chosen was precisely correct. But this did not bother us, for we only wished to establish that at least one specific two-chain complementary helix was stereochemically possible. Until this was clear, the objection could be raised that, although our idea was aesthetically elegant, the shape of the sugar-phosphate backbone might not permit its existence. Happily, now we knew that this was not true, and so we had lunch, telling each other that a structure this pretty just had to exist.

With the tension now off, I went to play tennis with Bertrand, telling Francis that later in the afternoon I would write Luria and Delbrück about the double helix. It was so arranged that John Kendrew would call up Maurice to say that he should come out to see what Francis and I had just devised. Neither Francis nor I wanted the task. Earlier in the day the post had brought a note from Maurice to Francis, mentioning that he was now about to go full steam ahead on DNA and intended to place emphasis on model building.

## Content Questions

1. Why must Watson and Crick find a "solution to the bases" before going forward with the polynucleotide backbone? (183)

2. Why is hydrogen bonding the central problem in finding a solution to the bases? (185)

3. Why were the initial tautomeric forms of guanine and thymine incorrect? (189)

4. What was the correct alternative to "like-with-like pairing"? (193)

5. Why must the "backbones of the two chains . . . run in opposite directions"? (194)

6. How does the double helix resemble a "spiral staircase"? (198)

7. Why did Watson and Crick, without the confirmation of x-ray evidence, believe that "a structure this pretty just had to exist"? (199)

## Application Questions

1. What is the "essential trick" of gene replication? (187) Explain how the Watson-Crick model for the structure of DNA accounts for the precise replication of genetic material.

2. What are the specific roles of the enzymes that catalyze DNA replication?

3. Explain how the sequence of bases in DNA determines the sequence in which amino acids are linked in protein synthesis.

4. Using the additional data that scientists have collected since the Watson-Crick discovery, explain why one strand of DNA is copied continuously while the other is copied in discontinuous segments.

5. Following the initial publication of Watson and Crick's conclusions, what kinds of experimental evidence helped to confirm their model for the structure of DNA?

6. What are the similarities and differences we now know to exist among prokaryotic, eukaryotic, and organelle DNA structure and replication?

7. What is our current understanding of how the sequence of bases in DNA determines the sequence in which amino acids are linked together in protein synthesis? How does DNA's control of protein synthesis allow it to regulate cellular structure and function?

## Discussion Questions

1. What do Watson's habits and concerns outside the lab reveal about him? About the scientific process?

2. Why are the intervals between laboratory work essential to progress?

3. Why does Watson include in his account the mistakes he made while working toward the solution to the structure of DNA?

4. When *The Double Helix* was published, it drew sharp criticism as well as praise. Some reviewers accused Watson of penning ungenerous portraits of his fellow researchers and taking too much credit for himself. Based on what you have read, do you think such criticisms are justified?

# Richard Dawkins

Richard Dawkins (1941– ) has been both credited with boldly explicating the realities
of gene-based behavior and criticized as a dogmatic reductionist with an overly mechanistic view of nature. His first book, *The Selfish Gene* (1976), became a bestseller
and has been translated into more than twenty languages. In it, Dawkins argues that
genes, not individuals, are the basic unit of evolution. His assertion was immediately
controversial and has remained so.

Dawkins was born in Nairobi, Kenya, where his family had moved from England
when his father joined the Allied forces during World War II. He studied zoology at
Oxford University, working for his doctorate with noted ethologist Nikolaas
Tinbergen. After a brief period teaching at the University of California, Berkeley,
Dawkins returned to Oxford, where he was named the first Charles Simonyi
Professor of Public Understanding of Science in 1995. Dawkins is the author of
six books, and he has won acclaim for his ability to explain difficult concepts
clearly to a nonscientific audience.

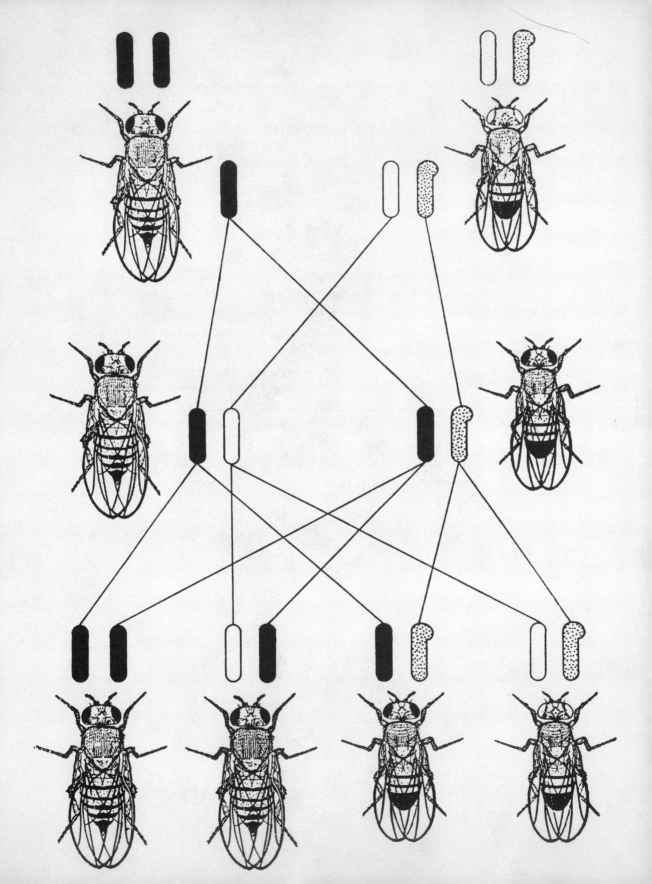

# The Selfish Gene

*(selection)*

I ntelligent life on a planet comes of age when it first works out the reason for its own existence. If superior creatures from space ever visit earth, the first question they will ask, in order to assess the level of our civilization, is "Have they discovered evolution yet?" Living organisms had existed on earth, without ever knowing why, for over three thousand million years before the truth finally dawned on one of them. His name was Charles Darwin. To be fair, others had had inklings of the truth, but it was Darwin who first put together a coherent and tenable account of why we exist. Darwin made it possible for us to give a sensible answer to the curious child whose question heads this chapter ["Why Are People?"]. We no longer have to resort to superstition when faced with the deep problems: Is there a meaning to life? What are we for? What is man? After posing the last of these questions, the eminent zoologist G. G. Simpson put it thus: "The point I want to make now is that all attempts to answer that question before 1859 are worthless and that we will be better off if we ignore them completely."

Today the theory of evolution is about as much open to doubt as the theory that the earth goes round the sun, but the full implications of Darwin's revolution have yet to be widely realized. Zoology is still a

*This selection is taken from chapter 1, "Why Are People?"; chapter 2, "The Replicators"; and chapter 3, "Immortal Coils."*

minority subject in universities, and even those who choose to study it often make their decision without appreciating its profound philosophical significance. Philosophy and the subjects known as "humanities" are still taught almost as if Darwin had never lived. No doubt this will change in time. In any case, this book is not intended as a general advocacy of Darwinism. Instead, it will explore the consequences of the evolution theory for a particular issue. My purpose is to examine the biology of selfishness and altruism.

Apart from its academic interest, the human importance of this subject is obvious. It touches every aspect of our social lives, our loving and hating, fighting and cooperating, giving and stealing, our greed and our generosity. These are claims that could have been made for Lorenz's *On Aggression*, Ardrey's *The Social Contract*, and Eibl-Eibesfeldt's *Love and Hate*. The trouble with these books is that their authors got it totally and utterly wrong. They got it wrong because they misunderstood how evolution works. They made the erroneous assumption that the important thing in evolution is the good of the *species* (or the group) rather than the good of the individual (or the gene). It is ironic that Ashley Montagu should criticize Lorenz as a "direct descendant of the 'nature red in tooth and claw' thinkers of the nineteenth century." As I understand Lorenz's view of evolution, he would be very much at one with Montagu in rejecting the implications of Tennyson's famous phrase. Unlike both of them, I think "nature red in tooth and claw" sums up our modern understanding of natural selection admirably.

Before beginning on my argument itself, I want to explain briefly what sort of an argument it is and what sort of an argument it is not. If we were told that a man had lived a long and prosperous life in the world of Chicago gangsters, we would be entitled to make some guesses as to the sort of man he was. We might expect that he would have qualities such as toughness, a quick trigger finger, and the ability to attract loyal friends. These would not be infallible deductions, but you can make some inferences about a man's character if you know something about the conditions in which he has survived and prospered. The argument of this book is that we, and all other animals, are machines created by our genes. Like successful Chicago gangsters, our genes have survived, in some cases for millions of years, in a highly competitive world. This entities us to expect certain qualities in our genes. I shall argue that a predominant quality to be expected in a successful gene is ruthless selfishness. This gene selfishness will usually give rise to selfishness in individual behavior. However, as we shall see, there are special circumstances in which a gene can achieve its own selfish goals best by fostering a limited form of altruism at the level of individual animals. "Special" and "limited" are important words in the last sentence. Much as we might wish to believe otherwise, universal love and the welfare of the species as a whole are concepts that simply do not make evolutionary sense.

This brings me to the first point I want to make about what this book is *not*. I am not advocating a morality based on evolution. I am saying how things have evolved. I am not saying how we humans morally ought to behave. I stress this, because I know I am in danger of being misunderstood by those people, all too numerous, who cannot distinguish a statement of belief in what is the case from an advocacy of what ought to be the case. My own feeling is that a human society based simply on the gene's law of universal ruthless selfishness would be a very nasty society in which to live. But unfortunately, however much we may deplore something, it does not stop it being true. This book is mainly intended to be interesting, but if you would extract a moral from it, read it as a warning. Be warned that if you wish, as I do, to build a society in which individuals cooperate generously and unselfishly toward a common good, you can expect little help from biological nature. Let us try to *teach* generosity and altruism, because we are born selfish. Let us understand what our own selfish genes are up to, because we may then at least have the chance to upset their designs, something that no other species has ever aspired to.

As a corollary to these remarks about teaching, it is a fallacy—incidentally a very common one—to suppose that genetically inherited traits are by definition fixed and unmodifiable. Our genes may instruct us to be selfish, but we are not necessarily compelled to obey them all our lives. It may just be more difficult to learn altruism than it would be if we were genetically programmed to be altruistic. Among animals, man is uniquely dominated by culture, by influences learned and handed down. Some would say that culture is so important that genes, whether selfish or not, are virtually irrelevant to the understanding of human nature. Others would disagree. It all depends where you stand in the debate over "nature versus nurture" as determinants of human attributes. This brings me to the second thing this book is not: it is not an advocacy of one position or another in the nature/nurture controversy. Naturally I have an opinion on this, but I am not going to express it, except insofar as it is implicit in the view of culture that I shall present in the final chapter. If genes really turn out to be totally irrelevant to the determination of modern human behavior, if we really are unique among animals in this respect, it is, at the very least, still interesting to inquire about the rule to which we have so recently become the exception. And if our species is not so exceptional as we might like to think, it is even more important that we should study the rule.

~ ~ ~

The account of the origin of life that I shall give is necessarily speculative; by definition, nobody was around to see what happened. There are a number of rival theories, but they all have certain features in common. The simplified account I shall give is probably not too far from the truth.

We do not know what chemical raw materials were abundant on earth before the coming of life, but among the plausible possibilities are water, carbon dioxide, methane, and ammonia: all simple compounds known to be present on at least some of the other planets in our solar system. Chemists have tried to imitate the chemical conditions of the young earth. They have put these simple substances in a flask and supplied a source of energy such as ultraviolet light or electric sparks—artificial simulation of primordial lightning. After a few weeks of this, something interesting is usually found inside the flask: a weak brown soup containing a large number of molecules more complex than the ones originally put in. In particular, amino acids have been found—the building blocks of proteins, one of the two great classes of biological molecules. Before these experiments were done, naturally occurring amino acids would have been thought of as diagnostic of the presence of life. If they had been detected on, say Mars, life on that planet would have seemed a near certainty. Now, however, their existence need imply only the presence of a few simple gases in the atmosphere and some volcanoes, sunlight, or thundery weather. More recently, laboratory simulations of the chemical conditions of Earth before the coming of life have yielded organic substances called purines and pyrimidines. These are building blocks of the genetic molecule, DNA itself.

Processes analogous to these must have given rise to the "primeval soup" which biologists and chemists believe constituted the seas some three to four thousand million years ago. The organic substances became locally concentrated, perhaps in drying scum round the shores, or in tiny suspended droplets. Under the further influence of energy such as ultraviolet light from the sun, they combined into larger molecules. Nowadays large organic molecules would not last long enough to be noticed: they would be quickly absorbed and broken down by bacteria or other living creatures. But bacteria and the rest of us are latecomers, and in those days large organic molecules could drift unmolested through the thickening broth.

At some point a particularly remarkable molecule was formed by accident. We will call it the *replicator*. It may not necessarily have been the biggest or the most complex molecule around, but it had the extraordinary property of being able to create copies of itself. This may seem a very unlikely sort of accident to happen. So it was. It was exceedingly improbable. In the lifetime of a man, things that are that improbable can be treated for practical purposes as impossible. That is why you will never win a big prize on the football pools. But in our human estimates of what is probable and what is not, we are not used to dealing in hundreds of millions of years. If you filled in pools coupons every week for a hundred million years you would very likely win several jackpots.

Actually a molecule that makes copies of itself is not as difficult to imagine as it seems at first, and it only had to arise once. Think of the replicator as a mold or template. Imagine it as a large molecule consisting of a complex chain of various sorts of building-block molecules. The small building blocks were abundantly available in the soup surrounding the replicator. Now suppose that each building block has an affinity for its own kind. Then whenever a building block from out in the soup lands up next to a part of the replicator for which it has an affinity, it will tend to stick there. The building blocks that attach themselves in this way will automatically be arranged in a sequence that mimics that of the replicator itself. It is easy then to think of them joining up to form a stable chain just as in the formation of the original replicator. This process could continue as a progressive stacking up, layer upon layer. This is how crystals are formed. On the other hand, the two chains might split apart, in which case we have two replicators, each of which can go on to make further copies.

A more complex possibility is that each building block has affinity not for its own kind, but reciprocally for one particular other kind. Then the replicator would act as a template not for an identical copy, but for a kind of "negative," which would in its turn remake an exact copy of the original positive. For our purposes it does not matter whether the original replication process was positive–negative or positive–positive, though it is worth remarking that the modern equivalents of the first replicator, the DNA molecules, use positive–negative replication. What does matter is that suddenly a new kind of "stability" came into the world. Previously it is probable that no particular kind of complex molecule was very abundant in the soup, because each was dependent on building blocks happening to fall by luck into a particular stable configuration. As soon as the replicator was born it must have spread its copies rapidly throughout the seas, until the smaller building-block molecules became a scarce resource, and other larger molecules were formed more and more rarely.

So we seem to arrive at a large population of identical replicas. But now we must mention an important property of any copying process: it is not perfect. Mistakes will happen. I hope there are no misprints in this book, but if you look carefully you may find one or two. They will probably not seriously distort the meaning of the sentences, because they will be "first generation" errors. But imagine the days before printing, when books such as the Gospels were copied by hand. All scribes, however careful, are bound to make a few errors, and some are not above a little willful "improvement." If they all copied from a single master original, meaning would not be greatly perverted. But let copies be made from other copies, which in their turn were made from other copies, and errors will start to become cumulative and serious. We tend to regard erratic copying as a bad thing, and in the case of human documents it is hard to think of examples where errors can be described as improvements. I suppose the scholars of the Septuagint could at least be said to have started something big when they mistranslated the Hebrew word for "young woman" into the Greek word for "virgin," coming up with the prophecy: "Behold a virgin shall conceive and bear a son. . . ." Anyway, as we shall see, erratic copying in biological replicators can in a real sense give rise to improvement, and it was essential for the progressive evolution of life that some errors were made. We do not know how accurately the original replicator molecules made their copies. Their modern descendants, the DNA molecules, are astonishingly faithful compared with the most high-fidelity human copying process, but even they occasionally make mistakes, and it is ultimately these mistakes that make evolution possible. Probably the original replicators were far more erratic, but in any case we may be sure that mistakes were made, and these mistakes were cumulative.

As miscopyings were made and propagated, the primeval soup became filled by a population not of identical replicas, but of several varieties of replicating molecules, all "descended" from the same ancestor. Would some varieties have been more numerous than others? Almost certainly yes. Some varieties would have been inherently more stable than others. Certain molecules, once formed, would be less likely than others to break up again. These types would become relatively numerous in the soup, not only as a direct logical consequence of their "longevity," but also because they would have a long time available for making copies of themselves. Replicators of high longevity would therefore tend to become more numerous, and other things being equal, there would have been an "evolutionary trend" toward greater longevity in the population of molecules.

But other things were probably not equal, and another property of a replicator variety that must have had even more importance in spreading it through the population was speed of replication or "fecundity." If replicator molecules of type A make copies of themselves on average once a week while those of type B make copies of themselves once an hour, it is not difficult to see that pretty soon type A molecules are going to be far outnumbered, even if they "live" much longer than B molecules. There would therefore probably have been an "evolutionary trend" toward higher "fecundity" of molecules in the soup. A third characteristic of replicator molecules which would have been positively selected is accuracy of replication. If molecules of type X and type Y last the same length of time and replicate at the same rate, but X makes a mistake on average every tenth replication while Y makes a mistake only every hundredth replication, Y will obviously become more numerous. The X contingent in the population loses not only the errant "children" themselves, but also all their descendants, actual or potential.

If you already know something about evolution, you may find something slightly paradoxical about the last point. Can we reconcile the idea that copying errors are an essential prerequisite for evolution to occur with the statement that natural selection favors high copying fidelity? The answer is that although evolution may seem, in some vague sense, a "good thing," especially since we are the product of it, nothing actually "wants" to evolve. Evolution is something that happens, willy-nilly, in spite of all the efforts of the replicators (and nowadays of the genes) to prevent it happening. Jacques Monod made this point very well in his Herbert Spencer lecture, after wryly remarking: "Another curious aspect of the theory of evolution is that everybody thinks he understands it!"

To return to the primeval soup, it must have become populated by stable varieties of molecule, stable in that either the individual molecules lasted a long time, or they replicated rapidly, or they replicated accurately. Evolutionary trends toward these three kinds of stability took place in the following sense: if you had sampled the soup at two different times, the later sample would have contained a higher proportion of varieties with high longevity/fecundity/copying fidelity. This is essentially what a biologist means by evolution when he is speaking of living creatures, and the mechanism is the same—natural selection.

Should we then call the original replicator molecules "living"? Who cares? I might say to you, "Darwin was the greatest man who has ever lived," and you might say, "No, Newton was," but I hope we would not prolong the argument. The point is that no conclusion of substance would be affected whichever way our argument was resolved. The facts of the lives and achievements of Newton and Darwin remain totally unchanged whether we label them "great" or not. Similarly, the story of the replicator molecules probably happened something like the way I am telling it regardless of whether we choose to call them "living." Human suffering has been caused because too many of us cannot grasp that words are only tools for our use and that the mere presence in the dictionary of a word like *living* does not mean it necessarily has to refer to something definite in the real world. Whether we call the early replicators living or not, they were the ancestors of life; they were our founding fathers.

The next important link in the argument, one that Darwin himself laid stress on (although he was talking about animals and plants, not molecules) is *competition*. The primeval soup was not capable of supporting an infinite number of replicator molecules. For one thing, the earth's size is finite, but other limiting factors must also have been important. In our picture of the replicator acting as a template or mold, we supposed it to be bathed in a soup rich in the small building-block molecules necessary to make copies. But when the replicators became numerous, building blocks must have been used up at such a rate that they became a scarce and precious resource. Different varieties or strains of replicator must have competed for them. We have considered the factors that would have increased the numbers of favored kinds of replicator. We can now see that less-favored varieties must actually have become *less* numerous because of competition, and ultimately many of their lines must have gone extinct. There was a struggle for existence among replicator varieties. They did not know they were struggling, or worry about it; the struggle was conducted without any hard feelings, indeed without feelings of any kind. But they were struggling, in the sense that any miscopying that resulted in a new higher level of stability or a new way of reducing the stability of rivals was automatically preserved and multiplied. The process of improvement was cumulative. Ways of increasing stability and of decreasing rivals' stability became more elaborate and more efficient. Some of them may even have "discovered" how to break up molecules of rival varieties chemically and to use the building blocks so released for making their own copies. These protocarnivores simultaneously obtained food and removed competing rivals. Other replicators perhaps discovered how to protect themselves, either chemically or by building a physical wall of protein around themselves. This may have been how the first living cells appeared. Replicators began not merely to exist, but to construct for themselves containers, vehicles for their continued existence. The replicators that survived were the ones that built *survival machines* for themselves to live in. The first survival machines probably consisted of nothing more than a protective coat. But making a living got steadily harder as new rivals arose with better and more effective survival machines. Survival machines got bigger and more elaborate, and the process was cumulative and progressive.

walls?

Was there to be any end to the gradual improvement in the techniques and artifices used by the replicators to ensure their own continuation in the world? There would be plenty of time for improvement. What weird engines of self-preservation would the millennia bring forth? Four thousand million years on, what was to be the fate of the ancient replicators? They did not die out, for they are past masters of the survival arts. But do not look for them floating loose in the sea; they gave up that cavalier freedom long ago. Now they swarm in huge colonies, safe inside gigantic lumbering robots, sealed off from the outside world, communicating with it by tortuous indirect routes, manipulating it by remote control. They are in you and in me; they created us, body and mind, and their preservation is the ultimate rationale for our existence. They have come a long way, those replicators. Now they go by the name of genes, and we are their survival machines.

We are survival machines, but "we" does not mean just people. It embraces all animals, plants, bacteria, and viruses. The total number of survival machines on Earth is very difficult to count and even the total number of species is unknown. Taking just insects alone, the number of living species has been estimated at around three million, and the number of individual insects may be a million million million.

Different sorts of survival machine appear very varied on the outside and in their internal organs. An octopus is nothing like a mouse, and both are quite different from an oak tree. Yet in their fundamental chemistry they are rather uniform, and in particular, the replicators that they bear, the genes, are basically the same kind of molecule in all of us—from bacteria to elephants. We are all survival machines for the same kind of replicator—molecules called DNA—but there are many different ways of making a living in the world, and the replicators have built a vast range of machines to exploit them. A monkey is a machine that preserves genes up trees, a fish is a machine that preserves genes in the water; there is even a small worm that preserves genes in German beer mats. DNA works in mysterious ways. . . .

I am using the word *gene* to mean a genetic unit that is small enough to last for a large number of generations and to be distributed around in the form of many copies. This is not a rigid all-or-nothing definition, but a kind of fading-out definition, like the definition of *big* or *old*. The more likely a length of chromosome is to be split by crossing over or altered by mutations of various kinds, the less it qualifies to be called a gene in the sense in which I am using the term. A cistron presumably qualifies, but so also do larger units. A dozen cistrons may be so close to each other on a chromosome that for our purposes they constitute a single long-lived genetic unit. . . . As the cistrons leave one body and enter the next, as they board sperm or egg for the journey into the next generation, they are likely to find that the little vessel contains their close neighbors of the previous voyage, old shipmates with whom they sailed on the long odyssey from the bodies of distant ancestors. Neighboring cistrons on the same chromosome form a tightly knit troupe of traveling companions who seldom fail to get on board the same vessel when meiosis time comes around.

To be strict, this book should be called not *The Selfish Cistron* nor *The Selfish Chromosome*, but *The slightly selfish big bit of chromosome and the even more selfish little bit of chromosome.* To say the least, this is not a catchy title, so, defining a gene as a little bit of chromosome which potentially lasts for many generations, I call the book *The Selfish Gene.*

We have now arrived back at the point we left at the end of chapter 1. There we saw that selfishness is to be expected in any entity that deserves the title of a basic unit of natural selection. We saw that some people regard the species as the unit of natural selection, others the population or group within the species, and yet others the individual. I said that I preferred to think of the gene as the fundamental unit of natural selection and therefore the fundamental unit of self-interest. What I have now done is to *define* the gene in such a way that I cannot really help being right!

Natural selection in its most general form means the differential survival of entities. Some entities live and others die, but in order for this selective death to have any impact on the world, an additional condition must be met. Each entity must exist in the form of lots of copies, and at least some of the entities must be *potentially* capable of surviving—in the form of copies—for a significant period of evolutionary time. Small genetic units have these properties: individuals, groups, and species do not. It was the great achievement of Gregor Mendel to show that hereditary units can be treated in practice as indivisible and independent particles. Nowadays we know that this is a little too simple. Even a cistron is occasionally divisible and any two genes on the same chromosome are not wholly independent. What I have done is to define a gene as a unit which, to a high degree, *approaches* the ideal of indivisible particulateness. A gene is not indivisible, but it is seldom divided. It is either definitely present or definitely absent in the body of any given individual. A gene travels intact from grandparent to grandchild, passing straight through the intermediate generation without being merged with other genes. If genes continually blended with each other, natural selection as we now understand it would be impossible. Incidentally, this was proved in Darwin's lifetime, and it caused Darwin great worry since in those days it was assumed that heredity was a blending process. Mendel's discovery had already been published, and it could have rescued Darwin, but alas he never knew about it: nobody seems to have read it until years after Darwin and Mendel had both died. Mendel perhaps did not realize the significance of his findings, otherwise he might have written to Darwin.

Another aspect of the particulateness of the gene is that it does not grow senile; it is no more likely to die when it is a million years old than when it is only a hundred. It leaps from body to body down the generations, manipulating body after body in its own way and for its own ends, abandoning a succession of mortal bodies before they sink in senility and death.

The genes are the immortals, or rather, they are defined as genetic entities that come close to deserving the title. We, the individual survival machines in the world, can expect to live a few more decades. But the genes in the world have an expectation of life that must be measured not in decades but in thousands and millions of years.

In sexually reproducing species, the individual is too large and too temporary a genetic unit to qualify as a significant unit of natural selection. The group of individuals is an even larger unit. Genetically speaking, individuals and groups are like clouds in the sky or dust storms in the desert. They are temporary aggregations or federations. They are not stable through evolutionary time. Populations may last a long while, but they are constantly blending with other populations and so losing their identity. They are also subject to evolutionary change from within. A population is not a discrete enough entity to be a unit of natural selection, not stable and unitary enough to be "selected" in preference to another population.

An individual body seems discrete enough while it lasts, but alas, how long is that? Each individual is unique. You cannot get evolution by selecting between entities when there is only one copy of each entity! Sexual reproduction is not replication. Just as a population is contaminated by other populations, so an individual's posterity is contaminated by that of his sexual partner. Your children are only half you, your grandchildren only a quarter you. In a few generations the most you can hope for is a large number of descendants, each of whom bears only a tiny portion of you—a few genes—even if a few do bear your surname as well.

Individuals are not stable things, they are fleeting. Chromosomes too are shuffled into oblivion, like hands of cards soon after they are dealt. But the cards themselves survive the shuffling. The cards are the genes. The genes are not destroyed by crossing over; they merely change partners and march on. Of course they march on. That is their business. They are the replicators and we are their survival machines. When we have served our purpose, we are cast aside. But genes are denizens of geological time: genes are forever.

Genes, like diamonds, are forever, but not quite in the same way as diamonds. It is an individual diamond crystal that lasts, as an unaltered pattern of atoms. DNA molecules don't have that kind of permanence. The life of any one physical DNA molecule is quite short—perhaps a matter of months, certainly not more than one lifetime. But a DNA molecule could theoretically live on in the form of *copies* of itself for a hundred million years. Moreover, just like the ancient replicators in the primeval soup, copies of a particular gene may be distributed all over the world. The difference is that the modern versions are all neatly packaged inside the bodies of survival machines.

What I am doing is emphasizing the potential near immortality of a gene, in the form of copies, as its defining property. To define a gene as a single cistron is good for some purposes, but for the purposes of evolutionary theory it needs to be enlarged. The extent of the enlargement is determined by the purpose of the definition. We want to find the practical unit of natural selection. To do this we begin by identifying the properties that a successful unit of natural selection must have. In the terms of the last chapter, these are longevity, fecundity, and copying fidelity. We then simply define a "gene" as the largest entity which, at least potentially, has these properties. The gene is a long-lived replicator, existing in the form of many duplicate copies. It is not infinitely long-lived. Even a diamond is not literally everlasting, and even a cistron can be cut in two by crossing over. The gene is defined as a piece of chromosome which is sufficiently short for it to last, potentially, for *long enough* for it to function as a significant unit of natural selection.

Exactly how long is "long enough"? There is no hard and fast answer. It will depend on how severe the natural selection "pressure" is. That is, on how much more likely a "bad" genetic unit is to die than its "good" allele. This is a matter of quantitative detail which will vary from example to example. The largest practical unit of natural selection—the gene—will usually be found to lie somewhere on the scale between cistron and chromosome.

It is its potential immortality that makes a gene a good candidate as the basic unit of natural selection. But now the time has come to stress the word "potential." A gene *can* live for a million years, but many new genes do not even make it past their first generation. The few new ones that succeed do so partly because they are lucky, but mainly because they have what it takes, and that means they are good at making survival machines. They have an effect on the embryonic development of each successive body in which they find themselves, such that that body is a little bit more likely to live and reproduce than it would have been under the influence of the rival gene or allele. For example, a "good" gene might ensure its survival by tending to endow the successive bodies in which it finds itself with long legs, which help those bodies to escape from predators. This is a particular example, not a universal one. Long legs, after all, are not always an asset. To a mole they would be a handicap. Rather than bog ourselves down in details, can we think of any *universal* qualities that we would expect to find in all good (i.e., long-lived) genes? Conversely, what are the properties that instantly mark a gene out as a "bad," short-lived one? There might be several such universal properties, but there is one that is particularly relevant to this book: at the gene level, altruism must be bad and selfishness good. This follows inexorably from our definitions of altruism and selfishness. Genes are competing directly with their alleles for survival, since their alleles in the gene pool are rivals for their slot on the chromosomes of future generations. Any gene that behaves in such a way as to increase its own survival chances in the gene pool at the expense of its alleles will, by definition, tautologously, tend to survive. The gene is the basic unit of selfishness.

## Content Questions

1. According to Dawkins, why does the theory of evolution supersede all previous efforts to understand the reason for humankind's existence? (205)

2. Why does Dawkins describe some genes as "successful Chicago gangsters"? (206) What qualities do these genes have?

3. Why will "gene selfishness" not always manifest itself in individual selfishness? (206)

4. Why is the evolution of the replicator, though "exceedingly improbable," nevertheless likely to be true, in Dawkins's view? (209)

5. Why did the existence of the replicator create "a new kind of 'stability'" in the world? (210)

6. What makes evolution possible at the genetic level? (210)

7. What three kinds of stability did evolutionary trends favor as life was beginning? (212)

8. According to Dawkins, why did the "survival machines" for genes get steadily bigger and more elaborate? (213)

9. What characteristics of individuals make them unable to serve as the basic unit of natural selection, in Dawkins's view? What characteristics of genes make them good candidates for the basic units of natural selection? (215–217)

10. What does Dawkins mean when he says that "the gene is the basic unit of selfishness"? (218)

## Application Questions

1. What is the basis for the current proposal that the first genetic material (the first replicator) was RNA? What is the evidence that nucleic acid genes were preceded by other, simpler systems?

2. One widely held approach in the study of biological systems posits that each level of biological structure has emergent properties—that with each step upward in the hierarchy of biological order, novel properties emerge that were not present at the simpler levels of organization. How would the adoption of this approach influence the analysis of Dawkins's argument?

## Discussion Questions

1. Does Dawkins intend his readers to draw moral conclusions from his argument? Why does he say that "this book is mainly intended to be interesting, but if you would extract a moral from it, read it as a warning"? (207)

2. Why does Dawkins refuse to state his position in the "nature/nurture controversy"? (207) Based on the selection you have read, what do you think his position is?

3. Would thinking of people as "survival machines" for genes affect your beliefs about what it means to be human? If so, how?

# Paul Colinvaux

Ecologist Paul Colinvaux (1930– ) has focused his work on the question of how the environment has determined the development of life. His 1980 book *The Fates of Nations* examines how ecological principles have affected human history from the Pleistocene era to the present. As a senior scientist at the Smithsonian Tropical Research Institute in Panama, Colinvaux investigated the ecological history of the Amazon River basin. In 1997, he and his colleagues used radiocarbon dating and pollen analysis of sediments from a small lake in Brazil to determine that during the last Ice Age, much of the basin was covered by a rain forest. This contradicted the widespread scientific belief that at that time the area was a dry grassland. Colinvaux received his Ph.D. from Duke University in 1962. He is professor emeritus at Ohio State University and currently heads a research laboratory at the Marine Biological Laboratory in Woods Hole, Massachusetts. Colinvaux has written ecology textbooks as well as works for general readers, including *Why Big Fierce Animals Are Rare*, from which the following selection is taken.

# Why Big Fierce Animals Are Rare

Animals come in different sizes, and the little ones are much more common than the big.

A typical small patch of woodland in any of the temperate lands of the North will contain hosts of insects and then nothing larger running about until we get to the size of small birds, which are much less numerous. Another size jump brings us to foxes, hawks, and owls, of which there may be only one or two. A fox is ten times the size of a songbird, which is ten times the size of an insect. If the insect is one of the predacious ground beetles of the forest floor, which hunt among the leaves like the wolf spiders, then it, in turn, is ten times bigger than the mites and other tiny things that they both hunt.

The animals in this system of living do indeed come in very distinct sizes. There are, of course, some in-between ones, but not many. Squirrels in the upper size range seem obvious, but I am hard put to find something between an insect and a small bird unless it is a newt or lizard, neither of them very prominent denizens of a temperate woodland. Slugs and snails are toward the size of caterpillars. Shrews and toads are near the size of songbirds. Even a snake can be thought of as an odd-shaped hawk.

In the wood as elsewhere there are distinctly different sizes, and the little ones are the most common. The same sort of thing exists in the sea in even odder form, for in the open sea the really tiny things are plants, the

223

microscopic diatoms and other algae. Ten times bigger than these (give or take a few times) are the animals of the plankton, the copepods, and the like. Bigger still are the shrimps and fish that hunt those copepods. Then another jump brings us to herrings, then to sharks, or killer whales. In any one place in the sea, this clumping of life into different sizes is the normal thing.

In the sea the rarity of the large is also most clearly shown. Great white sharks are extremely rare, and the other kinds of shark are scattered pretty thinly over the seas too. Fish of the herring size are vastly more common than sharks, but even so, the number that are seen in a casual dive in the sea is seldom immense. If you drift, and focus your eyes just outside the facemask, however, myriad darting specks of the smaller animals may become visible. If you later take some of that same water and spin it in a centrifuge, there is likely to be a thin green scum in the bottom made up of an almost uncountable multitude of independent, tiny plants.

The tiny things of woodland and sea are immensely common; bigger things are a whole jump bigger and a whole jump less common; and so on until we reach the largest and rarest animals of all. A like pattern can be found in tropical forests, Irish bogs, or just about anywhere else. It is an extraordinary thing but true that life comes in size fractions which, for all the blending and exceptions that can be found by careful scrutiny, are remarkably distinct. Animals in the larger sizes are comparatively rare.

Charles Elton of Oxford pointed out this strange reality half a century ago. Elton went adventuring on Spitsbergen, an Arctic island covered with treeless tundra, where the animals move about in the open and where particularly he could follow an arctic fox as it went about its daily affairs. Arctic foxes can be delightfully tame. On Saint George Island in the Bering Sea one tried to take sandwiches from my pocket as I sat upon a rock. Elton followed his foxes and pondered their activities through a summer that was to be one of the most important an ecologist ever spent.

The foxes caught the summer birds of the tundra—the ptarmigan, sandpipers, and buntings; and these birds were at once a size jump smaller than the foxes and much more numerous. The ptarmigan ate the fruit and leaves of tundra plants, but the sandpipers and buntings ate insects and worms, which were again a size jump smaller as well as more numerous. The foxes also ate seagulls and eider ducks, smaller and more numerous than the foxes, and these birds ate the tiny abundant life of the sea. Elton not only saw all this but, as Sherlock Holmes often lectured Watson, he *observed* it also. That small things are common and large things rare has been known by everybody since the dawn of thought, but Elton pondered it as Newton once pondered a falling apple, and knew he was watching something odd. Why should large animals be so remarkably rare? And why should life come in discrete sizes?

Elton's summer on Spitsbergen gave him the answer to the second of these questions even as he posed it. The discrete sizes came about from the mechanics of eating and being eaten. He had seen a fox eat a sandpiper and a sandpiper eat a worm. These animals of different sizes were linked together by invisible chains of eating and being eaten. Foxes had to be big enough, and active enough, to catch and eat the birds on which they preyed; and the birds likewise must overpower, and engulf at a single swallow, the animals on which they fed. The normal lot of an animal was to be big enough to vanquish its living food with ease, and usually to be able to stuff it down its throat whole or nearly so. As one moves from link to link of a food chain the animals get roughly ten times bigger. Life comes in discrete sizes because each kind must evolve to be much bigger than the thing it eats.

Elton's conclusions were obviously true in a very general way. The communities of woodland and ocean on which his thinking was based seemed to conform very nicely. Life in those communities did come in different sizes, and it seemed that the sizes had grown discrete because each kind had evolved to be much bigger than the thing it ate. But many exceptions to the general principle of food size come to mind: wolves, lions, internal parasites, elephants, and baleen whales. There are many animals that are either smaller than their food, such as wolves or parasites, or else absurdly bigger, like whales. But a closer look at any of these animals shows them to be instructive exceptions, if true exceptions to the rule all the same.

Land herbivores do not fit the Eltonian model, at least not completely, because land plants provide different-sized mouthfuls for different sizes of animals. You do not have to kill an entire land plant in order to eat it; you just tear off a suitable piece, a shoot, some grass blades, a berry, a bite out of a leaf. Food chains based on vegetation could start with many different sizes of plant-eating animal because squirrels, caterpillars, and elephants share the same food. Even so, there does not seem to be a complete continuum of sizes amongst vegetarians, at least in any one place. Both big and little plant-eaters exist in a forest or a prairie and there is not much difficulty in sorting them into sizes. This is because the predators of plant eaters do have to be size conscious when they look for food. A selection pressure acts downward along the food chains, as herbivores evolve sizes that let them escape even as carnivores evolve sizes that enable them to catch skillfully. It is as important to be of a size that does not fit in someone else's mouth as it is to have a mouth suited to the size of one's own prey. So natural selection tends to preserve size classes even when food chains start with a pabulum of meadow-forage or forest.

Wolves sometimes obey Eltonian principles, as when they hunt singly for rodents and small game, but they have evolved the trick of packing up to haul down bigger prey in winter, when they are freed from family cares and can go out in gangs. Other pack-hunting animals work variants on this method. And all large carnivores have had their sizes adjusted to the needs of killing, rather than of engulfing, so that a lion needs to be big enough to pull down an ailing zebra, but no bigger.

Parasites are smaller than their food, for obvious reasons, but their activities still tend to separate the animals on parasite food chains into different sizes with every link, as was described before the coming of ecology in a jingle by Jonathan Swift:

> Big fleas have little fleas
> Upon their backs to bite 'em
> And little fleas have lesser fleas
> And so *ad infinitum.*

Very special sea animals, such as whales, are even more instructive, and we discuss them at the end of this chapter. But otherwise in the sea the pattern of size tends to conform very well to the simplest interpretation of the workings of food size. This is because the sea plants are tiny, individual, and have to be hunted and killed by those who would live off them (seaweeds of the coasts are of trivial importance in the wide oceans). So in the sea a rather complete set of steps runs up the food chains from the smallest plants, through crustaceans and fish, to great white sharks.

Thinking these Eltonian thoughts brings up another of nature's conundrums, "Why are land plants big but sea plants small?" But that must wait for another chapter.

Now there was the matter of rarity. Elton showed that there had to be size jumps as one went up food chains and that the animals on the upper end had to be big. But why should the big be so rare? And very rare they are. One only has to compare the number of sharks to the number of herrings, or warblers to caterpillars, to see this. With every jump in size an even mightier loss occurs in numbers. Elton coined a term to describe this fact of life; he called it "the pyramid of numbers." He saw in his mind's eye a mighty host of tiny animals supporting on their backs a much smaller army of animals ten times as big. And this array supported, in turn, other animals ten times bigger still, but these were a select few. It was a graph of life he imagined with numbers of individuals along the horizontal axis, and position in the chain of eating, together with size, on the vertical. His vision saw the functioning of animal communities like the profile of Zoser's step pyramid at Saqqara, a triangular edifice built of stacked square-ended layers so that the summit could be reached by four or five giant steps. When ecologists forgather they call this result the "Eltonian pyramid." Now, why should there be pyramids of numbers in nature wherever we look, from the Arctic tundras to tropical forests and the open spaces of the sea? Why should large animals, particularly large hunting animals, always be so amazingly rare?

It is tempting to say that no problem exists, that it stands to reason that there cannot be as many big things as little. But this claim suggests that the Eltonian pyramid reflects no more than the elementary facts of spatial geometry. There is clearly no shortage of actual space to hold more big animals. On Spitsbergen, for instance, each fox had acres and acres to run around in, and the world oceans could hold mind-boggling quantities of the large sharks and killer whales who are the top carnivores of the sea. Large plants are crammed together on the earth in astounding numbers, so that we call the result a "forest." Only the large animals are discriminated against.

A second tempting argument is to say that there is a finite amount of flesh (what ecologists call biomass) to go round and that this chunk of flesh could be used either to make a few big bodies or to make very many little ones. The big are rare because they take large slices from their cake. This assertion is true as far as it goes, but it does not go nearly far enough. If, instead of counting the animals in the different size levels of the pyramid, one weighed them, one finds that there is vastly more flesh in the smaller classes, a greater standing crop of life as well as more numerous individuals. All the insects in a woodlot weigh many times as much as all the birds;

and all the songbirds, squirrels, and mice combined weigh vastly more than all the foxes, hawks, and owls combined. The pyramid of numbers is also a pyramid of mass, and the problem remains unsolved. Why is there so little living tissue in the larger animal sizes?

Elton did not have the answer. He thought it might be because little animals reproduced very quickly (true, they do—compare the egg output of butterflies with that of the birds that eat caterpillars) and that rapid reproduction was the key to vast populations. But this is to fall into the age-old error of biologists and theologians alike, the error that says numbers are set by breeding strategy.

. . . Numbers are set by the opportunities for one's way of life, not by the way one breeds. Professorships set the limit to the population of professors, not the productive output of graduate schools. The fact that large animals are rare cannot have anything to do with their reproductive drives. Elton's explanation will not do.

It took nearly twenty years for the corporate body of science to come up with the answer to the question Elton posed in 1927. Raymond Lindeman and Evelyn Hutchinson did so at Yale by thinking of food and bodies as calories rather than as flesh.

A unit of biomass, or flesh, represents a unit of potential energy that is measured in calories. If we burn a chunk of protein we liberate so many calories of heat, and if we burn a chunk of fat we get more calories still. This is now common knowledge to the affluent peoples of the West who worry about the calories in their food lest they become obese. In the 1930s and 1940s even illiterate Hollywood starlets knew this, but biologists wakened to the idea of the calorie rather more slowly. Yet in the use of food as calories lay the answer to the rarity of the large and fierce.

Measuring an animal's flesh in calories also alerts one's mind to the vital fact that bodies represent fuel as well as vessels for the soul. An animal continually burns up its fuel supply to do the work of living, puffing the exhaust gases out of the smokestacks of its mouth and nostrils and sending the calories off to outer space as radiant heat. The animal uses up its flesh, replacing the lost substance by eating more food, then burning most of this up too. This process of consuming matter by the fires of life goes on in every level of the Eltonian pyramids, and the fires are continually fresh stoked by the plants on which the animal pyramids rest. At each successive level in the pyramids, the animals have to make do with the fuel (food) that can be extorted from the level below. But they can only extort some fraction of what the level below had not itself used up, and with this tithe the denizens of the upper layers must both make their own bodies and fuel their lives. Which is why their numbers are only a fraction of the numbers below, which is to say why they are rare.

The ultimate furnace of life is the sun, streaming down calories of heat with never-fainting ray. On every usable scrap of the earth's surface a plant is staked out to catch the light, its green array of energy receptors and transducers tuned and directed to the glowing source like the gold-plated cells on the arms of a satellite. In those green transducers we call leaves, the plants synthesize fuel, taking a constant allotment of the streaming energy of the sun. Some of this fuel they use to build their bodies, but some they burn to do the work of living. Animals eat those plants, but they do not get all the plant tissue, as we know because the earth is carpeted brown with rotting debris that has not been part of an animal's dinner. Nor can the animals ever get the fuel the plants have already burned. So there cannot be as much animal flesh on the earth as there is plant flesh. It is possible for large plants to be vastly abundant and ranked side by side, but animals of the same size would have to be thinly spread out because they can only be a tenth as abundant.

This would be true even if all animals were vegetarian. But they are not. For flesh eaters, the largest possible supply of food calories they can obtain is a fraction of the bodies of their plant-eating prey, and they must use this fraction both to make bodies and as a fuel supply. Moreover, their bodies must be the big active bodies that let them hunt for a living. If one is higher still on the food chain, an eater of a flesh eater's flesh, one has yet a smaller fraction to support even bigger and fiercer bodies. Which is why large fierce animals are so astonishingly (or pleasingly) rare.

Thus was the grandest pattern of rarity and abundance in the world explained by two men at Yale in the 1940s. Ways of life were bumping against that most fundamental of physical restraints, the supply of energy.

As the realization of what Lindeman and Hutchinson had done for natural history percolated through the consciousness of biology in the fifties and sixties a thrill of self-respect began to throb in its younger practitioners. Here the pattern of field experience was linked to the fundamental laws of physics. We were talking of energy degraded step by step as it flowed down food chains, losing its power to do work and pouring steadily away to the sink of heat. The grand pattern of life that Elton had seen on Spitsbergen and that countless naturalists had intuitively known before was clearly and directly a consequence of the second law of thermodynamics.

We can now understand why there are not fiercer dragons on the earth than there are; it is because the energy supply will not stretch to the support of superdragons. Great white sharks or killer whales in the sea, and lions and tigers on the land, are apparently the most formidable animals the contemporary earth can support. Even these are very thinly spread. One may swim many lifetimes in the world oceans without encountering a great white shark, and an ancient Chinese proverb asserts that a hill shelters only one tiger. Evolutionary principle tells us that the existence of these animals creates a theoretical possibility for other animals to evolve to eat them, but the food calories to be won from the careers, or niches, of hunting great white sharks and tigers are too few to support a minimum population of animals as large and horribly ferocious as these would have to be. Such animals, therefore, have never evolved. Great white sharks and tigers represent the largest predators that the laws of physics allow the contemporary earth to support.

But here we run into what seems to be the first real difficulty of the argument. There are living animals that are much larger than tigers and sharks, and there have been some very big ones in the past. How does their existence square with our interpretation of the second law of thermodynamics?

Elephants and the big, cloven-hoofed animals are larger than tigers. In the past there have been even bigger mammals, such as giant ground-sloths and *Titanotherium*, a beast like an overgrown elephant and the largest land mammal ever. There have also been the largest reptiles of the Mesozoic, the ponderous dinosaurs: *Stegosaurus, Brontosaurus, Iguanodon*. None of these animals poses any difficulty for the model. They have all been plant eaters. In the strict Eltonian model the plant eaters are small, and indeed in life most of them actually are. In the open sea this rule that plant eaters must be small is strictly enforced because the drifting plants are so tiny that only very small animals can make a successful living by eating them. But on land, plants often appear as continuous mats of leaves, which we call vegetation, and it is possible for enormous sluggish animals to slurp them up without much nicety in the hunting. Masses of energy are available in the plant-eating niches at the bottom of the Eltonian pyramids, with the result that viable populations of even enormous animals can be supported. The brontosaur and the elephant alike, therefore, leave both our belief in the energy-flow model and the second law of thermodynamics intact.

That leaves two trickier kinds of animals to explain away: the great baleen whales of the contemporary oceans, which are the largest animals ever to have lived, and the flesh-eating dinosaurs such as *Tyrannosaurus rex*. These are both meat-eating animals, and they are impressively bigger than great white sharks or tigers.

The baleen whales have learned to cheat, hunting their food in non-Eltonian ways. Essential to the normal structure of the Eltonian pyramid was that every carnivorous animal should have a direct relationship to the size of its food, being big enough to catch and eat it but not so big that the food item should prove a trivial mouthful not worth the effort of hunting. On this model, the food of a blue or right whale should be several feet long. But it is not. The whales cheat with their sieves of baleen, which let them strain from the surface of the sea the tiny shrimps called krill in huge numbers and with little effort. The whales have cut out the middlemen, avoiding all the energy losses that would have accrued if the krill had been passed to a fish and that fish passed to a bigger fish before the whale had its chance at it like any other Eltonian feeder. So the whales, although not plant eaters, feed very low on food chains where the energy supply is still comparatively large. Floating as they do in the sea, they use little energy in their sluggish hunting, paddling quietly along with their mouths open, straining the meat out of the oceanic soup. So the apparent exception of the whales is no exception at all, and our model may stand.

*Tyrannosaurus rex* is more difficult for the argument. Tyrannosaurs were huge carnivorous dinosaurs, often pictured as a great green kangaroo-like form with a hideous toadlike head, nightmare teeth, and a pair of useless little flapping arms dangling below the ugly neck. An animal of this size answering to the name of *Tyrannosaurus* certainly existed, for we have specimens of all his bones. He was several times larger than lions or tigers, or indeed of any other recorded predator. What enabled it to escape the constraints apparently placed on all its successors by the second law of thermodynamics?

It is useful to note first that the tyrannosaur fed at the same level as its modern successors, the big cats, and at the same level as the baleen whales in the sea. It fed on plant eaters relatively low in the food chain, close to the bottom of the Eltonian pyramid, where there was still much energy to be won. A large body, therefore, does not seem hopelessly out of the question. We know that there were many kinds of very large herbivores about in the tyrannosaur's time, animals that, in the absence of pack-hunting predators such as dogs, could be overcome only by very powerful attackers. So we might conclude that the necessity for Mesozoic predators to be large and ferociously active is self-evident. There was nothing else to get at the meat so massively on the hoof, so natural selection provided *Tyrannosaurus rex*.

I have always been unhappy about this reasoning. If natural selection could fashion a tyrannosaur at that time, why not in all subsequent times? Why in particular was there nothing like a tyrannosaur in the great age of mammals, that later part of the Tertiary epoch when all the plains lands of the earth held herds of game that make the herds of modern Africa seem trivial by comparison? I have felt compelled to conclude that the constraints on the size of ferociously active predators that have been applied throughout the age of mammals ought to have applied to the reptiles of the Mesozoic era also. By thinking thus I maneuver myself into the position of saying that, on ecological grounds, the *Tyrannosaurus rex* did not exist. And yet there the bones are, indubitably the bones of a large, flesh-eating animal of the size claimed. It was with a sense of inward peace that I saw a drawing of a recent attempt to put the bones together differently.

The classic picture of the hopping, predacious tyrant lizard is derived from nineteenth-century reconstructions of the animal. The new reconstruction, first published in *Nature* in 1968, shows the animal to be a waddling, slow-moving beast, not at all the sort one can imagine dashing after a herd of galloping brontosauri. But it probably got them all the same, picking out the sick and the dying, often getting them only as carrion. The tyrannosaur was not a ferociously active predator. It did not stand upright, nor did it hop. It held that massive body horizontally, perhaps able to move swiftly for short periods as it balanced its motion with the long tail. But most of its days were spent lying on its belly, a prostration that conserved energy and from which it periodically roused itself, lifting its great bulk on those two little arms in front until it could balance on the thick walking legs. The tyrannosaur did indeed support a large mass by meat eating, but it escaped the energy-consuming price of being active in order to overcome prime specimens of the giant prey it ate. It managed on land essentially the same stratagem that the baleen whales manage in the sea; it found a non-Eltonian way of getting the meat of plant eaters without having to hunt them properly. Nothing like it has been seen since because the true active predators of the age of mammals were able to clean up the meat supplies before a sluggish beast such as a tyrannosaur could get to them. And active predators might even have eaten the tyrannosaur itself.

*Tyrannosaurus rex,* as popularly portrayed, is a myth. But it is probably safe to say that it will be as durable as any other myth in our culture. The size and ferocity of real-life predators is restricted to the scale of a tiger, and even these must always be rare. The second law of thermodynamics says so.

## Content Questions

1. How, specifically, did his fieldwork of following and observing the arctic fox lead Charles Elton to his conclusions about why large animals are rare? (224–225)

2. Why did Elton conclude that animals' differing sizes are related to "the mechanics of eating and being eaten"? (225)

3. Why is it that "natural selection tends to preserve size classes even when food chains start with a pabulum of meadow-forage or forest"? (226)

4. What "fact of life" does Elton's "pyramid of numbers" describe? (227)

5. Why are the explanations of lack of physical space, limitations of biomass, and the rapid reproduction of smaller creatures inadequate to answer the question of why large animals are rare? (227–228)

6. How did Raymond Lindeman and Evelyn Hutchinson, by thinking of food and flesh as calories, finally furnish a satisfying explanation of the rarity of large animals? (228)

7. In what way did the conclusions of Lindeman and Hutchinson change the way in which biologists view the regulation of population composition and size within a community? (229–230)

8. How does fierceness, as well as size, contribute to an animal's rarity? (229)

9. In the 1950s and 1960s, what relationship did some biologists articulate between Lindeman and Hutchinson's conclusions and the second law of thermodynamics? (229–230)

10. According to Colinvaux, why don't elephants or whales prove Lindeman and Hutchinson's hypothesis wrong? (230–231)

## Application Questions

1. Currently, there is considerable debate among paleontologists about whether *Tyrannosaurus rex* was a predator or a scavenger. Would Colinvaux's argument favor one of these ecological roles over the other? Why?

2. Using examples from sources other than Colinvaux, how do we explain the fact that the pyramid of biomass and the pyramid of numbers do not apply to all communities?

## Discussion Questions

1. In describing how Lindeman and Hutchinson modified Elton's conclusions, what point is Colinvaux making about the scientific process?

2. Is the force of Colinvaux's argument harmed by his mistaken assumptions about *Tyrannosaurus rex?* How would you modify his argument by taking into account newer findings about this dinosaur?

3. Based on Colinvaux's explanations of how animals evolve in relation to their sources of food, what conclusions can you draw about humankind's evolution as it relates to the food we eat?

4. Does Colinvaux's point of view alter the presumptions that we make about human beings? If so, how?

# Stephen Jay Gould

Stephen Jay Gould (1941–2002) combined a distinguished scientific career with great success as the author of books on science for a general audience. He wrote more than twenty books and hundreds of essays and reviews, and was a frequent lecturer on scientific topics. His most significant original theory was that of "punctuated equilibrium" in evolution, which he developed with Niles Eldredge in 1972. This theory asserts that evolution is not a gradual and continuous process, as it has usually been understood, but advances by relatively rapid and pronounced changes. In particular, the theory claims that structural changes in organisms can be preserved by natural selection only if they appear somewhat suddenly. Gould also addressed theories of human intelligence, and his book *The Mismeasure of Man* (1981) is an impassioned history and critique of the practice of ranking people according to their supposed genetic capabilities.

Gould was born in New York City and earned a Ph.D. from Columbia University in 1967. He then taught at Harvard University, where he was a professor of zoo-logy and geology, and was curator of invertebrate paleontology at Harvard's Museum of Comparative Zoology. In his own scientific fieldwork, he concentrated on fossil mol-lusks and snails in Bermuda. Gould was well known by the general public for his monthly column "This View of Life," which appeared in *Natural History* magazine from 1974 to 2000.

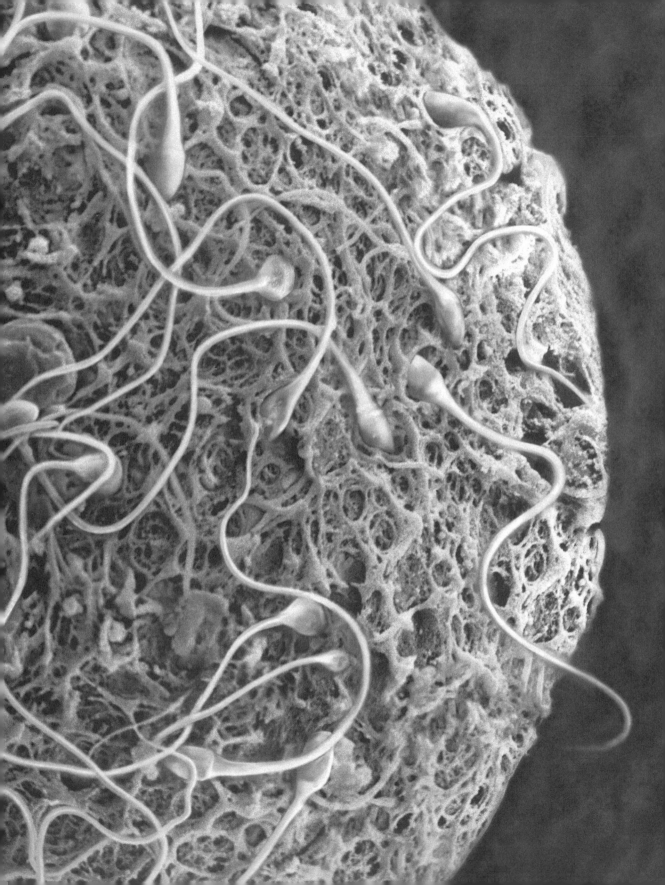

# Just in the Middle

The case for organic integrity was stated most forcefully by a poet, not a biologist. In his romantic paean *The Tables Turned*, William Wordsworth wrote:

> Sweet is the lore which nature brings;
> Our meddling intellect
> Misshapes the beauteous form of things:
> We murder to dissect.

The whiff of anti-intellectualism that pervades this poem has always disturbed me, much as I appreciate its defense of nature's unity. For it implies that any attempt at analysis, any striving to understand by breaking a complex system into constituent parts, is not only useless but even immoral.

Yet caricature and dismissal from the other side have been just as intense, if not usually stated with such felicity. Those scientists who study biological systems by breaking them down into ever smaller parts, until they reach the chemistry of molecules, often deride biologists who insist upon treating organisms as irreducible wholes. The two sides of this oversimplified dichotomy even have names, often invoked in a derogatory way by their opponents. The dissectors are "mechanists" who believe that life is

239

nothing more than the physics and chemistry of its component parts. The integrationists are "vitalists" who hold that life and life alone has that "special something" forever beyond the reach of chemistry and physics and even incompatible with "basic" science. In this reading you are, according to your adversaries, either a heartless mechanist or a mystical vitalist.

I have often been amused by our vulgar tendency to take complex issues, with solutions at neither extreme of a continuum of possibilities, and break them into dichotomies, assigning one group to one pole and the other to an opposite end, with no acknowledgment of subtleties and intermediate positions—and nearly always with moral opprobrium attached to opponents. As the wise Private Willis sings in Gilbert and Sullivan's *Iolanthe*:

> I often think it's comical
> How nature always does contrive
> That every boy and every gal
> That's born into the world alive
> Is either a little Liberal
> Or else a little Conservative!
>   Fal la la!

The categories have changed today, but we are still either rightists or leftists, advocates of nuclear power or solar heating, pro-choice or against the murder of fetuses. We are simply not allowed the subtlety of an intermediate view on intricate issues (although I suspect that the only truly important and complex debate with no possible stance in between is whether you are for or against the designated hitter rule—and I'm agin it).

Thus, the impression persists that biologists are either mechanists or vitalists, either advocates of an ultimate reduction to physics and chemistry (with no appreciation for the integrity of organisms) or supporters of a special force that gives life meaning (and modern mystics who would deny the potential unity of science). For example, a popular article on research at the Marine Biological Laboratory of Woods Hole (in the September–October 1983 issue of *Harvard Magazine*) discusses the work of a scientist with a physicist's approach to neurological problems:

In the parlance of philosophers of science, [he] could be considered a "reductionist" or "mechanist." He believes that fundamental laws of mechanics and electromagnetism suffice to account for all phenomena at this level. Vitalists, in contrast, maintain that some vital principle, some spark of life, separates living from nonliving matter. Thomas Hunt Morgan, a confirmed vitalist, once remarked acidly that scientists who compared living organisms to machines were like "wild Indians who derailed trains and looked for the horses inside the locomotive." Most mechanists, in turn, regard their opponents' vital principle as so much black magic.

But this dichotomy is an absurd caricature of the opinions held by most biologists. Although I have known a few mechanists, as defined in this article, I don't think that I have ever met a vitalist (although the argument did enjoy some popularity during the nineteenth century). The vast majority of biologists, including the great geneticist T. H. Morgan (who was as antivitalist as any scientist of our century), advocate a middle position. The extremes may make good copy and a convenient (if simplistic) theme for discussion, but they are occupied by few, if any, practicing scientists. If we can understand this middle position and grasp why it has been so persistently popular, perhaps we can begin to criticize our lamentable tendency to dichotomize complex issues in the first place. I therefore devote this essay to defining and supporting this middle way by showing how a fine American biologist, Ernest Everett Just, developed and defended it in the course of his own biological research.

The middle position holds that life, as a result of its structural and functional complexity, cannot be taken apart into chemical constituents and explained in its entirety by physical and chemical laws working at the molecular level. But the middle way denies just as strenuously that this failure of reductionism records any mystical property of life, any special "spark" that inheres in life alone. Life acquires its own principles from the hierarchical structure of nature. As levels of complexity mount along the hierarchy of atom, molecule, gene, cell, tissue, organism, and population, new properties arise as results of interactions and interconnections emerging at each new level. A higher level cannot be fully explained by taking it apart into component elements and rendering their properties in the absence of these interactions. Thus, we need new, or "emergent," principles to encompass life's complexity; these principles are additional to, and consistent with, the physics and chemistry of atoms and molecules.

This middle way may be designated "organizational," or "holistic"; it represents the stance adopted by most biologists and even by most physical scientists who have thought hard about biology and directly experienced its complexity. It was, for example, espoused in what may be our century's most famous book on "what is life?"—the short masterpiece of the same title written in 1944 by Erwin Schrödinger, the great quantum physicist who turned to biological problems at the end of his career. Schrödinger wrote:

> From all we have learnt about the structure of living matter, we must be prepared to find it working in a manner that cannot be reduced to the ordinary laws of physics. And that not on the ground that there is any "new force" or whatnot, directing the behavior of the single atoms within a living organism, but because the construction is different from anything we have yet tested in the physical laboratory.

Schrödinger then presents a striking analogy. Compare the ordinary physicist to an engineer familiar only with the operation of steam engines. When this engineer encounters, for the first time, a more complicated electric motor, he will not assume that it works by intrinsically mysterious laws just because he cannot understand it with the principles appropriate to steam engines: "He will not suspect that an electric motor is driven by a ghost because it is set spinning by the turn of a switch, without boiler and steam."

Ernest Everett Just, a thoughtful embryologist who developed a similar holistic attitude as a direct consequence of his own research, was born one hundred years ago in Charleston, South Carolina.[1] He graduated as valedictorian of Dartmouth in 1907 and did most of his research at the Marine Biological Laboratory of Woods Hole during the 1920s. He continued his work at various European biological laboratories during the 1930s and was briefly interned by the Nazis when France fell in 1940. Repatriated to the United States, and broken in spirit, he died of pancreatic cancer in 1941 at age fifty-eight.

Just began as an experimentalist, studying problems of fertilization at the cellular level, and in the great tradition of careful, descriptive research

1. I wrote this essay in 1983, for the centenary of Just's birth.

242

so characteristic of the "Woods Hole school." As this work developed, and particularly after he left for Europe, his career entered a new phase: he became fascinated with the biology of cell surfaces. This shift emerged directly from his interest in fertilization and his particular concern with an old problem: How does the sperm penetrate an egg's outer membrane, and how does the egg's surface then react in physical and chemical terms? At the same time, Just's work took on a more philosophical tone (although he never abandoned his experiments), and he slowly developed a holistic, or organizational, perspective midway between the caricatured extremes of classical mechanism and vitalism. Just expounded this biological philosophy, a direct result of his growing concern with the properties of cell surfaces considered as wholes, in *The Biology of the Cell Surface*, published in 1939.

Just's early work on fertilization was a harbinger of things to come. He was not particularly interested in how the genetic material of egg and sperm fuse and then direct the subsequent architecture of development—a classical theme of the reductionist tradition (an attempt to explain the properties of embryology in terms of genes housed in a controlling nucleus). He was more concerned with the effects that fertilization imposes upon the entire cell, particularly its surface, and on the interaction of nucleus and cytoplasm in subsequent cell division and differentiation of the embryo.

Just had an uncanny knack for devising simple and elegant experiments that spoke to the primary theoretical issues of his day. In his very first paper, for example, he showed that, for some species of marine invertebrates at least, the sperm's point of entry determines the plane of first cleavage (the initial division of the fertilized egg into two cells). He also proved that the egg's surface is equipotential—that is, the sperm has an equal probability of entering at any point. At this time, biologists were pursuing a vigorous debate (here we go with dichotomies again) between preformationists, who held that an embryo's differentiation into specialized parts and organs was already prefigured in the structure of an unfertilized egg, and epigeneticists, who argued that differentiation arose during development from an egg initially able to form any subsequent structure from any of its regions.

By showing that the direction of cleavage followed the happenstance of a sperm's penetration (and that a sperm could enter anywhere on the egg's surface), Just supported the epigenetic alternative. This first paper already contains the basis for Just's later and explicit holism—his concern with properties of entire organisms (the egg's complete surface) and with inter-actions of organism and environment (the epigenetic character of develop-ment contrasted with the preformationist view that pathways of later development lie within the egg's structure).

I believe that Just's mature holism had two primary sources in his earlier experimental work on fertilization. First, Just distinguished himself at Woods Hole as the great "green thumb" of his generation. He was a stickler for proper procedure and cleanliness in the laboratory. He had an uncanny rapport with the various species of marine invertebrates that inhabit the waters about Woods Hole. He knew where to find them and he understood their habits intimately. He could extract eggs and keep them normal and healthy under laboratory conditions. He became the chief source of techni-cal advice for hotshot young researchers who had mastered all the latest techniques of experimentation but knew little natural history.

Just therefore understood better than anyone else the importance of healthy normality in eggs used for experiments on fertilization—the integrity of whole cells in their ordinary conditions of life could not be compromised. Over and over again, he showed how many famous experiments by eminent scientists had no validity because they used moribund or abnormal cells, and their results could be traced to these "unlifelike" conditions, not to the experimental intervention itself. For example, Just refuted an important set of experiments on abnormalities of development produced when eggs are fertilized by sperm of another species. He proved that the peculiar patterns of embryology must be traced, not to the foreign sperm itself, but to the moribund state of eggs produced by environmental conditions (of tempera-ture and water chemistry) necessary to induce the abnormal fertilization, but uncongenial for the eggs' good health.

Just derided the lack of concern for natural history shown by so many experimenters who knew all the latest about fancy physics and chemistry, but ever so little about organisms. They referred to their eggs and sperm as "material" (I have the same reaction to modern reductionists who call the living cells and organs of their experiments a "preparation") and accepted their experimental objects in any condition because they couldn't distin-guish normality from abnormality: "If the condition of the eggs is not taken into account," Just wrote, "the results obtained by the use of subnormal eggs in experiments may be due wholly or in part to the poor physiological condition of the eggs."

Second, and more important, Just's twenty years of research on fertilization led directly, almost inexorably, to his interest in the cell's surface and to his holistic philosophy. Since his work, as previously mentioned, centered upon the changes that cell surfaces undergo during fertilization, Just soon realized that the cell's surface was no simple, passive boundary, but a complex and essential part of cellular organization:

> The surface cytoplasm cannot be thought of as inert or apart from the living cell substance. The ectoplasm [Just's name for the surface material] is more than a barrier to stem the rising tide within the active cell substance; it is more than a dam against the outside world. It is a living mobile part of the cell.

Later, pursuing a common concern of holistic biology, Just emphasized that the cell surface, as the domain of communication between organism and environment, embodies the theme of interaction—an organizational complexity that cannot be reduced to chemical parts:

> It is keyed to the outside world as no other part of the cell. It stands guard over the peculiar form of the living substance, is buffer against the attacks of the surroundings and the means of communication with it.

Moreover, as his major experimental contribution, Just showed that the cell surface responded to fertilization as a continuous and indivisible entity, even though the sperm only entered at a single point. If the surface has such integrity and if it regulates so many cellular processes, how can we meaningfully interpret the functions of cells by breaking them apart into molecular components?

> Under the impact of a spermatozoon the egg surface first gives way and then rebounds; the egg membrane moves in and out beneath the actively moving spermatozoon for a second or two. Then suddenly the spermatozoon becomes motionless with its tip buried in a slight indentation of the egg surface, at which point the ectoplasm develops a cloudy appearance. The turbidity spreads from here so that at twenty seconds after insemination—the mixing of eggs and spermatozoa—the whole ectoplasm is cloudy. Now like a flash, beginning at the point of sperm attachment, a wave sweeps over the surface of the egg, clearing up the ectoplasm as it passes.

As his work progressed, Just claimed more and more importance for the cellular surface, eventually going too far. He wisely denied the reductionistic premise that all cellular features are passive products of directing genes in the nucleus, but his alternative view of ectoplasmic control over nuclear motions cannot be supported either. Moreover, his argument that the history of life records an increasing dominance of ectoplasm, since nerve cells are most richly endowed with surface material and since brain size increases continually in evolution, reflects the common misconception that evolution inevitably yields progress measured by mental advance as a primary criterion. The following passage may reflect Just's literary skill, but it stands as confusing metaphor, not enlightening biology:

> Our minds encompass planetary movements, mark out geological eras, resolve matter into its constituent electrons, because our mentality is the transcendental expression of the age-old integration between ectoplasm and nonliving world.

Finally, Just's work also suffered because he had the misfortune to pursue his research and publish his book just before the invention of the electron microscope. The cell surface is too thin for light microscopy to resolve, and Just could never fathom its structure. He was forced to work from inferences based upon transient changes of the cell surface during fertilization—and he succeeded brilliantly in the face of these limitations. But within a decade of his death, much of his painstaking work had been rendered obsolete.

Thus, Just fell into obscurity partly because he claimed too much and alienated his colleagues, and partly because he knew too little as a consequence of limited techniques available to him. Yet the current invisibility of Just's biology seems unfair for two reasons. First, he was basically right about the integrity and importance of cell surfaces. With electron microscopy, we have now resolved the membrane's structure—a complex and fascinating story worth an essay in its own right. Moreover, we accept Just's premise that the surface is no mere passive barrier, but an active and essential component of cellular structure. The most popular college text in biology (Keeton's *Biological Science*) proclaims:

> The cell membrane not only serves as an envelope that gives mechanical strength and shape and some protection to the cell. It is also an active component of the living cell, preventing some substances from entering it

and others from leaking out. It regulates the traffic in materials between the precisely ordered interior of the cell and the essentially unfavorable and potentially disruptive outer environment. All substances moving between the cell's environment and the cellular interior in either direction must pass through a membrane barrier.

Second, and more important for this essay, whatever the factual status of Just's views on cell surfaces, he used his ideas to develop a holistic philosophy that represents a sensible middle way between extremes of mechanism and vitalism—a wise philosophy that may continue to guide us today.

We may epitomize Just's holism, and identify it as a genuine solution to the mechanist-vitalist debate, by summarizing its three major premises. First, nothing in biology contradicts the laws of physics and chemistry; any adequate biology must conform with the "basic" sciences. Just began his book with these words:

> Living things have material composition, are made up finally of units, molecules, atoms, and electrons, as surely as any nonliving matter. Like all forms in nature they have chemical structure and physical properties, are physicochemical systems. As such they obey the laws of physics and chemistry. Would one deny this fact, one would thereby deny the possibility of any scientific investigation of living things.

Second, the principles of physics and chemistry are not sufficient to explain complex biological objects because new properties emerge as a result of organization and interaction. These properties can only be understood by the direct study of whole, living systems in their normal state. Just wrote in a 1933 article:

> We have often striven to prove life as wholly mechanistic, starting with the hypothesis that organisms are machines! Thus we overlook the organo-dynamics of protoplasm—its power to organize itself. Living substance is such because it possesses this organization—something more than the sum of its minutest parts. . . . It is . . . the organization of protoplasm, which is its predominant characteristic and which places biology in a category quite apart from physics and chemistry. . . . Nor is it barren vitalism to say that there is something remaining in the behavior of protoplasm which our physicochemical studies leave unexplained. This "something" is the peculiar organization of protoplasm.

In striking metaphor, Just illustrates the inadequacy of mechanistic studies:

> The living thing disappears and only a mere agglomerate of parts remains. The better this analysis proceeds and the greater its yield, the more completely does life vanish from the investigated living matter. The state of being alive is like a snowflake on a windowpane which disappears under the warm touch of an inquisitive child. . . . Few investigators, nowadays, I think, subscribe to the naive but seriously meant comparison once made by an eminent authority in biology, namely that the experimenter on an egg seeks to know its development by wrecking it, as one wrecks a train for understanding its mechanism. . . . The days of experimental embryology as a punitive expedition against the egg, let us hope, have passed.

Third, the insufficiency of physics and chemistry to encompass life records no mystical addition, no contradiction to the basic sciences, but only reflects the hierarchy of natural objects and the principle of emergent properties at higher levels of organization:

> The direct analysis of the state of being alive must never go below the order of organization which characterizes life; it must confine itself to the combination of compounds in the life unit, never descending to single compounds and, therefore, certainly never below these. . . . The physicist aims at the least, the indivisible, particle of matter. The study of the state of being alive is confined to that organization which is peculiar to it.

Finally, I must emphasize once again that Just's arguments are not unique or even unusual. They represent the standard opinion of most practicing biologists and, as such, refute the dichotomous scheme that sees biology as a war between vitalists and mechanists. The middle way is both eminently sensible and popular. I chose Just as an illustration because his career exemplifies how a thoughtful biologist can be driven to such a position by his own investigation of complex phenomena. In addition, Just said it all so well and so forcefully; he qualifies as an exemplar of the middle way under our most venerable criterion—"what oft was thought, but ne'er so well expressed."

This essay should end here. In a world of decency and simple justice it would. But it cannot. E. E. Just struggled all his life for judgment by the intrinsic merit of his biological research alone—something I have tried so uselessly (and posthumously) to grant him here. He never achieved this recognition, never came close, for one intrinsically biological reason that should not matter, but always has in America. E. E. Just was black.

Today, a black valedictorian at a major Ivy League school would be inundated with opportunity. Just secured no mobility at all in 1907. As his biographer, M.I.T. historian of science Kenneth R. Manning, writes: "An educated black had two options, both limited: he could either teach or preach—and only among blacks." (Manning's biography, *Black Apollo of Science: The Life of Ernest Everett Just,* was published in 1983 by Oxford University Press. It is a superbly written and documented book, the finest biography I have read in years. Manning's book is an institutional history of Just's life. It discusses his endless struggle for funding and his complex relationships with institutions of teaching and research, but says relatively little about his biological work per se—a gap that I have tried, in some respects, to fill with this essay.)

So Just went to Howard and remained there all his life. Howard was a prestigious school, but it maintained no graduate program, and crushing demands for teaching and administration left Just neither time nor opportunity for the research career that he so ardently desired. But Just would not be beaten. By assiduous and tireless self-promotion, he sought support from every philanthropy and fund that might sponsor a black biologist—and he succeeded relatively well. He garnered enough support to spend long summers at Woods Hole and managed to publish more than seventy papers and two books in what could never be more than a part-time research career studded with innumerable obstacles, both overt and psychological.

But eventually, the explicit racism of his detractors and, even worse, the persistent paternalism of his supporters wore Just down. He dared not even hope for a permanent job at any white institution that might foster research, and the accumulation of slights and slurs at Woods Hole eventually made life intolerable for a proud man like Just. If he had fit the mold of an acceptable black scientist, he might have survived in the hypocritical world of white liberalism in his time. A man like George Washington Carver, who upheld Booker T. Washington's doctrine of slow and humble self-help for blacks, who dressed in his agricultural work clothes, and who spent his life in the practical task of helping black farmers find more uses for peanuts, was paraded as a paragon of proper black science. But Just preferred fancy suits, good wines, classical music, and women of all colors. He wished to pursue theoretical research at the highest levels of abstraction, and he succeeded with distinction. If his work disagreed with the theories of eminent white scientists, he said so, and with force (although his general demeanor tended toward modesty).

The one thing that Just so desperately wanted above all else—to be judged on the merit of his research alone—he could never have. His strongest supporters treated him with what, in retrospect, can only be labeled a crushing paternalism. Forget your research, de-emphasize it, go slower, they all said. Go back to Howard and be a "model for your race"; give up personal goals and devote your life to training black doctors. Would such an issue ever have arisen for a white man of Just's evident talent?

Eventually, like many other black intellectuals, Just exiled himself to Europe. There, in the 1930s he finally found what he had sought—simple acceptance for his excellence as a scientist. But his joy and productivity were short-lived, as the specter of Nazism soon turned to reality and sent him back home to Howard and an early death.

Just was a brilliant man, and his life embodied strong elements of tragedy, but we must not depict him as a cardboard hero. He was far too fascinating, complex, and ambiguous a man for such simplistic misconstruction. Deeply conservative and more than a little elitist in character, Just never identified his suffering with the lot of blacks in general and considered each rebuff as a personal slight. His anger became so deep, and his joy at European acceptance so great, that he completely misunderstood Italian politics of the 1930s and became a supporter of Mussolini. He even sought research funds directly from Il Duce.

Yet how can we dare to judge a man so thwarted in the land of his birth? Yes, Just fared far better than most blacks. He had a good job and reasonable economic security. But, truly, we do not live by bread alone. Just was robbed of an intellectual's birthright—the desire to be taken seriously for his ideas and accomplishments. I know, in the most direct and personal way, the joy and the need for research. No fire burns more deeply within me, and no scientist of merit and accomplishment feels any differently. (One of my most eminent colleagues once told me that he regarded research as the greatest joy of all, for it was like continual orgasm.) Just's suffering may have been subtle compared with the brutalization of so many black lives in America, but it was deep, pervasive, and soul destroying. The man who understood holism so well in biology was not allowed to live a complete life. We may at least mark his centenary by considering the ideas that he struggled to develop and presented so well.

## Content Questions

1. According to Gould, what is the "middle position" on the nature of life? Why is understanding it so important? (241–242)

2. How is the "middle way" Gould outlines "organizational" or "holistic"? (242–244)

3. How did Just's experiments with fertilization lead him to a holistic understanding of the nature of life? (244–245)

4. What point is Gould making about science and scientists when he discusses Just's theory of "ectoplasmic control over nuclear motions"? (246)

5. How did the invention of the electron microscope affect Just's scientific legacy? (246)

6. What two reasons does Gould give for considering Just's current obscurity unfair? (246–247)

7. What are the three major premises of Just's holistic view of life, as presented by Gould? (247–248)

8. What specific obstacles does Gould say that Just faced because of his race? (248–250)

9. What is the "intellectual's birthright" of which Just was robbed, according to Gould? (250)

## Application Questions

1. Gould describes how Just's research led him to the conclusion that "the cell's surface was no simple, passive boundary, but a complex and essential part of cellular organization." (245) How does current information about the structure of cell membranes lend strong support to Just's conclusion?

2. In what important ways is the structure of the cell membrane related to its function? Specifically, how is the structure of the cell membrane related to the regulation of the passage of materials into and out of the cell?

3. What is our current understanding of the events triggered by the penetration of an egg by a sperm? What do we know about the actual process of fertilization (defined as the fusion of the two gamete nuclei)? What prevents more than one sperm from fertilizing an egg?

4. What roles did the transmission electron microscope and the scanning electron microscope have in developing our current understanding of cell structure?

## Discussion Questions

1. What larger point about human thinking is Gould making when he discusses the tendency to divide biologists into "vitalists" and "mechanists"? (240–241) Do you agree with his point?

2. What does Gould mean when he says that his essay "should end here. In a world of decency and simple justice it would"? (248)

3. Why does Gould say that we must not make Just "a cardboard hero"? (250)

4. Does a scientist who is a member of a minority group still face the same kind of obstacles that Just did? Does he or she face different obstacles or only the obstacles common to all in the field?

# Edward O. Wilson

Edward O. Wilson (1929– ) has earned a reputation as a scientist and writer with a unique ability to synthesize insights from separate fields of knowledge and generate new ideas as a result. As the leading proponent of sociobiology, Wilson has expounded the controversial theory that all human behavior is genetically based and subject to natural selection. While evolutionary theory has usually focused on the adaptation and survival of individual organisms, Wilson, like Konrad Lorenz, is concerned with the behavioral characteristics of groups and how those characteristics affect survival. His detailed studies of insect behavior, particularly that of ants, formed the germ of his theory of human group behavior.

Wilson has been seriously interested in entomology since he was seventeen, and as a child in Alabama he was a dedicated explorer of the Gulf Coast's natural environment. He earned his Ph.D. at Harvard University in 1955 and began teaching in 1956 as a professor of zoology and later as a professor of science. Wilson currently is Pellegrino University Research Professor at Harvard and Honorary Curator in Entomology at the university's Museum of Comparative Zoology. The author of several books, Wilson is the only person to have won both the National Medal of Science and the Pulitzer Prize (for general nonfiction). He was awarded the Pulitzer twice, for *On Human Nature* (1978) and for *The Ants* (1990).

# The Diversity of Life

*(selection)*

Than no trace of the biosphere could be seen with the naked eye. Yet life

The most wonderful mystery of life may well be the means by which it created so much diversity from so little physical matter. The biosphere, all organisms combined, makes up only about one part in ten billion of the earth's mass. It is sparsely distributed through a kilometer-thick layer of soil, water, and air stretched over a half billion square kilometers of surface. If the world were the size of an ordinary desktop globe and its surface were viewed edgewise an arm's length away, no trace of the biosphere could be seen with the naked eye. Yet life has divided into millions of species, the fundamental units, each playing a unique role in relation to the whole.

For another way to visualize the tenuousness of life, imagine yourself on a journey upward from the center of the earth, taken at the pace of a leisurely walk. For the first twelve weeks you travel through furnace-hot rock and magma devoid of life. Three minutes to the surface, five hundred meters to go, you encounter the first organisms, bacteria feeding on nutrients that have filtered into the deep water-bearing strata. You breach the surface and for ten seconds glimpse a dazzling burst of life, tens of thousands of species of microorganisms, plants, and animals within horizontal line of sight. Half a minute later almost all are gone. Two hours later only

*This selection is taken from chapter 4, "The Fundamental Unit."*

the faintest traces remain, consisting largely of people in airliners who are filled in turn with colon bacteria.

The hallmark of life is this: a struggle among an immense variety of organisms weighing next to nothing for a vanishingly small amount of energy. Life operates on only 10 percent of the sun's energy reaching Earth's surface, that portion fixed by the photosynthesis of green plants. The free energy is then sharply discounted as it passes through the food webs from one organism to the next: very roughly 10 percent passes to the caterpillars and other herbivores that eat the plants and bacteria, 10 percent of that (or 1 percent of the original) to the spiders and other low-level carnivores that eat the herbivores, 10 percent of the residue to the warblers and other middle-level carnivores that eat the low-level carnivores, and so on upward to the top carnivores, which are consumed by no one except parasites and scavengers. Top carnivores, including eagles, tigers, and great white sharks, are predestined by their perch at the apex of the food web to be big in size and sparse in numbers. They live on such a small portion of life's available energy as always to skirt the edge of extinction, and they are the first to suffer when the ecosystem around them starts to erode.

A great deal can be learned quickly about biological diversity by noticing that species in the food web are arranged into two hierarchies. The first is the energy pyramid, a straightforward consequence of the law of diminishing energy flow as noted: a relatively large amount from the sun's energy incident on earth goes into the plants at the bottom, tapering to a minute quantity to the big carnivores on top. The second pyramid is composed of biomass, the weight of organisms. By far the largest part of the physical bulk of the living world is contained in plants. The second largest amount belongs to the scavengers and other decomposers, from bacteria to fungi and termites, which together extract the last bit of fixed energy from dead tissue and waste at every level in the food web, and in exchange return degraded nutrient chemicals to the plants. Each level above the plants diminishes thereafter in biomass until you come to the top carnivores, which are so scarce that the very sight of one in the wild is memorable. Let me stress that point. No one looks twice at a sparrow or squirrel, or even once at a dandelion, but a peregrine falcon or mountain lion is a lifetime experience. And not just because of their size (think of a cow) or ferocity (think of a housecat), but because they are rare.

The biomass pyramid of the sea is at first glance puzzling: it is turned upside down. The photosynthetic organisms still capture almost all the energy, which is discounted in steps by the 10 percent rule, but they have less total bulk than the animals that eat them. How is this inversion possible? The answer is that the photosynthetic organisms are not plants in the traditional land-bound sense. They are phytoplankton, microscopic single-celled algae carried passively by water currents. Cell for cell, planktonic algae fix more solar energy and manufacture more protoplasm than plants on the land, and they grow, divide, and die at an immensely faster pace. Small animals, particularly copepods and other small crustaceans carried in the sea currents, hence called zooplankton, consume the algae. They harvest huge quantities without exhausting the standing photosynthetic crop in the water. Zooplankton in turn are eaten by larger invertebrate animals and fish, which are then eaten by still larger fish and marine mammals such as seals and porpoises, which are hunted by killer whales and great white sharks, the top carnivores. The inversion of the biomass pyramid is why the waters of the open ocean are so clear, why you can look into them and spot an occasional fish but not the green plants—algae—on which all the animals ultimately depend.

We have arrived at the question of central interest. The larger organisms of Earth, composing the visible superstructures of the energy and biomass pyramids, owe their existence to biological diversity. Of what then is biodiversity composed? Since antiquity biologists have felt a compelling need to posit an atomic unit by which diversity can be broken apart, then described, measured, and reassembled. Let me put the matter as strongly as this important issue merits. Western science is built on the obsessive and hitherto successful search for atomic units, with which abstract laws and principles can be derived. Scientific knowledge is written in the vocabulary of atoms, subatomic particles, molecules, organisms, ecosystems, and many other units, including species. The metaconcept holding all of the units together is hierarchy, which presupposes levels of organization. Atoms bond into molecules, which are assembled into nuclei, mitochondria, and other organelles, which aggregate into cells, which associate as tissues. The levels then progress on upward as organs, organisms, societies, species, and ecosystems. The reverse procedure is decomposition, the breaking of ecosystems into species, species into societies and organisms, and so on downward. Both theory and experimental analysis in science are predicated on the assumption—the trust, the faith—that complex systems can be cleaved into simpler systems. And so the search proceeds relentlessly for natural units until, like the true grail, they are found and all rejoice. Scientific fame awaits those who discover the lines of fracture and the processes by which lesser natural units are joined to create larger natural units.

So the species concept is crucial to the study of biodiversity. It is the grail of systematic biology. Not to have a natural unit such as the species would be to abandon a large part of biology into free fall, all the way from the ecosystem down to the organism. It would be to concede the idea of amorphous variation and arbitrary limits for such intuitively obvious entities as American elms (species: *Ulmus americana*), cabbage white butterflies *(Pieris rapae)*, and human beings *(Homo sapiens)*. Without natural species, ecosystems could be analyzed only in the broadest terms, using crude and shifting descriptions of the organisms that compose them. Biologists would find it difficult to compare results from one study to the next. How might we assess, for example, the thousands of research papers on the fruit fly, which form much of the foundation of modern genetics, if no one could tell one kind of fruit fly from another?

## Content Questions

1. What does Wilson mean when he refers to the "tenuousness of life"? (255) How do the two metaphors he uses (the desktop globe and the journey from the center of the earth through the atmosphere) develop this idea?

2. What process determines that life on Earth can access only 10 percent of the sun's energy that reaches the planet? (256)

3. Why are "top carnivores" the first to go hungry when an ecosystem is damaged? (256)

4. How are the energy and biomass pyramids that Wilson describes related? (256)

5. According to Wilson, why is the sea's biomass pyramid inverted? (256–257)

## Application Questions

1. What is the biological definition of a species?

2. Explain the geographic isolation model of divergent speciation, taking into account the roles of mutation, recombination, natural selection, and the gene pool. What are the roles of intrinsic and extrinsic isolating mechanisms in this process?

## Discussion Questions

1. When Wilson refers to the "hitherto successful search for atomic units," is he saying that this type of search is no longer successful? (257)

2. How much doubt does Wilson intend to cast on the search for "atomic units" and the understanding of aggregation and decomposition that he describes in the last section? Is he saying that such an understanding is wrong, or that there are limits to its usefulness? (257–258)

3. According to Wilson, what would happen if we stopped thinking of species as distinct? (258)

4. What effect would it have on science "to concede the idea of amorphous variation and arbitrary limits" for natural entities? (258)

# Lynn Margulis

Lynn Margulis (1938– ) is the proponent of a theory that has revolutionized the way many scientists think about the origins of life. Her assertion that living cells evolved as a result of microorganisms joining together and working cooperatively reverses the traditional view of microorganisms as competitors. When Margulis first articulated her theory in the early 1970s, it posed such a challenge to scientific orthodoxy that she had difficulty getting her work published or discussed at conferences. She also had trouble obtaining grants for further research. But by 1981, when Margulis published her book *Symbiosis in Cell Evolution,* a number of scientists had come to agree with her that chloroplasts and mitochondria developed in symbiosis. While still controversial, her serial endosymbiosis theory, concerning early development of the cell, has won sufficient acceptance to be covered in many high school biology textbooks.

Margulis grew up in Chicago and was a precocious student, enrolling at the University of Chicago when she was fourteen. She cites her immersion in the university's Great Books program, with its emphasis on discussing original works and tracing the development of ideas, as a formative influence on her approach to science. Margulis received her Ph.D. in genetics from the University of California, Berkeley, and currently teaches at the University of Massachusetts. She also has collaborated with British chemist James E. Lovelock on the Gaia hypothesis, which posits that the earth is a single organism that maintains and regulates itself. Margulis was awarded the 1999 National Medal of Science for her "outstanding contributions to the understanding of the structure and evolution of living cells, and for extraordinary abilities as a teacher and communicator of science to the public."

# Life from Scum

What mystery pervades a well!
That water lives so far— . . .
Like looking every time you please
In an abyss's face!

—Emily Dickinson

Whether bacterial or nucleated, the units of life are cells. All visible organisms are composed of nucleated cells, and, as we have seen, the first nucleated cell evolved by bacterial cell merger. But how did that elusive unit, the parent of all Earth life, originate? What accounts for the beginning of the ur-cell? How did the very first bacterial cell originate? This question is exactly equivalent to the question "How did life originate?" To appreciate SET [serial endosymbiosis theory], which only recombines, merges, and integrates exceedingly diverse bacteria, we first have to understand where these diverse bacteria came from. In short, we need to try to understand life from scum.

*This selection is taken from* Symbiotic Planet, *chapter 5, "Life from Scum"; chapter 2, "Against Orthodoxy"; and chapter 3, "Individuality by Incorporation."*

263

In search of the ecological setting of the earliest cells on Earth, every few years my students and I make a pilgrimage to San Quintín Bay, in Baja California Norte, Mexico. We seek the shifting shores of Laguna Figueroa, a lagooned complex festooned with salt flats. Here we find laminated, brightly striped sediments underlain by gelatinous mud. These colorful seaside expanses, called "microbial mats," enchant me—a living landscape just where the sea meets and rolls back and forth over the land. Luckily for our studies, the scene is inhospitable to the vast majority of large life-forms, humans included. I put my hands in the mud of fragrant microbial tissues and whiff the exchanging gases. Here, as in the human sphere, but neither by commandment nor of necessity, death is part of life. Population growth potential is alternately checked and realized. These seaside communities have persisted for over three billion years. Many inhabitants die daily but the community itself never overgrows its bounds. This is an evolutionary Eden more primal than the greenest grassland. Here, in this Earth tissue, animals and plants are all but absent. Even protists and fungi are rare. Mostly bacteria thrive. Standing at the microbial mat, I feel privileged. I delight in escape, thrilled to abandon the urban sprawl of human hyperactivity and exhilarated with the freedom to contemplate life's most remote origins.

The origin of life is a mythical concept, not in the sense of being untrue but rather in stirring a deep sense of mystery. Even scientists need to narrate, to integrate their observations into origin stories. How did the earliest life, the first bacterial cell, begin? How did the ur-bacteria differ from the environment from which they are alleged to have emerged? Not only is such a question within the province of scientific inquiry, but an adequate answer is essential for SET. We must know how bacteria started and what they became before we can understand how separate bacteria merged to create our cells. Answers to the "origin of life" problem are woven from the lifework of scholars in many nations. The scientific story of the first life on Earth is the least parochial of the world's origin myths. It is freely available to all who care to learn about it.

The properties of minimal bacterial life, first life, can be inferred by several approaches. First, one compares all living beings to see what they share in common. Common and absolutely required aspects of all life are deduced to have persisted from our earliest bacterial ancestor. The chain of life has not once been broken since its formation.

A second approach to origins is via paleobiology: studies of microfossils, the remains of early life. Ages can be assigned to some microfossils. They may be dated by direct measurement of the age of the surrounding volcanic rocks with which they are associated.

A third avenue to illuminate life's origins attempts to remake a cell. The minimal ancestral state of nature is chemically imitated in the laboratory. Some components of life have been synthesized from simpler compounds in this way, but so far nothing close to a laboratory re-creation of a bacterial cell has been achieved. Of course, even if it were, we could not conclude that our clumsy imitation was the way cells really originated in the first place.

Through a combination of methods, I have come to agree with other scientists on the most likely, and investigable, scenario for the origin of the first cell on Earth. Before cells there were cell-like systems. Today, no piece of DNA, no gene, replicates outside the cell of which it is a part. Nor does any virus make more of itself without inhabiting a live cell. The bacterial cell, today's minimal unit of life, self-maintenance, and reproduction, is where we must begin.

No one claims to have "solved" the origin of life problem. Yet, although we cannot create cells from chemicals, cell-like membranous enclosures form as naturally as bubbles when oil is shaken with water. In the earliest days of the still lifeless Earth, such bubble enclosures separated inside from outside. Prelife, with a suitable source of energy inside a greasy membrane, grew chemically complex. Harold J. Morowitz, distinguished professor at George Mason University, Fairfax, Virginia, and director of the Krasnow Institute for the Study of Evolution of Consciousness, argues this eloquently in his amusing mayonnaise book. These lipidic bags grew and developed self-maintenance. They, through exchange of parts, maintained their structure in a more or less increasingly faithful way. Energy, of course, was required. Probably solar energy at first moved through the droplets; controlled energy flow led to the selfhood that became cell life. By definition, the most stable of these droplets survived longest and eventually, at random, retained their form by incessant interchange of parts with the environment. After a great deal of metabolic evolution, which I believe occurred inside the self-maintaining greasy membrane, some, those containing phosphate and nucleosides with phosphate attached to them, acquired the ability to replicate more or less accurately.

However the first bacteria happened we can only guess. Yet the oldest fossils we have today are interpreted to be remains of fossil bacteria. Over 3.5 billion years old, probably the best preserved come from southern Africa. The very existence of these Swaziland microspheres, as they are called, shows us that life was already thriving, reproducing, and growing, just 1.1 billion years after the Earth's origin as a solid rocky body with atmosphere and ocean. No one today doubts that life on this planet is very old. Since the universe itself, exploding into existence from the "singularity" of the big bang, is usually dated at only 12,000 to 15,000 million years, the greater-than-3,000-million-year tenure of life on Earth suggests life's presence for a quarter of the time span of the universe. Nor does anyone doubt that the earliest life was neither plant nor animal.

As the material stuff from which all living bodies are made, we have in another sense been around since the origin of the universe. The matter in the bodies of all life-forms, including, of course, mammals like us, can be traced to the carbon, nitrogen, oxygen, and other elements that were made in the supernova explosions of stars.

At first it may seem improbable to you that all life on Earth today, inhabitants of cities, jungles, oceans, forests, and grasslands, is the progeny of an ancient bacterium. How could one or a few bacteria have been so prodigious? Remember that you, yourself, were once a single cell: the fertilized egg, the zygote, that reproduced by division to become an embryo in your mother's womb. Later you became a crying infant in her arms. If in nine months a single fertile egg can become a human, albeit a pudgy, defenseless, and uncoordinated one, is it not easily conceivable that all life-forms today arose from a single bacterium over 3,000 million years ago?

The minimal cells, those of the tiniest bacteria, about one ten-millionth of a meter in diameter, never, never stop their metabolism. This simply means they continuously undergo hundreds of chemical transformations. They are fully alive. Recent work has revealed that the tiniest, most simple bacteria are very much like us. They continuously metabolize, using the same components we do: proteins, fats, vitamins, nucleic acids, sugars, and other carbohydrates. Even the simplest bacterium is extremely complex. Yet its inner workings are still like those of larger life. All the DNA of one of the simplest cells, a bacterium called *Mycoplasma geniticulum*, has already been sequenced. This means we know all the details of its genes. The more closely we study gene sequences and metabolism, the more we realize that all life since its origin has been similar to its brethren, all other life. *Mycoplasma*, like all the other bacteria, never stop using energy to take up food; balance their salts; make DNA, RNA, and proteins; and convert one chemical to another to keep themselves going. They emphatically differentiate themselves from their surroundings. The simplest bacterial cell on the early Earth, like the smallest ones today, already had integrity. The tiniest first bacterium was already so complicated that Sir Francis Crick, one of the discoverers of the structure of DNA, made an astounding claim. Crick wrote an influential book, *Life Itself,* arguing that life, because of its overwhelming complexity, must have been brought to Earth from outer space. He suggested that bacterial life was sent here by an extraterrestrial civilization bent on seeding planet Earth. Crick, with uninterpretable seriousness, claims that just as a human gardener introduces seeds into the soil of her backyard, propagules were planted on Earth eons ago. This idea—called directed panspermia or pangenesis and put forth for centuries—that life came in seed form from outer space seems to me to stem from ignorance of evolution on Earth.

To transfer the problem of life's origin to outer space is intellectually unsatisfactory. Why should it have been easier for life to originate elsewhere than on Earth? Wherever cellular life began, it faced the same problems of origin. This idea of spontaneous generation shows not the origin of species but the origin of the specious.

For generations, Europeans believed that life appears spontaneously in scum and muck. Rotting meat was thought to generate maggots. Old rags grew mice. Close observation and experiment, however, revealed intermediates. Maggots, we know, do not appear from messes no matter how chemically complex. They grow from sperm-fertilized eggs laid by flies. Yet maggots wriggling in stinking meat, in the minds of Louis Pasteur's predecessors, meant that life arose from the decay itself. In the 1860s Pasteur exposed boiled meat extract to the air. He used a long flask, whose thin, downward-pointing neck admitted air but not bacteria or any other propagule. Another flask, open to the air, putrefied with growing bacteria and fungi within a few days. Pasteur's "control," the closed flask with its spout facing down, has never spoiled. The uncontaminated broth is still on display at the Pasteur Institute in Paris. The last of believers in spontaneous generation, Pasteur proved dramatically, were incorrect. Puppies come from dogs and bitches; babies come from men and women. Flies come from maggots; mice come from inseminated mother mice. Like them all, microbes come from pre-existing microbes, or at least one unisex parent microbe.

However, there is some irony in this tale: Pasteur, a serious Catholic, interpreted his finding, as we all still do, to mean that all life must arise from preexisting life of the same type. But for Pasteur this showed that evolution does not occur and that only God made the many types of life. Today's scientists turn the argument around: all life came not from the hand of almighty God, they argue, but ultimately from first life, and first life originated from nonliving solar system matter. This is the irony.

Bacteria, Pasteur convinced us, are just as alive as we are. Bacterial presence is correlated with disease and food contamination. Pasteur's brilliant experiments enjoy a great legacy. He established the prevalent view: infectious, indeed near-diabolical, bacteria are "germs" that need to be destroyed. The great successes of modern medicine reinforce the idea of microbes as enemy. Cleanliness, sterilization of surgical instruments, and especially antibiotics are all described as weapons of war against microbial aggressors.

The more balanced view of microbe as colleague and ancestor remains almost unexpressed. Our culture ignores the hard-won fact that these disease "agents," these "germs," also germinated all life. Our ancestors, the germs, were bacteria.

Whence came the first bacteria?

Spontaneous generation, as Pasteur and others triumphantly demonstrated, does not occur nowadays. But this Pasteurian observation is misinterpreted by creationists and other dogmatists to argue that life *never* came from nonlife. Some information theorists suggest that the chance that life would organize itself from nonlife by random interactions of molecules is so improbable as to constitute a "mathematical proof" that the origin of life was divine. But to me their assumption that life originated as a result of molecules mixed at random is flawed.

Direct experiments on the "origins of life problem" began in 1953. Stanley L. Miller, then a twenty-two-year-old graduate student of the Nobel laureate Harold C. Urey at the University of Chicago, filled laboratory glassware with gases floating over a surface of sterilized water. For a week he exposed this miniature diorama of the chemistry of early Earth to periodic electricity, mimicking lightning. Through the technique of paper chromatography he separated some of the many organic compounds that spontaneously formed. He recognized among these alanine and glycine, two amino acids found in all proteins and in all cells of living bodies. Miller and Urey gleefully concluded that such "spontaneous generation" of the chemical components of life was a natural result of chemical interaction.

In space, or on the early Earth, we think organic compounds like those found by Stanley Miller spontaneously formed from simpler precursors. Miller and Urey, of course, could only guess about the chemical characteristics of the early Earth's surface environment. The gases Miller used in his glass apparatus—hydrogen, water vapor, ammonia, and methane—seem reasonable. These gases are all hydrogen-rich. Hydrogen, the main element in the sun, forms more than 90 percent of the matter in the entire universe. Miller reasoned that hydrogen probably was abundant on the inner planets early in the history of the solar system. Thus arose the notion of a "primordial soup," that life emerged from a "gemish," a complex structure like that which floated in or stuck to the sides of Miller's flask. Earth, we think, was steeped in organic compounds synthesized by sunlight and other energy sources long before life. A Miller-like experiment probably occurred on a planetary scale. If twenty-two-year-old humans like Stanley could produce amino acids in the laboratory in only a few days, why could not the laboratory of Earth, in an experiment over the course of a thousand or a million years, produce life?

More recent experiments confirm that precursors of life can be produced naturally in the laboratory under conditions simulating the environment of the early Earth. Molecules, however, do not combine at random: carbon, hydrogen, nitrogen, phosphorus, oxygen, sulfur, and the other elements of life interact according to the rules of chemistry. The science of heat and energy, called thermodynamics, has laws that molecules obey. Certain chemical reactions are far more likely than others; the notion that all chemical combinations are equally likely may be convenient for calculating life's improbability, but it is not accurate. Moreover, if we assume that life evolved from the beginning in cell-like lipid droplets, the odds for the emergence of startlingly self-maintaining systems increase. A tendency toward complexity ensues.

To me the most exciting research now under way concerning life's origins is that of my friend Harold Morowitz. To space, time, and causality in biology, Morowitz adds "memory." Biology, he claims, is the bridge between physics and history. The oldest rocks on Earth, including those from the Isua formation in Greenland, are nearly four billion years old. All life has chemical memory that cannot be dated by direct measurement.

The metabolic memory of modern cells most likely even predates the most ancient rocks. Some metabolic pathways, such as the enzymatic steps leading from fatty compounds to steroids like cholesterol, Morowitz notes, are limited to animals. Others, however, are components of "primary metabolism": metabolic pathways common to all living beings. Because certain carbon-chemical metabolic pathways are absolutely necessary for all metabolism, the earliest ones that underlie the cellular phenomenon of self-maintenance and were present from the beginning, the chemical interactions of carbon, nitrogen, sulfur, and phosphorus upon which all metabolism is based, must be retained in all cells at all times. Any cell dies if its universally required metabolism is hampered by environmental restraints, lethal DNA mutation, or other interference.

Chemical systems in nature that become more and more complex, even if they are capable of making more of themselves, are not necessarily alive. Such systems are called *autocatalytic*. An autocatalytic system is a cyclical series of interlocking reactions whose end product is the same as its starting point. Some such reactions have been referred to as "chemical clocks" because they do not quickly reach a steady state; rather, they persist and repeat. The Belousov-Zhabotinsky system is a colorful series of self-sustaining reactions. Malonic acid is oxidized by bromate in a sulfuric acid solution containing cerium, iron, or manganese atoms. As these chemicals react with each other and then react again and again, concentric and rotating spiral waves are produced that often endure for hours before reaching a final stable pattern. A thermodynamic analysis of these reactions interprets them as dissipative structures, as described by the Belgian Nobel laureate Ilya Prigogine. A *dissipative structure* is any system that maintains its function through assimilating useful energy and dissipating useless energy, usually heat. Reactions of dissipative structures share certain traits with life and the chemical systems that evolved into life. But all chemical systems, dissipatively structured or not, only continue to operate and make more ordered matter for a short time. Then they fall apart.

From thermodynamic analysis and scientific experience, we infer that perpetual-motion machines cannot exist: although energy itself does not disappear, it is irretrievably transformed. Dissipated heat cannot be recovered. High-quality energy, energy that can do work, tends to disappear over time. Snowmen melt and do not re-form. Cups and glasses are broken far more frequently than they are put back together. Messing up a room is far easier than tidying it. In thermodynamics, messiness rules. That energy is lost and things fall apart, never to reunite, is an inescapable fact, a law, of nature. Life, with its complex order, does not violate the thermodynamic law of inexorable tendency toward disorder. Life always requires its specific source of high-quality energy. Sunlight moves through life, empowering cyclic work, in much the same way that chemical energy channels through a Belousov-Zhabotinsky reaction. But because cells grow and reproduce to form more cells like them, once life evolved the life chemistry never ceased. Cyclic life, if provided a continuous source of energy and nutrients, will indefinitely make more of itself. Chemical systems lack selves: they cannot make more *selves*. Life is a series of selves—organisms or cells. These must expend energy to continue to exist, but they do so in unseverable connection to past life. Life has been, since inception and with no discontinuity, chemically connected to its past.

Morowitz points out that the cumulative metabolic chart of living organisms, worked out by hundreds of scientists, mainly since the beginning of this century, is one of the greatest and most underappreciated intellectual achievements of humankind. Several Nobel Prizes have been awarded for deciphering significant fragments of metabolism, the intertwined chemical reactions of cells. Only Morowitz, as far as I know, tries to organize the massive details of metabolic information into a single coherent whole, a lens to peer into life's ancient history.

Because life is intrinsically a memory-storing system, some scenarios advanced to explain its origin seem unlikely to me. Crystals, glasses, coacervates, clay, and iron pyrite (fool's gold) have all been claimed to be keys to the earliest prelife chemical systems. Advocates tout rock crevices or clay particles as the sites of the origin of life. Cavities filled with fluid exist in the membrane-bounded cells of nearly all living beings. Similar cavities, chemical bags called *liposomes*, also arise naturally. Such liposomes, membrane vesicles, appear spontaneously in so-called origin-of-life experiments. These sorts of droplets appear to me to be far more likely to represent life's original natural architecture than iron pyrite, clay, or glass. A principle of life's continuity, of life's memory, can be invoked here. I think the proverbial primordial soup of free-floating DNA or RNA never existed, because nucleic acids (DNA, RNA) are far more easily destroyed than they are spontaneously formed. Membranous structures are the sine qua non of life. Today the membrane-bounded entities with identity and integrity are cells. Life arose in its cellular wholeness. The cells of today are, as Morowitz says, "virtual fossils."

271

In all of today's cells, genes are made of DNA. RNA, quite similar to DNA, is needed by all cells to synthesize protein. The precise amino-acid sequence gives a protein much of its structure and so determines what it will do, just as the sequence of letters gives the written word its meaning. Proteins exist in many sizes and shapes with hundreds of functions. Some proteins pump ions: sodium, hydrogen, phosphate, potassium, and others. Other proteins, attached to pigments, provide energy absorbers in dark eyes, spotted skin, green cyanobacteria, and algal plastids. Muscles are primarily protein; blood, skin, and tongues are complexes of many proteins packed in cells.

Cells work by a two-part system. First, they copy or "replicate" their genes. This gene-making step is DNA synthesis. DNA is copied, and one copy of the hereditary information is put on reserve. The other copy is "translated": identical base sequences of selected parts of the genome are made into RNA. Inside the cell, on tiny "factories" called ribosomes, the RNA directs the fabrication of long-chain proteins. Proteins of different kinds, some three thousand to ten thousand per cell, form most of an organism's body. Growth ultimately means protein synthesis (and, of course, water uptake). Together in a fluid-filled membranous bag DNA, RNA, and protein make the self-maintaining structure of cells. The RNA molecule, however, is more versatile than its DNA complement. Given the appropriate chemical milieu, but without any protein, RNA can autocatalytically make more of itself. DNA, on the other hand, requires both RNA and enzyme proteins to complete its work of replication; DNA by itself is dead. The capacity of RNA both to accelerate chemical reactions and to replicate suggests that RNA preceded DNA in the history of life. We can use RNA as an index of proximity to prelife. Nothing smaller than a live cell maintains its identity and produces greater numbers of itself. From the beginning, life was a cell, a mutual interaction between gene molecules (like RNA) and the oily membrane that segregated them from their environment.

The physicist Freeman Dyson suggests that the first life arose from a molecular symbiosis, a coming together of relatively amorphous "protein creatures" and the supermolecule RNA. Like most of us Dyson is impressed with RNA as a supermolecule, which, like DNA, replicates itself but which, unlike DNA, also directs amino acids into protein sequences. Although I think Dyson misuses the word *symbiosis*, his story of independent development of macromolecular sequences followed by strong interaction has merit.

As Dyson knows, the unique talents of the RNA molecule are confirmed by laboratory experiment. In the late 1960s, at the Göttingen Institute in Germany, the Nobel Prize–winning physicist Manfred Eigen showed RNA molecules that replicate in test tubes by themselves. He and his colleagues, including Don Mills at Columbia University and the late Sol Spiegelman of the University of Illinois at Urbana-Champaign, showed that test-tube RNA could mutate into new RNA molecules that replicated more rapidly than their "parents." Test-tube RNA molecules by themselves, like viruses, proteins, or DNA, in solution are dead. Yet molecular systems can proliferate and mutate in the test tube when provided proper support.

Thomas Cech of the University of Colorado and Sidney Altman of Yale University, both very young in the early 1980s, made the key discovery. Certain RNA molecules not only replicate but act like proteins: they splice themselves. They thus rearrange their own molecular form. Cech and colleagues proved without a shadow of a doubt—that is, without contaminating proteins—that RNA behaves as the kind of protein that can rearrange and reorganize genetic material. This kind of RNA is dubbed a "ribozyme." Given ribozymes, bits of RNA, with small spare parts (chemicals called ribonucleotides), evolve by themselves in a test tube. Let me emphasize that the RNA mix—whether or not enclosed in a liposome—is still not a cell. RNA and/or DNA molecules in a bottle are in no way alive. If left unmanipulated, neither test-tube RNA nor DNA alone is even a virus. They are food for enterprising bacteria, protists, and fungi. But RNA molecules do evolve in the test tube, suggesting that biochemical evolution may have preceded life. Gerald Joyce and Jack W. Szostak, at the University of California, San Diego, engineer ribozymes that accelerate RNA replication. A Harvard University scientist, Wally Gilbert, a Nobel laureate, coined the catchy term *RNA world*. Gilbert drew attention to RNA potency, suggesting among other good ideas that RNA acting as replicating ribozyme formed the kernel of the first living cell. I quite agree with Wally that RNA metabolism-accelerating reactions and replicating molecules preceded any DNA-based molecules. However, *both* RNA and DNA types of metabolism, as Morowitz emphasizes, live *inside* cells.

No life-form exists outside a self-maintaining, self-reproducing cell. The most stripped-down minimal form of life on Earth is still extraordinarily complex. Just a tiny membrane-bounded sphere, a wall-less bacterial cell requires a cadre of molecular interactions, more than fifteen kinds of

DNA and RNA, nearly five hundred different types of protein and usually closer to five thousand kinds. RNA by itself, DNA by itself, any virus alone, is not alive. All living cells, even in principle, are much more complicated than any gene or virus. Cells interchange their parts; they maintain themselves continuously from nutrients and energy drawn from their surroundings. I agree with Morowitz: the first life-forms were membrane-bounded self-maintaining cells, like those still alive today.

Using the principle of continuity, Morowitz casts autotrophs, bacteria that make their own food and generate their own energy from inorganic materials, as the original membrane-bounded cells. Photoautotrophs do not have to eat; they use sunlight for energy. Chemotrophs do not have to eat; they use hydrogen-rich chemicals without the aid of light for energy. Both photoautotrophs and chemotrophs derive carbon from the atmosphere's carbon dioxide ($CO_2$). Neither eats organic compounds; that is, neither eats food. Plants, cyanobacteria, and ammonia-, sulfide-, and methane-oxidizing bacteria are all autotrophs. The opposite of an autotroph is a heterotroph: any organism (herbivore, algivore, bacterivore, carnivore, or cannibal) that eats food. "Eating food" is the same as taking in preformed organic matter. All heterotrophs eat organic molecules made by autotrophs. Autotrophs "eat" air for food. They "eat" sunlight or employ the mephitic power of hydrogen-rich compounds, such as hydrogen gas ($H_2$), methane ($CH_3$), hydrogen sulfide ($H_2S$), or ammonia ($HN_3$), to make more of themselves. The energy of autotrophs is the same as fire: the hydrogen-rich compounds react with oxygen. Morowitz thinks the autotrophs still close to Earth's original nonliving geochemistry were the original type from which the rest of us sprang. Reasoning that autotrophs are closer to life's original thermodynamic cycles, Morowitz postulates that the chemoautotrophic way of life even antedates the photoautotrophic.

In seminars, Morowitz unveils the chemical layers of the onion step by step. We just converse and listen to him. My students and I enjoy working with Morowitz and others to trace life's history from its living present to its inert chemical past. We need to know the transition from prebiotic chemistry to cell-based life so that we can figure out how organelles evolved. Did they emerge directly from prelife and complexify, or are they stripped-down bacteria? I think and read about this extensively, but what I do with students and colleagues, in the laboratory and the classroom, is different. We deal directly with life: microbes and other live cells and their parts. Bacteria, protoctists, plants, or fungi are our objects of study. With my students and colleagues I trace life's history from its microbial antecedents. We observe growth and reproduction; we spy on protoctist sexuality and physical maturation; we measure the responses of bacteria and protists to environmental "insults." We are especially concerned with these microbes' behavior, rich social lives, and interaction with sediments as they form persistent community structures.

The origin of cells from scummy chemicals may have occurred once or many times. In any case, the first cells in our lineage were membrane-bounded, RNA- and DNA-based, self-maintaining protein systems. In details of cell structure and metabolic behavior they very much resembled us. Their material constituents continuously exchanged themselves with the external environment. They vented waste as they acquired food and energy. Their patterns persisted as they replenished their innards with chemicals taken from the surroundings. Indeed, metabolizing ancient bacteria were so effective at remaking themselves when threatened with disintegration and thermodynamic demise that the insides of our bodies today are chemically more akin to the external environment of the early Earth, in which life originated, than they are like our present oxygen-rich world. Life, always made of cells that grow and divide, literally has preserved its past as chemistry. The book of life is written in neither mathematics nor English: it is written in the language of carbon chemistry. "Speaking" the language of chemistry, the bacteria diversified and talked to each other on a global scale. Those that swam attached to those that degraded glucose, the sugar, and so generated power for swimming. The swimming, glucose-degrading partnership led to protists. The rest is history—my SET vision of history.

~ ~ ~

My earliest complete statement of "serial endosymbiosis theory" was published after fifteen or so assorted rejections and losses of an early, painfully convoluted, and poorly written manuscript. Called "Origin of Mitosing Cells," it was finally accepted for publication in 1966 through the personal intervention of James F. Danielli, then editor of the daring *Journal of Theoretical Biology*. Of course, the article, when it finally appeared in print in late 1967, carried my first married name, Lynn Sagan. The theory was dubbed SET, the acronym for *serial endosymbiosis theory* (not to be confused with SETI—the search for extraterrestrial intelligence), by another protist aficionado, Professor Max Taylor of the University of British Columbia.

Not until I was well into my second marriage and pregnant with my daughter Jennifer (in 1969) was I obliged to stay home for extended periods. Enforced home leave permitted uninterrupted thought. This, in turn, stimulated me to document the expanded version of my four-part SET narrative clearly. The story of the origin of cells begun in my 1967 paper sprouted, expanded, and eventually was pruned into a book-length manuscript. I typed late into many nights, determined to make the deadline required by contract. Of course, as a virtual unknown I was given neither advance nor compensation for the many illustrations I commissioned. All help came from home. Finally I completed what I thought was the final draft. With pride and care, even earlier in the morning than the voices of children, I boxed up and then mailed off the heavily illustrated work to the publisher who held the contract: Academic Press in New York City. The receipt of the box was not acknowledged. I waited. I continued to wait, for about five months. One day my box, without explanation, sent by surface book rate, reappeared at my mailbox. Much later I was informed, not even by the editor, that extremely negative peer review had led Academic Press to hold the manuscript for months. From the press finally I received a form letter of rejection. No explanation, in fact not even a personal letter signed by the Academic Press editor, accompanied the formal rejection. More than a year later, after far more painful and far longer labor than Jenny ever caused me, the book finally was nicely edited, produced, and published by Yale University Press. Because of commentary and criticism by Max Taylor and other generous colleagues the serial endosymbiosis theory prevailed. Eventually the pain of the Academic Press rejection subsided.

SET attracted experimental contributions by many scientists and graduate students unknown to me throughout the 1970s and 1980s. Molecular biological, genetic, and high-powered microscopic studies all tended to confirm the once-radical nineteenth-century idea that the cells of plants and of our animal bodies (as well as those of fungi and all other organisms composed of cells with nuclei) originated through a specific sequence of mergers of different types of bacteria. Joint residence prevails and proliferates. My most current version of SET is shown in [the figure on the right]. Today I am amazed to see a watered-down version of SET taught as revealed truth in high school and college texts. I find, to my dismay if not to my surprise, that

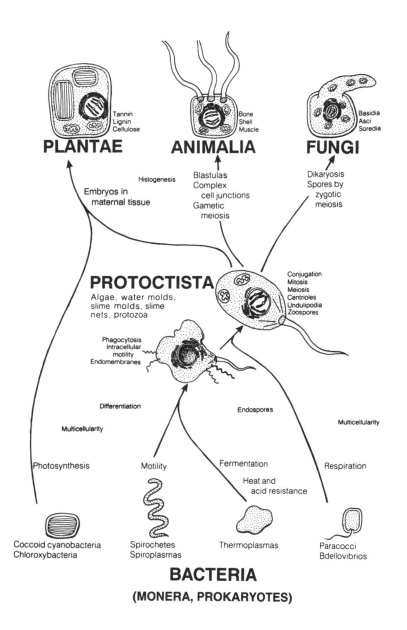

**PLANTAE**      **ANIMALIA**      **FUNGI**

Tannin
Lignin
Cellulose

Bone
Shell
Muscle

Basidia
Asci
Soredia

Histogenesis

Blastulas
Complex
cell junctions
Gametic
meiosis

Dikaryosis
Spores by
zygotic
meiosis

Embryos in
maternal tissue

**PROTOCTISTA**

Algae, water molds,
slime molds, slime
nets, protozoa

Conjugation
Mitosis
Meiosis
Centrioles
Undulipodia
Zoospores

Phagocytosis
Intracellular
motility
Endomembranes

Differentiation

Endospores

Multicellularity

Multicellularity

Photosynthesis

Motility

Fermentation

Respiration

Heat and
acid resistance

Coccoid cyanobacteria
Chloroxybacteria

Spirochetes
Spiroplasmas

Thermoplasmas

Paracocci
Bdellovibrios

**BACTERIA**

**(MONERA, PROKARYOTES)**

*SET (serial endosymbiosis theory) phylogeny*

the exposition is dogmatic, misleading, not logically argued, and often frankly incorrect. Unlike the science itself, SET now is uncritically accepted. So it goes.

SET is a theory of coming together, of merging of cells of different histories and abilities. Before serial endosymbiosis and the establishment of the aerobic nucleated cell, no cell-fusion sex existed. Meiotic sex, like that of the egg fertilized by the sperm, came later. Serial endosymbiosis made our kind of fusion sex possible. Sex, too, is the coming together, the merging of cells of different histories and abilities. In sex the cells that fuse are closely related and the fusion is reversible; in serial endosymbiosis the cells that fuse are only distantly related, and the fusion is permanent.

~ ~ ~

Symbiosis, the term coined by the German botanist Anton deBary in 1873, is the living together of very different kinds of organisms; deBary actually defined it as the "living together of differently named organisms." In certain cases cohabitation, long-term living, results in symbiogenesis: the appearance of new bodies, new organs, new species. In short, I believe that most evolutionary novelty arose, and still arises, directly from symbiosis. This is not the popular idea of the basis of evolutionary change in most textbooks.

Symbiogenesis, an idea proposed by its Russian inventor Konstantin Merezhkovsky (1855–1921), refers to the formation of new organs and organisms through symbiotic mergers. As I will show it is a fundamental fact of evolution. All organisms large enough for us to see are composed of once-independent microbes, teamed up to become larger wholes. As they merged, many lost what we in retrospect recognize as their former individuality.

My theory of the symbiogenetic origin of plant, animal, and other cells with nuclei employs four provable postulates. All four involve symbiogenesis, incorporation, and body fusion by symbiosis. The theory precisely outlines the steps that must have occurred in the past, especially in relation to the bright green cells of plants. Cells, of course, are familiar units of structure in mosses, ferns, and all other plants. The slender stamen hairs particularly visible in *Zebrina* and *Tradescantia* ("wandering Jew") flowers are made of rows of such plant cells. Large, walled green cells preceded plants: they were already fully formed in the green algae, water-dwelling ancestors of plants. That nucleated organisms evolved by merger is best appreciated in plants because in their large and beautiful cells, the integrity of their component organelles is easily observed. The idea is straightforward: four once entirely independent and physically separate ancestors merged in a specific order to become the green algal cell. All four were bacteria. Each of the four bacteria types differed in ways we can still infer. In both merged and free-living forms the descendants of all four kinds of bacteria still live today. Some say the four types are mutually enslaved, trapped both in the plant and as the plant. Today each of the types of former bacteria provides clues about its ancestry; life is chemically so conservative that we can even deduce the specific order in which they merged. The term *serial* in *serial endosymbiosis theory* refers to the order in the merger sequence.

# Content Questions

1. What does serial endosymbiosis theory (SET) "only" do, according to Margulis? (263) Why is an understanding of the origins of bacteria needed to fully appreciate SET? (263–264)

2. Why does Margulis conclude that "the bacterial cell, today's minimal unit of life . . . is where we must begin" to investigate the origins of life? (265) How does this conclusion follow from the three approaches to inferring the origins of life that she explains? (264–265)

3. What aspects of the beginning of life are there no doubts about, according to Margulis? (266) What actions do the simplest bacteria perform that are characteristic of all life? (266)

4. Why does Margulis find the theory that life on Earth originated in outer space "intellectually unsatisfactory"? (267)

5. How does Margulis answer the objection that it is extremely unlikely for molecules to have combined as proponents of the life-from-nonliving-matter school claim they did? (268–269)

6. Why does Margulis believe that RNA preceded DNA in the history of life? (272)

7. What characteristics does a ribozyme have that distinguish it from other types of RNA? What does the ability of RNA molecules to evolve in a test tube suggest about the chronology of life's development on Earth? (273)

8. Why does Margulis conclude that free-floating DNA or RNA never existed? (271–274)

9. Why are autotrophs the most likely candidates for being "the original membrane-bounded cells"? (274)

10. According to Margulis, what characteristics did the first cells in our lineage have? In what ways did they resemble the cells in our bodies today? (275)

11. How does Margulis use the concepts of symbiosis and symbiogenesis to arrive at SET? (278–279)

## Application Questions

1. Explain why the results of Pasteur's experiment disproved the idea of spontaneous generation. What was the role of the control flask in his experiment?

2. What can living cells do that chemical systems cannot, even if some chemical systems are capable of making more of themselves or maintaining their functions by assimilating energy?

3. What three elements, working together in "a fluid-filled membranous bag," enable a cell to maintain its life? (272) Why is the function of each of these elements essential?

## Discussion Questions

1. According to Margulis, why is it important to attempt to understand the early steps in the origin of life?

2. What does Margulis mean when she says that in the microbial mat "death is part of life," though "neither by commandment nor of necessity"? (264)

3. Why does Margulis find SET intellectually satisfying? Do you agree?

4. How do Margulis's accounts of her work with her students and her own delight in investigating microbes contribute to the effect of her discussion of life's origins?

5. Why does Margulis present the history of her efforts to publish her work on SET, rather than discuss only the work itself?

6. Why is Margulis not surprised that the exposition of SET in high school and college texts is "dogmatic, misleading, not logically argued, and often frankly incorrect"? (276–278)

# Comparative
# Discussion Questions

1. How would two of the scientists in this anthology define "life"? (Choose two whose answers differ substantively.)

2. Is there a difference between what Aristotle, Lucretius, and Bacon mean by "nature"?

3. Would Bacon say that Aristotle, in "Parts of Animals," moves from particulars to axioms? If so, are they what Bacon calls "true and solid and living axioms"?

4. How does Mendel display the qualities of the ant, the spider, and the bee as described by Bacon?

5. Would Bacon say that Mendel was establishing an axiom "framed to the measure of those particulars only from which it is derived," or one that is "larger and wider"?

6. How would Aristotle or Bernard view Mendel's admittance of chance into his explanation? How much of a threat would Mendel's view of chance pose to either scientist's view of determinism?

7. How do Aristotle's and Bernard's explanations of, and arguments for, scientific method compare?

8. How would Bernard reply to Aristotle's discussion of necessity and final causes?

9. Compare Lucretius's ideas about heredity to those of Mendel or Darwin.

10. In the terms that Gould outlines in "Just in the Middle," could you consider Lucretius a "vitalist" and Bernard a "mechanist"? Why or why not?

11. How might Bacon, Eiseley, or Lorenz respond to Carson's critique of thoughtless technological development?

12. How do the results of Pasteur's experiment, described by Margulis, contrast with the views expressed by Lucretius?

13. To what extent do Dawkins or Margulis lend credence to Lucretius's assertion that "things which we see are sentient / . . . have their origin in things / Quite without sentience"?

14. How does Eiseley's view of evolution compare to that of Darwin or Dawkins?

15. What is uniquely human, according to two of the scientists whose works you have read?

16. How would you compare the view of the human relationship to and responsibility toward the natural world, as presented by two of the scientists whose works you have read?

17. Compare Just's view of the nature of life to the view Bernard expresses.

18. Compare Dawkins's competitive view of life's evolution with Margulis's symbiotic one. To what extent is there room for compromise between the two?

19. How would you define "good" science, after reading what you have read? What distinguishes good science from bad science?

20. What responsibility do scientists have to communicate their ideas to nonscientists? To speak out on ethical considerations that arise from their scientific work?

21. To what extent is science an arena open to all, in which work is judged solely on its merit? To what extent is science affected by prejudice, favoritism, and other considerations?

22. Compare Dawkins's approach to the problem of the origin of life with that of Margulis. Does Gould's point about adopting a "middle position" apply as we attempt to understand these divergent approaches? Why or why not?

23. What are the essential differences in the ways that Lucretius, Darwin, Mendel, Dawkins, and Margulis approach the theme of continuity and change?

24. What are the essential differences in the ways that Aristotle and Eiseley approach the theme of relationship of structure to function?

25. Darwin's ideas profoundly transformed biology. Choose one of the scientists in this anthology who wrote before the mid-1800s and one who wrote after, and describe the ways in which their approaches are different due to Darwin's influence.

# Bibliography

## For further reading

Barlow, Connie, ed. *From Gaia to Selfish Genes: Selected Writings in the Life Sciences*. Cambridge: MIT Press, 1992.

Carey, John, ed. *Eyewitness to Science*. Cambridge: Harvard University Press, 1997.

Dampier, William C., ed. *Readings in the Literature of Science; Being Extracts from the Writings of Men of Science to Illustrate the Development of Scientific Thought*. New York: Harper, 1959.

Gardner, Martin, ed. *Great Essays in Science*. Buffalo, NY: Prometheus Books, 1994.

Harris, Henry. *The Birth of the Cell*. New Haven: Yale University Press, 1999.

Mayr, Ernst. *The Growth of Biological Thought: Diversity, Evolution, and Inheritance*. Cambridge: Harvard University Press, Belknap Press, 1982.

Miller, Gordon L., ed. *Nature's Fading Chorus: Classic and Contemporary Writings on Amphibians*. Washington, D.C.: Island Press, 2000.

Nussbaum, Martha, and Cass R. Sunstein, eds. *Clones and Clones: Facts and Fantasies About Human Cloning*. New York: W. W. Norton, 1998.

Quammen, David. *The Flight of the Iguana: A Sidelong View of Science and Nature*. New York: Delacorte Press, 1988.

Souder, William. *A Plague of Frogs: The Horrifying True Story*. New York: Hyperion, 2000.

Thomas, Lewis. *The Lives of a Cell: Notes of a Biology Watcher*. New York: Viking Press, 1974; New York: Penguin, 1995.


## By and about authors represented in this collection

### Aristotle

Adler, Mortimer J. *Aristotle for Everybody: Difficult Thought Made Easy*. New York: Macmillan, 1978.

Lloyd, G. E. R. *Early Greek Science: Thales to Aristotle*. New York: W. W. Norton, 1974.

### Bacon

Eiseley, Loren. *The Man Who Saw Through Time*. Rev. and enl. ed. of *Francis Bacon and the Modern Dilemma*. New York: Scribner, 1973.

Urbach, Peter. *Francis Bacon's Philosophy of Science: An Account and a Reappraisal*. La Salle, IL: Open Court, 1987.

### Darwin

Browne, Janet. *Charles Darwin: A Biography*. Princeton: Princeton University Press, 1996.

Darwin, Charles. *The Autobiography of Charles Darwin, 1809–1882: With Original Omissions Restored*. Edited by Nora Barlow. Rev. ed. New York: W. W. Norton, 1993.

### Mendel

Henig, Robin Marantz. *The Monk in the Garden: The Lost and Found Genius of Gregor Mendel*. New York: Houghton Mifflin, 2000.

### Eiseley

Christianson, Gale E. *Fox at the Wood's Edge: A Biography of Loren Eiseley*. New York: Henry Holt, 1990.

Pitts, Mary Ellen. *Toward a Dialogue of Understandings: Loren Eiseley and the Critique of Science*. Bethlehem, PA: Lehigh University Press, 1995.

**Carson**

Carson, Rachel. *The Sea Around Us*. New York: Oxford University Press, 1951.

Lear, Linda J. *Rachel Carson: Witness for Nature*. New York: Henry Holt, 1997.

**Lorenz**

Nisbett, Alec. *Konrad Lorenz*. New York: Harcourt Brace Jovanovich, 1977.

**Watson**

Sayre, Anne. *Rosalind Franklin and DNA*. New York: W. W. Norton, 1978.

Watson, James D. *A Passion for DNA: Genes, Genomes, and Society*. Cold Spring Harbor, NY: Cold Spring Harbor Laboratory Press, 2000.

**Dawkins**

Dawkins, Richard. *River Out of Eden: A Darwinian View of Life*. New York: Basic Books, 1995.

**Gould**

Gould, Stephen Jay. *The Mismeasure of Man*. Rev. and expanded. New York: W. W. Norton, 1996.

**Margulis**

Margulis, Lynn, and Dorion Sagan. *Microcosmos: Four Billion Years of Evolution from Our Microbial Ancestors*. New York: Summit Books, 1986.

Margulis, Lynn, and Dorion Sagan. *Slanted Truths: Essays on Gaia, Symbiosis, and Evolution*. New York: Copernicus, 1997.

McDermott, Jeanne. "A Biologist Whose Heresy Redraws Earth's Tree of Life." *Smithsonian* 20 (August 1989): 72–81.

# Acknowledgments

All possible care has been taken to trace ownership and secure permission for each selection in this book. The Great Books Foundation wishes to thank the following authors, publishers, and representatives for permission to reprint copyrighted material:

*Parts of Animals,* reprinted by permission of the publishers and the Trustees of the Loeb Classical Library from ARISTOTLE: PARTS OF ANIMALS, VOLUME XII, Loeb Classical Library Volume L 323, translated by A. L. Peck, Cambridge, Mass.: Harvard University Press, 1937, revised 1961. The Loeb Classical Library is a registered trademark of the President and Fellows of Harvard College. All rights reserved.

*Novum Organum,* from THE NEW ORGANON AND RELATED WRITINGS, edited by Fulton Anderson. Reprinted by permission of Pearson Education, Inc.

*Experiments in Plant Hybridization,* by Gregor Mendel, from READINGS IN THE LITERATURE OF SCIENCE, edited by William C. Dampier. Reprinted with the permission of Cambridge University Press.

*An Introduction to the Study of Experimental Medicine,* from AN INTRODUCTION TO THE STUDY OF EXPERIMENTAL MEDICINE, by Claude Bernard, translated by Henry Copley Greene. Reprinted by permission of Dover Publications, Inc.

*The Snout,* from THE IMMENSE JOURNEY, by Loren Eiseley. Copyright 1950 by Loren Eiseley. Reprinted by permission of Random House, Inc.

## Art Credits

**Front cover** Photograph of hamadryas by James Balog. © 1989 James Balog.
**22** Claude Perrault, *Description anatomique de divers animaux dissequez dan l'Académie Royale des Sciences,* 1687. Bibliothèque publique et universitaire, Geneva. **30** Theodore de Bry and Jacques de Morgues, *Brevis Narratio,* 1563. Engraving. © Giraudon/Art Resource, NY. **42** Hieronymus Cock and F. Floris, *Geometry.* Engraving. © Musee Nat. du Château de Malmaison, Rueil-Malmaison/Lauros-Giraudon, Paris/SuperStock. **56** *Sky & Water I* by M. C. Escher. © 2001 Cordon Art-Baarn-Holland. All rights reserved. **98** Giorgio Liberale and Wolfgang Meyerpeck, *Broad Bean* (plant from pea family Leguminosae), c. 1564. Engraving. **116** Anatomical study, from Gautier d'Argoty's *Planches anatomiques,* c. 1750. Bibliothèque Nationale, Paris. **126** Zdenek Burian, *Marshy Wood of the Carboniferous Period* (detail), 1950. Senckenberg Natural History Museum, Frankfurt. **138** DDT protester, 1969. © Ted Streshinsky/Corbis. **158** Ephraim Moshe Lillien, *Adam and Eve Driven from the Garden of Eden.* Engraving. **182** © Corbis. **204** Diagram showing the transmission of a sex-linked characteristic in the fruit fly. Bibliothèque de Genève. **222** © Renee Lynn/Stone. **238** Scanning electron micrograph of human egg surrounded by sperm. © Yorgos Nikas/Stone. **254** Melchior d'Hondecoeter, *The Menagerie of Prince William III at the Château du Loo.* Mauritshuis, The Hague. **262** © Corbis. **Back cover** Photograph of chimpanzee by James Balog. © 1989 James Balog.